TALKING TO TWEENIES

TALKING TO
TWEENIES

Getting it Right Before it Gets Rocky
With Your 8–12 Year Old

ELIZABETH HARTLEY-BREWER

HODDER
MOBIUS

Hodder & Stoughton

600063402

Copyright © 2004 by Elizabeth Hartley-Brewer

First published in Great Britain in 2004 by Hodder and Stoughton
A division of Hodder Headline
This paperback edition published in 2005

The right of Elizabeth Hartley-Brewer to be identified as the Author
of the Work has been asserted by her in accordance with the
Copyright, Designs and Patents Act 1988

A Mobius paperback

1 3 5 7 9 10 8 6 4 2

A CIP catalogue record for this title is available from the British Library

ISBN 0 340 734426

Typeset in Sabon by Palimpsest Book Production Limited,
Polmont, Stirlingshire

Printed and bound by Clays Ltd, St Ives plc

Hodder Headline's policy is to use papers that are natural,
renewable and recyclable products and made from wood grown in
sustainable forests. The logging and manufacturing processes are
expected to conform to the environmental regulations of the
country of origin

Hodder and Stoughton Ltd
A division of Hodder Headline
338 Euston Road
London NW1 3BH

For
Emma and Emily
who are almost there

Acknowledgements

I AM GRATEFUL TO SO many people for direct assistance and wider support in writing this book. It has covered such a spread of topics that I have had to rely on the specialist knowledge of a number of friends, colleagues and professionals, as well as young people, to ensure I covered genuine concerns in a relevant and informed way. The longstanding gap in research on and awareness of eight to twelve-year-olds' experience is at last being filled so there was much to locate and learn.

I should like to thank, in particular, John Coleman, Director of the Trust for the Study of Adolescence, for his thorough comments on an early draft, and Ruth Beedle, friend and experienced personal, social and health education teacher of boys across this age range and beyond, for much in-depth discussion of a number of issues and chapters. Her insight, knowledge, stories and guidance were especially valuable. In addition, Adrienne Katz, founder of the organisation Young Voice, was most supportive and as instructive as ever. Others who made my task considerably easier were Anna Kassman-McKerrell, of the Children's Play Information Service; Liz Atkins, Head of Policy at NSPCC; Simon Blake, Assistant Director of Child Development at the National Children's Bureau; Rosalind Edwards, of South Bank University, Professor Seth Love, consultant neuropathologist, Laurence Buckman, general practitioner; and Don Rowe, of the Citizenship Foundation. Hilary Wareing, from Public Management Associates, shared her experiences of talking to young people about their early sexual activity, drug taking and smoking. Sarah Molloy, my agent, was enthusiastic from the start and always ready to be dumped on and to re-inspire and my editor, Emma Heyworth-Dunn, ensured that I kept a coherent, finished product in mind at all times. I am also very appreciative of the eight- to twelve-year-olds who agreed to talk to me about their lives. Special thanks, then, go to Alex, Alice, Caitlin, Emma, Gaby, Freddie, Julie, Lucy, Molly, Paris and Simon, as well as to all those with whom I have spoken in the past whose stories I have revisited. Lucy and Lauren helped me, too, by reflecting back on their recent memories of these years. I am indebted to academics Audrey Mullender, Bren Neale and Amanda Wade for permission to draw from their important work and to quote the young people they interviewed as part of their research.

On a more personal level, I must thank my children who always give me strength. And I would not have been as continuously cheerful and optimistic throughout without the joyful company of Freda and Richard, two treasured friends.

Contents

Introduction

WHEN I TOLD A TEACHER friend I was writing another book for parents, this time on raising eight to twelve-year-olds, and admitted I was not sure quite where to start, he joked that I had probably written it already. Whatever you have put on paper about teenagers, he said, you can reuse because it all happens two years earlier now.

He was only half joking, but the point was well made. The term 'tweenies' was initially created by the marketing industry to describe those children who fell between childhood and adolescence – not quite children but not yet teenagers. The emergence of a new name to describe the eight to twelve-year-olds is significant. Tweenies suffer from eating disorders, are exposed to intense peer pressure, want to go places on their own, keep up with fashion and watch videos certified for older children, just as teenagers do. But the similarity between tweenies and teenagers goes only so far. Many twelve-year-olds are indeed teenage wannabes, but most of our eight-year-olds are not there yet. None the less, they expect different treatment to mark their growing sense of confidence and independence, and have certainly been targeted by the advertising and marketing industry as a new and distinct group to exploit, with huge success.

The scary thing about being a parent today is that everything changes so fast. We seem to spend our time stumbling in the dark, constantly facing new issues and responding to new situations and changing expectations. We accept, now, that our own childhood experiences shed little light on what to do with our own children. What does come as a shock, unless our children are very close together in age, is that what worked for one child cannot be applied with any certainty to the next, because the ground shifts so quickly. This is on top of the sensitivity we have to develop to each of our children's differing personalities. My own experience as an active stepmother of two children, which began more than thirty years ago, was not always useful thirteen years later when my son was growing up; and what I applied then I had to recast for his sister who is seven years younger because she wanted different things and expected more. And girls do grow up earlier. It was hard enough to deal with the commercialism, consumerism and peer pressure she faced as a tweenie, but I can see it would be far harder now, only five years later. When we are in the thick of coping with intense and endless demands, and equally intense demonstrations of disappointment when demands are stymied, it can be hard to keep a sense of perspective, to trust our judgement and stick to clear and relevant principles. 'But so and so is allowed to . . .' must be the most commonly heard gripe, and it's hard not to be swayed by it. Most of us do not have the opportunity or, perhaps, luxury to be parents over a long enough period to acquire the quiet confidence children delight in. When society is stable, experience comes quickly and stays relevant. When it slips into fast-forward, the benefit of hindsight usually comes too late to be put to practical use, which is where a book can offer support.

A new way forward

As a new phenomenon, the tweenie period raises issues that are not addressed in most of the standard child-rearing texts. There are books on babies, books on toddlers and books on teenagers, but nothing on understanding the world and state of mind of our tweenies. Whether the issue is holding the line against the fashion alternatives to sensible clothes and shoes; whether to let ten-year-olds play out, walk to school alone or go to the park with friends; whether we should allow our child to host the ultim-ate, film-première-style party to go one better than the last birthday boy or girl, to have every fad going regardless of cost; or whether the issue is simply when to renegotiate the rules around eating or bedtimes, many parents are asking for guidance through these pre-teen years.

It is important to get it right before the rocky teenage times take over, so the teen years are less fraught. Having the benefit of hindsight gained from many years as a parent and step-parent; having reflected on family relationships and written for parents and the professionals they encounter for the last decade; and living currently with a post-tweenie teenager who is grappling with today's temptations, I offer you a new perspective on rais-ing our eight- to twelve-year-olds. I believe this perspective will help you to decide what's best for your own tweenie and estab-lish a durable relationship that will work for the longer term. The 'bottom line' of this approach is both to nurture each child's individual strengths and sense of self to enable each one to develop a clear direction and positive outlook; and to keep the parent-tweenie relationship active and healthy through listening carefully, ensuring appropriate increases in autonomy, and a very gradual loosening of the reins while staying communicative, attentive and present. In other words, we should stay close while beginning to let go. It's hard to reel back freedom, so if we let them have too much of what they want too soon we may have little authority left to monitor, supervise and guide during adolescent exploration and risk-taking.

But keeping everything tightly controlled in the tweenie period is not the answer either: following that course can result in a frustrated, pent-up teenager who rockets off with her new-found freedom and orbits dangerously out of range. But how can we identify and then follow the desirable middle course? It is easier to spot once we have appreciated the crucial difference between autonomy and freedom, which is explained in chapter one.

Throughout the book, ways are suggested in which we can increase appropriately our tweenies' experience of autonomy without agreeing to a degree of personal liberty we might later regret or that puts them at risk. If we respect, talk, listen and respond to our tweenie as a maturing person during these five years, yet maintain a clear framework of expectations and boundaries that adjusts over this time, we are more likely to be treated respectfully in return by them in the teenage years that follow.

Using the book with your tweenie

As all parents know only too well, it is one thing to know the theory and quite another to apply it. Too many parenting handbooks fall short either because they fail to take account of the very real difficulties and challenges that many families face or because they do not offer enough detail when translating the theory into practice. *Tweenies* is different — it focuses on practical advice, with the issues and suggestions firmly rooted in the real world. In addition, the underlying approach is founded on a clear understanding of what is now known about children's physical, emotional and neurological development. There are plenty of tips to choose from, but no reader should follow every single one to the letter. Each family has different values and experiences based on culture, religion or previous history, and certain issues will be more pressing for some than for others. And children, of course, have different personalities. Only the parent can decide which advice will work best in relation to their family's situation or for their child. Variation is inevitable, as different people will find success in different approaches. Trying something that we are not comfortable with will not benefit our family in the long term. Indeed, taking the time to evaluate what is right for our own family and to select the best option is important, necessary and healthy because it helps us to define our own position and thereby take a clearer, more consistent line that a tweenie will appreciate.

The key themes and messages

Much as we would like to, we cannot cocoon our tweenies from all outside influences. Cigarettes and alcohol, commercialism and peer pressure increasingly feature in any tweenie's world. It is natural that we should worry about the impact of these, and the book offers advice on how to help our tweenie negotiate a safe route through these particular attractions and temptations. But it also promotes a core message, backed up by practical suggestions, that the most powerful way to protect and strengthen any child is to concentrate on helping her to feel secure, significant and with a strong sense of belonging. When a child feels secure in her relationships, is treated as significant and important by people who matter to her, feels successful and experiences a strong, common thread of connection to her family and other familiar groups, she will be happier, more creative, have more friends, be more likely to do justice to her potential, develop a more sensible attitude to taking risks and be more resistant to pressure. In other words, a tweenie with a strong identity and a stable and positive sense of self and belonging will be far less likely to self-destruct. In contrast, a child who feels insecure, insignificant, neglected and isolated will be vulnerable not only to temptation as she attempts to find an alternative significance, but also to mental health problems that stem from her sense of self-doubt.

The book's chapters mirror the increasingly diverse spheres of a tweenie's life and encourage parents and carers to see the world from their tweenie's progressively more independent point of view. We take a look at our eight- to twelve-year-olds at home, in the shops, with their friends, at work and play, out on the streets and in school and consider how our bond with them in relation to each of these spheres should adapt and grow. We consider what changes their impending puberty will bring, how to encourage physical and mental health during these important years and how we might encourage appropriate moral values and maintain good standards of behaviour. Wherever practical and relevant, suggestions are informed by research and steered by the views and voices of tweenies themselves. Each chapter focuses on three or four selected issues within the area, offers taster tips mid-chapter, and concludes with ten further take-out tips: a summary of possible points for action.

The central message is that time invested in getting it right during this crucial In-between period will bestow long-term benefits – for us as parents, for our tweenie and for the relationship. It will not be five years of hard slog or guilt: on the contrary, tweenies' developing sense of humour, their newly acquired, fresh-faced wisdom, their excitement and enthusiasm and their growing confidence in their stronger bodies and more capable minds make tweenies a delight to watch and be with. There is a lot of fun to be had. We will be kept on our toes because they are more able to judge and no longer view us as demi-gods, but our reward will be a fulfilling, loving and mutually supportive and maturing relationship that can sustain them for years – so enjoy!

POSTSCRIPT ON GENDER
Most of the comments in the book refer to boys as well as girls. Where the gender differences are significant, separate sections are included to apply to each sex as indicated. Outside these sections, 'he' or 'she' is used in turn in alternate chapters for balance.

I
A SEPARATE STAGE
Understanding Tweenies

A S A PARENT, ONE OF the most discouraging yet common situations to find ourselves in is to believe either that our child is uniquely trying or that we are the only one with the problem. Either way, we readily believe it has something to do with us, so we feel useless, blame ourselves and feel guilty; perhaps worse, we might blame and reject our child. Being a parent is so much easier when we know what behaviour to expect given our child's age and stage of development, and how their needs change during childhood.

This knowledge helps us to prepare, adapt and stay confident. It means we can avoid the trap of basing decisions on our require-ments, giving our children what *we* feel able to give, what *we* feel we missed out on or what *we* need to prove we can achieve. Alternatively, we may simply guess what is in their best interests, not appreciating the pressurised world eight- to twelve-year-olds now face. Hitherto, people have been working largely in the dark. Little has been written in detail about this stage of develop-ment for professionals, let alone parents, largely because it was considered to be uneventful and glossed over. Researchers and policy makers have only recently decided to look deeper, realis-ing that pre-teen children experience significant changes and real challenges, that these five years constitute a separate and important developmental stage and that we should really understand more – and start by consulting them.

This chapter tries to convey what life is like for many eight- to twelve-year-olds today. It describes the social pressures and difficulties tweenies face and how they typically deal with them; it then reviews the significant physiological and psychological milestones of this period – significant physical changes associated with puberty, and the mental and emotional changes that strengthen children's sense of self, self-esteem and thirst for autonomy – and considers the implications of all this for parents. Of course, if tweenies' needs change, we need to change too, to adjust our expectations and offer more scope for self-management. Armed with both knowledge and insight, we are less likely to rely on hit-and-miss guesswork or put our needs before theirs.

Once we understand the theory, it is easier to change our practice. Reading this chapter before tackling any specific topic covered later in the book will help anyone caring for a tweenie both to reflect sensitively on any single issue and make it easier to devise a consistent overall approach that will suit them and their particular child.

New expectations, hopes and demands

Up to about ten years ago, most parents seemed to find living with an eight- to twelve-year-old child unproblematic. The phase passed unremarkably. 'Middle childhood', the term used by psychologists to describe these youngsters, was a time of relative peace. A child's identity was supposedly established, enabling these boys and girls to live through a stable period in which they were happy to be 'responsible' children intent on pleasing their parents, exploring their particular talents and skills, getting on with their school work and being generally co-operative.

The story now is rather different. Tweenies are gaining in confidence, expecting more freedoms and becoming less compliant, not least because they are being increasingly targeted and exploited commercially. Tweenies today seem to be in a big hurry to grow up, as if childhood is no longer an acceptable place to be. They are the young sophisticates, eager to parade their growing sense of self and need to belong to groups unrelated to their family through a stronger commitment to clothes, pop bands and friends. They are becoming a force to be reckoned with, at home and outside.

Far from experiencing five years of innocent, quiet, confident and happy stability, our would-be teenagers are now, without doubt, fidgety 'In-betweenies,' living in a kind of no-man's-land, with an urge to occupy territory that seems to offer greater meaning, a clearer purpose and more excitement. As parents we are puzzled. We know that they are still children, but we are confused as to whether we should hold our tweenies back to preserve their innocence and safety or allow them to go with the flow, which is quickening. Tweenies' life today is characterised by change: school changes (most will change twice); family change, for many will have parents who separate and then re-partner; physiological change, because their bodies and brains alter fundamentally as they approach puberty even if this is not yet obvious from the outside; and they face a bewildering array of shifting choices, leisure opportunities and expectations.

Naturally, an eight-year-old tweenie will be very different from a twelve-year-old. At eight, children are unambiguously children, relying heavily on their parents and family for both their core security and their daily routines. But by the age of twelve, most are looking forward to greater independence – to an increasingly separate social life with friends and to travelling independently to schools further away. Molly, aged eleven, said, 'I feel that I have really matured in the last year, I've grown up a lot because I have learned from my experiences. I can understand things. I can talk more openly about opinions, I've learned to apologise when I'm wrong. It feels like I've shed a skin.'

These children still need their families as a foundation for their sense of security and confidence, but they depend increasingly on friends and on their own wits to help them cope with unfamiliar situations. Many are also more able and ready to take on responsibility for themselves and others. In other cultures and in other times, thirteen- and fourteen-year-olds have been viewed as virtual adults. Girls in their early teens have been considered marriageable and at twelve will have been betrothed. Boys might have been apprenticed to a trade, and would probably have lived away from home. Today, it is very different. Young people stay in education for far longer, partly to acquire the knowledge-based and thinking skills today's jobs increasingly require. This practice prolongs dependency and appears to postpone adulthood. Perhaps it is no surprise that tweenies want to chart clear progress through the seemingly endless years we define as childhood.

NEW PRESSURES AND CONTRADICTIONS

Our tweenies now have to respond to a growing array of both external and internal pressures of increasing intensity. Academically, far more is expected of tweenies now than was the case even five years ago. They are being tested, measured and monitored against specific targets throughout this period, so many may find it hard to relax. Social pressure invades more areas of a tweenie's life, and one form of this, peer pressure, is the driver to changing fashions and fads through which tweenies must pick their way, with parents firmly in tow. And at either end of these crucial in-between years, tweenies have two significant school changes. Moving from infant to junior school, and junior to secondary is not new, of course, but each transition has been made more tortuous because it is accompanied by national school tests, measures of achievement and, at eleven, up to six months of uncertainty over which secondary school will be attended and whether or not it is well regarded, given its position in local league tables. Internal pressures are those that are self-imposed, so they seem more natural. However, when a child hears enough times from others that it is important to have, or to do, or achieve certain things or to look a certain way, it is understandable if he turns these external pressures into personal objectives and targets, particularly when he's keen to fit in.

On top of these pressures, tweenies now also experience many contradictions that mirror their 'in-between' status. We give them more freedom to demand and consume material things but considerably less freedom than many of us experienced to play and explore the wider world. They are the immobile, mobile phone generation, speaking to or texting their friends rather than going out to play or visit: they let their fingers (or thumbs) do both the walking and the talking as they key in their conversations via mobile phones and computers from the safety of their homes. We ask for more responsibility from our tweenies for doing well at school but, by and large, less domestic and personal responsibility at home. Consumer choice should help to highlight individual identity, yet fashion and commercialism tempt tweenies to ignore their individuality and opt for conformity instead. That same commercialism flaunts sex to sell clothes and magazines to tweenies, yet our teenagers get pilloried when they use it as a badge of maturity and experiment too early. The 'traditional' boundaries of childhood seem to be withering away. We should not be surprised, then, if our tweenies do not know quite where to pitch themselves in terms of image or age, or simply how to be: whether to feel confident about what they can do, or uncertain because they are increasingly made aware of what or who they are not, or what they do not have.

These intense and varied pressures and tensions are likely to combine and affect children's general behaviour. We know that when we feel overwhelmed, we tend to fall short of our own standards, lose our cool more often and sometimes make any pressures worse, perversely, by ignoring them. Worries can interrupt our sleep, and tiredness increases irritability and chips at confidence. Children are the same. They may stop concentrating in school, argue more with their siblings or become more defensive and less accommodating. By understanding the underlying issues, we put ourselves in a stronger position to empathise, offer emotional support and devise practical ways that will help them through.

Taster tips to appreciate and relieve the impact of pressure

✓ With our own child in mind, list the particular pressures he may face currently to get a measure of the extent of personal uncertainty experienced.

✓ Identify all the features that offer stability – the routines, any rituals, and any little personal pleasures that give joy. It is important that these are sustained as far as possible to counteract the pressures.

✓ Consider which, if any, times in which you have clashed recently could be due to him feeling tense and whether you can let up a little to show understanding.

Key developmental milestones

A combination of growing social and academic pressure, the contradictions listed above and the family changes experienced by many children by the time they reach twelve years old is creating another challenge for tweenies – to hold on to their sense of self and self-esteem that would normally blossom at this time.

Developmental psychologists agree that the age of eight marks a leap in most children's confidence, sense of identity and self-awareness, including gender awareness. The growth in confidence is one of the key developmental pluses of the tweenie years. Tweenies' growing potential for social and emotional maturity is further enhanced by a renewed quest for independence and autonomy, combined with a greater reliance on friends, who can take individuals that little bit further. 'My friends have made me a lot more confident than I used to be,' said Molly, eleven. 'They encouraged me to do more things, like to sing in the school choir in front of people.' Pre-teen friendships are so important that a separate chapter has been allocated to the subject.

Of course, no account of developmental milestones can ignore the profound impact on eight- to twelve-year-olds of puberty. As part of puberty, children's bodies and brain functioning change dramatically and girls, of course, change in different ways and at different times from boys. The earliest physical changes are subtle and go almost unnoticed, but by the time girls in particular reach eleven or twelve years of age, the transformation is obvious and dramatic – verging on the traumatic. Puberty is the bridge to adolescence and thence to adulthood. Twelve-year-olds are, then, very different from eight-year-olds: in terms of how they look (much taller, much chunkier and with a different body shape), how they see themselves, how they think (more comparatively, reflectively and comfortable with abstract ideas), what they can understand, what they want and how they behave. The physical aspects of puberty are discussed in a later chapter on health, though tweenies' growing gender awareness is addressed as a key aspect of identity, below.

NURTURING SELF-ESTEEM AND IDENTITY
The tweenie years present a crucial time in which we can help to reinforce and set a positive self-image for our child. Before

the age of eight, the sense of self is growing and developing, aided and substantially influenced by parents and the immediate family. From eight until twelve or thirteen, a child's self-esteem typically flowers, a measure of his new confidence and separating identity. Children then look increasingly to people and friends outside the family to check themselves out and refine the assessment they have made based on their family's feedback. They say, in effect, 'This is me; I have this to offer. I think I am like you in this way or that way; do you agree and do you like me?' They need to know if they are likeable. An affirmative response will boost their self-esteem, which will help them to be open and outgoing.

Tweenies will check out their identity with their peers whether their self-assessment is positive or negative. A tweenie who has learned to see himself as 'trouble' or 'a bit of a clown', for example, will seek a fellow troublesome spirit to bond with as surely as someone who defines himself by more positive traits will look for confirmation from similar types. Any negative reactions from the self-selected friendship group – whether the friends are wayward or more conformist – can be especially hurtful and cause a confidence collapse, whereas continued loyalty and support will help them to fly. It may appear that they need friends more and us less, but our role remains important. It is vital that we stand close by and stay involved, not only to strengthen our tweenie's self-belief and self-esteem if these become undermined by hostile 'friends' or specific events, but also to help him develop a more positive and robust identity rooted in a variety of skills, clearly appreciated personal attributes, the experience of independence and a prevailing certainty that we notice and care. On both sides of the Atlantic, come the age of fourteen, girls in particular suffer a dramatic drop in their self-esteem and an increase in self-doubt. But if we make the most of the pre-teen years, enabling our tweenie to enter adolescence with clear identity and a strong sense of self, he is more likely to withstand the ravages of teenage angst or the pull of the peer group.

What is 'self-esteem'?

The term 'self-esteem' is now so widely used that it might seem to need no explanation. In fact, it is so widely used that it is sometimes misused, which is why there are doubters who think the concept is ridiculous and flawed. Most people understand that if someone has high, or positive, self-esteem it means they feel good about themselves. This is correct, but it means a great deal more than this. If it were only this, it could, indeed, mean that a parent's job would be to indulge their child at every moment with goodies and an easy life to ensure uninterrupted happiness; but that way would lead to disaster. Over-indulged children can find it hard to cope with setbacks, may become friendless because they're used to getting their way and can become over-reliant on possessions as status symbols.

'Self-esteem' is often used as a convenient catch-all word. However, for our purposes it helps to understand the separate strands that, when combined, will encourage our tweenie to develop that crucial overall positive sense of self.

Our tweenie will feel good about himself when he:

- Feels we value him as a person, trust him and take account of his interests.
- Can see that he possesses a range of skills that help him to be capable and successful.
- Knows he is special to us because we think about him often, and regularly notice and appreciate his efforts and achievements.
- Feels up to the challenge when faced with a simple or more demanding task to fulfil.
- Feels comfortable and confident with family and friends.

- Has faith in his general ability to achieve things and carry things through.
- Feels worthwhile because we have demonstrated to his satisfaction that he is worthy of our care and attention.
- Is clear about who he is; what he likes and doesn't like, what he is good at and what things are simply 'not for him' so he does not have to pretend.

Self-esteem, then, is related to such notions as self-worth, self-confidence, self-belief, self-respect, self-awareness, self-image, self-efficacy and self-reliance. It is important because research tells us that children with positive self-esteem are more likely to do well in school and to have a wide range of interests, less likely to become teenage parents, less likely to become depressed, develop an eating disorder or self-harm and more likely to be able to make and keep friends and establish close emotional bonds as adults. We even know that they tend to earn more and experience less unemployment in their working life. It is certainly worth making the effort to nurture and preserve our tweenie's self-esteem.

The ups and downs of self-esteem
Self-esteem is a bit like a helter-skelter. Someone who stands at the top feeling fine but gets pushed unexpectedly from behind can slide down fast. It is hard to grab a hold and stop in full flight, especially if they were unprepared and it was a big shove. They can attempt to scramble up again but it takes longer and is better achieved step-by-step, using the stairs on the inside. Superficial adjustments still leave them prone to slip again as they try to pull themselves back up against the powerful gravitational force of self-doubt. The more times someone slides, the shinier their seat becomes so the faster they fall each time.

This image shows that none of us is locked into high or low self-esteem for life. Our feelings about ourselves can get topped up or drawn down. And if adults are fragile at times, which we certainly are, pre-teen children will be more so: they have less experience to help them realise things will improve and fewer friends or favourite activities that can bolster self-belief; if one thing goes wrong, their whole self can appear to collapse. There are a number of types of situations that typically challenge self-belief and rock confidence. These include bullying, illness or death in the family, losing a close friend or changing school. How best to help our child deal with these situations is covered in later chapters. In fact, any change that involves new situations and new expectations will present as a challenge; and we have seen that tweenies are living through many changes and are therefore likely to feel wobbly quite often. We can act to preserve our child's positive feelings about himself if we offer extra love and support during times of particular upheaval.

Information points: What makes children feel good about themselves?

Girls say they feel good about themselves when parents and friends:

- Are supportive.
- Treat them as equals and responsible.
- Give reassurance and hugs.
- Praise them.
- Say something positive.
- Listen to them.
- Notice helpful deeds or when something has been done well.

They don't like it when parents:

- Don't say well done.

- Are sarcastic and critical.
- Compare them unfavourably with friends or siblings.

And girls can also feel down when they:

- Believe they do not look as good as they want to.
- Feel they have no special talents.

Boys say they feel good about themselves when:

- People give them positive recognition for things they are good at.
- Adults appreciate when they have tried hard.
- Mates want to spend time with them and they all do things they enjoy.
- Friends respect their privacy and don't go talking to others about personal things.
- They feel accepted and recognised for who they are.
- They know and feel it is all right to be different and that different is normal.
- They sense they're good at relationships.
- They have someone to talk to who will listen, understand and not judge.

They don't like it when parents:

- Put pressure on them.
- Don't say well done.
- Tease and belittle them.

And boys can also feel down when they:

- Are laughed at and teased by peers and other adults.
- Feel isolated and alone.

> – Feel locked into a gender stereotype – get blamed for
> everything that goes wrong or are judged against fixed
> expectations, e.g. 'Your handwriting's neat for a boy!'

Young children sense whether the people around them are friendly or hostile, approving or disapproving, accepting or rejecting, responsive or neglectful. These impressions are absorbed and generate feelings of pride and contentment, or shame and confusion. Parents, key carers and other family members will have most influence early on, but by the age of eight the influence of others grows. Clumsy, hostile or rejecting schools, teachers and friends can and do rock the most stable of children. We are not responsible for everything our child feels, though it is our job to pick up the pieces and support our child should he feel undermined. The best news is that an uncertain tweenie, destabilised following one or even several difficult experiences, can recover and regain his true spirit, with our help.

Taster tips on raising, maintaining and regenerating a tweenie's self-esteem

✓ Strengthen their sense of self by listening to their views and offering choices to help them determine their own mind.

✓ Acknowledge what they're good at through giving plenty of honest praise and appreciation. Let them impress you.

✓ Sharpen their personal identity by accepting any gender-specific or cross-gender interests.

✓ Allow them to work to their strengths – and to follow self-chosen activities and skills, but love them for who they are, not for what they can do.

> ✓ Give them plenty of time and attention: if we don't show we value them, how can they value themselves?
> ✓ Reinforce their sense of belonging and connection by demonstrating care, sharing activities and talking together.
> ✓ Provide a physically and emotionally safe environment that offers a measure of routine and predictability.
> ✓ Meet their need for unconditional approval: keep criticism to a minimum.
> ✓ Top up their self-respect, constantly, by trusting that they can manage greater autonomy.

What is identity?

There is an important difference between self-esteem and identity. Self-esteem involves judgement and evaluation. We look at ourselves and decide whether we like and value what we see. Our evaluation will be either positive or negative, leading to either high, or low, self-esteem, or somewhere in-between. Identity, on the other hand, does not involve judgement; it is descriptive. It relates to someone's sense of who he is, how he would describe himself (I am like this, I belong to this family, I can do this, I can't do that). Before any of us can assess how much we value or esteem ourselves, we have to know who we are – what it is we are measuring. A clear sense of identity is, then, a prerequisite for self-esteem. And if a clear sense of identity has to come first, it makes it more important than self-esteem. Our self-descriptions tend to be based on a combination of self-knowledge (I like football, I don't like the colour red, I am shy) and the attachment of labels (I belong to this group, that religion, I have this number of brothers, my name is, and so on). Value doesn't come into it. Of course, self-esteem and identity are related in practice, because if our self-concept is based more on 'can-do' rather than 'can't-do' descriptions, we are more likely to evaluate ourselves positively. And if we are a member of a religion, or a racial or cultural group that experiences hostility and discrimination, that particular label may, from time to time, have negative consequences for our self-esteem. In general, a clear self-concept helps a tweenie say, 'I know who I am'. It roots him and therefore has a stabilising effect, making him less susceptible to peer and other pressures.

That's not the only advantage. A clear sense of identity will help our tweenie to make decisions and choices and to have a sense of agency. Knowing who he is helps him to define his preferences and what it is he wants to and can achieve. He can be more realistic, self-directed and independent. It therefore contributes to the development of maturity and responsibility – and success, because children with accurate self-knowledge tend neither to overshoot nor to undershoot. When children are encouraged to offer views and opinions, or become members of different clubs and groups, it creates additional strands of identity and deepens self-knowledge. On the other hand, when children feel neglected and isolated they experience themselves as a non-person: if nobody takes any notice, they may question if they exist; and if you don't know who you are, you cannot know who you can become. Neglect, therefore, threatens identity and motivation as well as self-worth. Parents therefore can and do influence the nature and range of descriptions that help to create identity. Children experience, define and redefine themselves throughout their childhood, especially at key developmental moments. It is important that we help our tweenie to maintain a clear sense of who he is and where he belongs as he makes his transitions.

Taster tips on creating a strong sense of identity

✓ Tell stories about the family: when we were a child and when they were babies, about aunts, uncles for example, to connect them to a common, family past.

✓ Offer appropriate choices so they can identify their likes and dislikes and increase their self-knowledge.

✓ Describe what it is we like and admire about them and what they are good at; avoid blanket terms such as 'good', or 'lovely'.

✓ Fully support their school or teacher: split loyalties can undermine the benefits of 'belonging' to other groups or institutions.

✓ Keep promises to prove our respect and help them to feel important to us.

The role of gender in identity

Although children begin to accept and understand that they are a girl or boy from roughly the age of two, they do not experience those of the other gender as radically different and they play together happily. This peaceful coexistence does not last for long, however. Around the age of eight, boys and girls become sufficiently aware of their differences that children regroup. Each gender may begin to see the other as a near alien, and often a distinctly inferior one at that. Girls generally look down on boys as being immature, rowdy and aggressive, and boys sneer (in public anyway) at girls for being wimps and goody-goodies, only interested in gossip. The last thing most of them want is to have anything to do with each other. As they become more self-conscious about who they are, gender awareness becomes a more significant part of how each sex sees themselves. They may still play with selected individuals from the other camp, but these friends tend to be hand picked. Lucy, aged nine, said, 'I have a friend who's a boy. He's mister brainy. He's not like the other boys, not showy offy. Other boys think, You're a girl – why should I play with you? He thinks about you as a friend, not a girl friend. He does play some fighting games but he doesn't like hurting people like the other boys.' Freddie, aged ten, said, 'I play out with girls in my village and in school but mostly only with those who like to play football.' Paris, aged twelve, said he was also happy to join in any mixed ball game back home after school and often played tennis with girls. The trend for boys and girls to gravitate to same-sex groups for work and play, and for their activities increasingly to conform to gender stereotype, consciously or unconsciously, has been observed worldwide.

It seems, then, that the tweenie years are used to explore and crystallise gender identity. Certainly, watching girls and boys in their separate gender groups highlights the extent to which they can have very different approaches to work and play. It is almost as though, until boys and girls are clear and confident about their different gender-related roles, they feel uncomfortably similar. As with magnets that present like poles, many seem unsettled in each other's force field, so keep their distance. Later, of course, they present as magnetic opposites, and begin to attract as powerfully as they were previously repelled – aided, of course, by irresistible hormones!

'In-between' boys also have different experiences from girls at home, and at about eight will undergo another major shift. Until the age of seven or eight boys generally enjoy being emotionally close to their mother as well as their father. As with their sisters, their prime need is for love, trust, warmth, respect, kindness, togetherness, enjoyment and security – universal human needs that ignore gender and even age. At eight, boys around the world have been noticed to switch their focus to their father or other male role model, presumably to help them develop further the male aspect of themselves. Robin Skynner, the author and psychologist, wrote of boys 'crossing the bridge' at this time, seeking greater independence from mothers to join and identify more closely with the impressive men in their lives. Ten- to twelve-year-old boys may not experience the same degree of hormonal upheaval as girls, given their later onset of puberty, but their 'identity crisis' could be greater than girls', especially if there is not an available father or father figure close by on whom to model themselves as they make the transition to greater independence and towards adulthood.

AUTONOMY AND INDEPENDENCE

Tweenies need growing opportunities to manage themselves in limited and appropriate ways because these will help them to feel more capable, more trustworthy and more grown-up. Their thirst for autonomy makes them want to make more decisions; in effect they say, 'This is me, I know who I am, I now know better what I want so please let me choose and decide. How can you know me better than I know myself?' Very young children are clearly unstoppable in their desire to feed themselves, do their own buttons, wash their face and, of course, walk. Tweenies will feel no less intensely about equivalent advances in their march to maturity.

Autonomy is different from freedom or liberty. In fact, too much of either freedom or liberty may be counter-productive. If our pre-teen child is given too much responsibility for managing himself and is put in situations he is neither ready for nor comfortable with, far from increasing his confidence and sense of independence, he could either feel abandoned and neglected or question his ability to cope and become more fearful of the unknown, not less, even though he may pretend otherwise.

We can more easily identify the safe way to give our tweenie the psychological and practical space desired if we understand what these various terms mean. Liberty is the right, or power, to do as one pleases, or living without the constraint of laws or, more relevant to children, boundaries. But eight-year-olds, and twelve-year-olds too, clearly still need rules and boundaries, and need to learn to think about other people's needs and wishes and not be entirely selfish. Perhaps more important, inside or outside the home, no tweenie can have the experience or maturity to anticipate or deal safely with any unexpected problem that unfettered liberty might present. Freedom relates to the power of self-determination, the right to do something. It refers, then, to 'doing', rather than to the state of being totally free to do. Tweenies, the same as other children, need freedom within boundaries; they should not yet be offered unrestricted freedom. But we should understand they are likely to be pushing for fewer restrictions, and we should be ready either to hold the line or to redraw the boundaries according to the particular issue at stake.

There is, we should note, an important difference between 'freedom from' and 'freedom to'. Tweenies must have the right to be totally free *from* physical, sexual and emotional abuse and assaults. They do not have an automatic right, however, to be free *to do* anything without our involvement as judge and gatekeeper of what is, at any one time, appropriate.

Getting the balance right between the two

The notion of autonomy becomes useful and important when thinking about achieving a good balance. Autonomy refers to freedom of the will: being in charge of yourself, being able to influence and determine the things that happen to you. So for parents, giving children more autonomy involves treating children as a source of authority about themselves, allowing them to express a preference, involving them in decisions that affect them, and leaving it to them to decide exactly how they do the things that they have to do, provided, of course, that the tasks get done. This is very different from giving them open-ended freedom.

So what should we let tweenies do more of? It is hard to give unqualified directions about this. So much depends on whether our tweenie is eight, ten or twelve, whether he generally takes sensible decisions or likes to challenge, perhaps to a point where health and safety are at risk, whether there are relevant cost implications, and so on. If we're not sure, we should start with small things and work up to the more important decisions as we assess how our tweenie responds and copes. However, decisions such as how hungry they are, how cold they feel, where they do their homework, how many after-school clubs and activities they attend, who they choose as friends, what colour sweater to have, should normally be theirs. We can put decisions, tasks and activities into three categories: those that are entirely their business; those they should have some control over; and those that are for us to decide, in general after consulting them.

Tuning in to tweenies

'When my mum and me go out shopping, she always picks clothes she wants me to wear. She goes on and on about it, so I don't have the heart to tell her I like something else.' Sandy, ten

'Here at this school it's fun, and they let you think things over, not just do what they tell you to do. We can choose what order to do things in.' Harry, nine

'If I'd been told all this information about alcohol, I'd have taken no notice, but because I've found it out and done it myself it's been really good.' Paul, eleven

'I'm getting so fed up with them forgetting to give me any pocket money, I sometimes think I'll just steal it from them.' Lucy, nine

---

Paul was clear that doing the research himself, looking at leaflets, books and the Internet, had made him sit up and take notice. And he felt good about what he had achieved. Having autonomy helps children to feel competent. Doing everything for children can sap their confidence and give them little opportunity to grow.

How autonomy links with identity and self-esteem

Autonomy presupposes a sense of self and clear identity as well as the opportunity to decide things: if you don't know who you are or what you like, you can't know what to do when put in charge. It can seem as if the person within has gone missing. As children decide more things, their confidence in their ideas and their ability to act decisively grows, which gives them a stronger sense of agency as well as deeper self-knowledge. It is a virtuous circle. Autonomy is, then, central to developing a child's identity and positive self-esteem.

But autonomy goes further than this. Having a say in what happens helps us to feel alive: a significant, involved human being. It contributes to self-respect and staves off disappointment and depression that often result from neglect and inactivity. As Vijay, ten, complained, 'I hate it when adults ignore me. It makes me feel like an ant.' Without that sense of being through doing, children can feel like they're nothing.

The importance of autonomy for future success

Researchers at the London School of Economics looked at the results of interviews of a group of adults now in their late twenties undertaken when they were aged ten, to see what contributes to career success and high pay. They found that those earning most were notable at the age of ten for having not only higher self-esteem but also a stronger 'sense of agency' – feeling that they can control and influence events. Academic qualifications were important but, other things being equal, not as important as these psychological factors. As children, the successful adults had good friendships, supportive and non-critical parents, felt they were in control of themselves and believed they could sort out problems.

Drawing this together

Tweenies' attitudes and outlook are coloured by several key developmental milestones reached around the age of eight: their growing sense of self as they begin to separate from parents and explore the characteristics they associate with their gender; the onset and progress of puberty; parallel changes in cognitive thinking; a much greater focus on friends as an alternative source of fun and identity; and an increasing desire for autonomy – chances to explore and express their likes and dislikes and to demonstrate their burgeoning confidence. These changes combine to create the underlying fresh self-assurance and optimism that has characterised tweenies hitherto. Now, though, there is a real possibility that the pressures and contradictions they confront will hamper the natural growth of hope and openness. In the light of these pressures, our responsibility is to reinforce our child's self-belief and self-esteem wherever possible, and to convince each one they have an important place in our lives.

Ten top take-out tips

- Help to preserve their self-respect: don't put them down or let them down.
- Help them reach their full potential: catch them doing something right.
- Children don't generally resist change, they resist being

changed so involve them as much as possible and problem-solve together.

- We often bring about that which we fear. Let them be who they are, and trust them.
- Possessions and clothes are part of them and should be respected. Don't throw anything out or pass anything on without asking first – even if it hasn't been touched or worn for ages.
- Cut down on blame and criticism, which makes children feel they can never succeed.
- Children need to be noticed, enjoyed and appreciated. Give plenty of praise: appreciate what they do and love them for who they are.
- Let them be a source of authority on themselves – who they want to play with, how they want to spend their time, how hungry or cold they are, how they best approach their home-work.
- In order to feel significant, tweenies should be seen and heard.
- Be aware of the pressures tweenies face, and take the pressure off whenever possible.

And Remember!

Don't hold them back, but don't let them rush through a key stage of childhood.

When we demand too much, we add to their pressures.

Autonomy is different from freedom: it is about choosing how to live and being able to make a difference.

2
CREATING A LOVING BASE:
Balancing Attention and Autonomy

HOME REMAINS HUGELY IMPORTANT TO tweenies, despite their growing focus on friends and their need to grow wings. Home is, of course, both the physical building in which a child lives and the web of close and important family relationships associated with it. Home needs to be the safe, tethering point from which our tweenie will venture forth and explore her personal potential and wider freedoms. The more stable, caring and dependable the home base, the more measured and sensible will be the first forays into freedom. And the more secure and confident a tweenie is, the more she is likely to take advantage of opportunities to explore a range of possible talents and pleasures.

One of the challenges that face parents of tweenies is getting the balance somewhere near right between apparently contradictory needs. For example, a tweenie's desire to be different, to strike out more on her own, to check out and develop her identity and gain confidence in herself, has to be balanced against the continuing need to feel secure and connected, contained as part of the family. In a similar way, tweenies may want to claim more rights, freedoms and space as a badge of maturity, but they also need to learn more about their capacity for deeper dependability through a matched increase in responsibilities in the home. And family conversation, gossip, debate, fun, attention and enquiry should never be sacrificed on the altar of growing independence: tweenies need all of these. In summary, we need to stay close while letting go, to loosen the reins gently yet ensure the communication still flows. This objective should guide us as we negotiate and renegotiate the rules and boundaries over such domestic essentials as bed and wake-up times, personal care and tidiness, mealtimes, family outings, and, most important, rights and responsibilities. This chapter also looks at how having at least one tweenie in the family can change the nature of sibling rivalry and may also lead us to reassess our childcare needs. Home, of course, can present potential dangers to children as well as succour. This chapter also considers how to calculate these afresh to make home safe as older tweenies begin to spend small amounts of time unsupervised, home alone.

Family time

Families and relationships with children never stand still. They grow and change as the children grow and as we change our commitments, ideas and circumstances. Our tweenie will want to be treated differently and to have more time to herself over the In-between years because 'I'm not a little kid any more'. Rather than make ad hoc changes to family organisation and routines under pressure, or simply refuse to budge, it is better to think ahead to focus on the principles that should guide the negotiation and compromise. It is not possible to address every domestic issue here, but a review of a few should illustrate that rules and routines need to be adjusted carefully to ensure there remains plenty of time for the family to do things and be together at the same time as enabling our tweenie to have more space and time to herself.

ATTENTION, TIME AND QUALITY TIME

All children need to be noticed. They visibly flourish when they have our attention and wilt when they feel ignored. When a child makes the move from infant to junior school, we often judge it to be a good moment to start or take on more work. After all, our seven- or eight-year-old appears to need us less. But if we take this step, it puts pressure on us to make something more of the time we have together at home. We place our faith in 'quality time' – the expectation that we do something special, if possible one-to-one, with each of our children that can compensate for being around less. Quality time is thought to be fun time, action-packed time, a period of fairly intense, personalised talking and doing. That may be appropriate for younger children, but by the time they reach eight, and certainly by twelve, they have their own pace and plans and may not be as willing to dance to our tune. They may prefer us to be around but seen rather than heard, though tweenies still value family time.

Researchers at Cardiff University asked nearly 500 eleven- and twelve-year-olds about family time. Close to three-quarters of them agreed that they enjoyed spending time with their family – girls slightly more than boys. They said they enjoyed this more than the time they spent with friends or on their own.

Information points: 'Quality' time is . . .

These eleven- and twelve-year-olds valued the following qualities of time spent at home:

- Family time as ordinariness and routine.
- Family time as someone being around and there for them.
- Having a say over one's time.

- Having time that is peaceful and quiet.
- Having a chance to plan one's own time.

Features associated with typical adult ideas of 'quality time' were not significant. Children were not asking for more outings, games or shopping trips arranged by parents, or more 'special time' for intimate conversation or active togetherness. What home and family was valued for most, in contrast to both school and time with friends, was rest and relaxation – having unpressured time in which *they* controlled what they did. At school, they felt dictated to, and time with friends was seen as busy. Home was the place for repose. 'Ordinariness' and 'routine' help to build a sense of security; 'having someone around for you' contributes to their sense of significance; the freedom to plan and use that time adds to their sense of self; and the family and surroundings deepen their sense of belonging. Action-packed, adult-led 'quality time' will be less effective at meeting any of these objectives.

Some nine-year-olds were asked on television recently what made them happy. The majority mentioned very simple things, such as cuddles, family walks, when a parent is proud of them and says well done, playing family games together. None of them mentioned presents or possessions. They were happier with 'doing' than with 'having'. This suggests that any tendency to assuage our guilt by buying things is not really appreciated. Presents are no substitute for our presence. So if we have time at home with our tweenie, it can be more important to use it to keep things ordinary and familiar and to do simple, fun things there than to inject special excitement, especially if this happens erratically. To create tweenie-sensitive quality time, we should:

• Allow them the choice of whether they do something special with us or not.

- If they agree, they should be invited to select the activity.
- If they would prefer to flop about at home playing on the computer, we might offer to learn about the currently favoured game, or provide a special lunch to demonstrate our commitment to them in an alternative way.
- We can also invite them to chat to us while we get tea ready, use bath time as a time to catch up (provided they feel comfortable with this), or do any paperwork jobs close by as they watch TV.

FAMILY FUN AND OUTINGS

But we can't always let them flop around at home 'doing their own thing'. They're part of the family, too, and we have just seen that they enjoy family fun and the occasional outing that help children to feel they belong. They may moan and groan, but these outings often become embedded in family legend – rain-drenched rows and all. Especially during the later tweenie years, our child may begin to resent being dragooned to join these jolly jaunts. It is part of daring to be different: she may state she hates walking, she hates picnics, is fed up with museums, or even theme parks. The local 'visitor attraction' will have been visited to death; and we hear the place she would *really* like to visit is the extreme adventure park the other end of the country. What do we do? We can't leave her at home; none the less, the thought of having a reluctant tourist ruining the day for everyone – dragging her feet, picking on her siblings, finding fault in the boring sandwiches, slagging off history – is not an attractive prospect. How do we balance her desire to be left behind with our wish or need for her to join in?

One tactic is to discuss possible options and preferred choices for outings some time ahead. It might then be possible to agree a compromise such that every other outing or every one in three, depending on any other person's right to choose, is her choice. The reluctant tourist could go to a friend's house occasionally rather than trek with the rest – but not too often. It is also important for our tweenie to realise that sometimes what we expect to be boring can be great fun so she should not 'trash' every option without thought. But another effective tactic is to suggest our tweenie takes responsibility for organising and managing the timings and finances of the day. Instead of merely tagging along, she becomes the key player. A trip out will then be a challenge and encourage responsibility, not be a 'drag' or a 'pain'. A follow-up challenge could be to plan an outing that, apart from any transport, costs nothing. Tweenies are certainly old enough to learn to judge the value of money and discover that fun can be had without it.

Taster tips for turning tweenies into project managers for family outings

We can suggest that our tweenie:

✓ Uses the telephone or goes on the web to find out opening times and costs.

✓ Takes charge of the budget and decides whether there are other places nearby that can be visited at the same time at reasonable cost.

✓ Decides what sort of lunch could be afforded within the budget, and if money is saved eating sandwiches, suggests how to spend what's left over.

✓ Produces a schedule for the day – covering the journey time to the destination, how long it will take to view it or do it, how much time to give to lunch.

✓ Plans the route there and back by consulting maps, timetables etc.

MEALTIMES

Mealtimes are a microcosm of family life – sometimes functional, sometimes great fun, sometimes spiky and difficult. Like trips and outings, they pull the family together but can be a source of endless arguments. How can we help to ensure that eating together is a congenial experience? Lots of families get in a tangle over table manners, and this is looked at in chapter four. Striving to ensure our children eat healthily can be another bone of contention, considered in the chapter on health. Here, we look at why it is important for tweenies that we retain mealtimes as family time.

As children grow older, who eats what, where and when become bigger issues. The more they become used to having choices and independence, the harder it can be to persuade them that sharing the same food, eating together as a family in one place and the one time, and preferably somewhere quiet so people can actually talk to each other and be heard, is a good idea. Tweenies may well prefer to eat what momentarily takes their fancy, to finish their homework while they're in the mood or to watch a television programme rather than sit at the collective meal. Perhaps some will want to eat when they get in from school and not later when everyone else has returned; and others may wish to reject aspects of their cultural and religious food-related customs. Should we be flexible and concede, or hold firm to the routines? Is it not easier, given microwaves, fast foods and heavy commitments all round, to cut down on the arguments and let everyone do their own thing? Whatever arrangement would seem to work best for our family, we should bear in mind an important objective: to have regular times when the whole family can share their experiences and views. A daily family meal is not always possible; but as eating together helps to maintain family bonds, the event should not be dropped entirely. Established mealtimes will also create a structure for the day and make everyone feel well looked after.

TWEENIES AND SIBLINGS: PEACE RULES, KO!

When two sisters aged ten and twelve were asked what they fought over, the answer was, 'Everything, really.' They cited using the phone, what time to turn the light off at night (they shared a bedroom), what music to have on. They agreed that the squabbles seemed endless because each one tried to get her own back after the previous 'defeat', 'So it seems like she hasn't won', said one of them. In other words, their arguments were about getting even, about pecking orders, about power and self-respect. More generally, possessions get fought over, too. 'How come my socks are in your drawer? Thief!' 'But it's *mine*. I said you weren't to use my X box when you have friends over.' And space is another key battleground as siblings enter the In-between years. '*I* was sitting in that chair first – get out of it now!' or, 'It's *my* turn to have the early bathroom slot / the front seat in the car, this week. Why are *you* in there?'

Whereas early sibling rivalry stems largely from competition for a parent's attention, with raw jealousy fuelling the fury, the prime concerns for tweenies seem to be space, possessions, fair treatment (including equal spending on main presents and occasional gifts) and friends. Chloe, eleven, was worried that 'my friends are going to like my older sister more than me'. Pre-teen boys may belittle sisters as they try to dominate family space, and both brothers and sisters can come to blows as they assert physical superiority or explode with frustration or fury. Jealousy may remain underneath, but tweenies' instinctive response is to protect their identity, influence, ownership and self-respect in any battles over territory and possessions so they feel 'in charge' and capable, not exploited or put upon.

The positive aspect of sibling jousting in the pre-teen years is that we can afford to, and should, try to stand back to let them solve the problem. When we intervene, we imply that they cannot be trusted to do so and our imposed solutions often miss the point. Sibling spats are normal, healthy and teach some important lessons:

- Through hating someone safely, children learn what they love and value and what is enduring. (As a brother and sister agreed enthusiastically after a tetchy conversation, 'Oh, we love each other; we just don't *like* each other!')
- Through the experience of active disagreement, and being left to find their own solution, they can learn how to compromise and manage conflict.
- Through regular comparison with their nearest (and mostly dearest), children learn what makes them unique and eventually to tolerate and value other people's quirks.

We cannot demand that our children be friends, either as children or as adults, though it's great when this happens. If we accept that it is for each of them to evolve an independent relationship with a brother or sister that works for them, the pressure is off us to create eternal happiness.

Taster tips on peace rules and learning to compromise

✓ Ask if they want to be left to sort it themselves or if they need you.

✓ Ask how important the issue is to both of them. Sometimes, they get worked up over nothing by accident and find it hard to call a halt.

✓ Avoid jumping to conclusions and allocating blame. If we try to find out whose 'fault' it was, we so often get it wrong. Apparent favouritism causes resentment and can fuel fights.

✓ If you have to get involved, mediate rather than adjudicate: don't pronounce on the rights or wrongs, but

---

encourage each to identify their preferred solution then explore the scope for compromise so each gets some of what was wanted.

✓ Explain that it should not be necessary to 'win' each skirmish.

✓ Encourage sharing, for example of favourite breakfast cereals; split the contents of each box rather than buy multiples.

✓ But sharing isn't always the answer, if the issue is territorial or about belongings. Tweenies will need their rights and wishes respected.

✓ Encourage them to use 'I' statements, not 'You' statements. To say, 'I felt this, I wanted that, I thought that he . . .' will avoid either child feeling attacked and prolonging the argument with aggressive defences.

✓ Suggest the 'white rabbits' tactic, whereby either child uses an agreed phrase, for example 'white rabbits', to call a halt without losing face when an argument escalates. When this phrase is used, the row's over and further verbal swipes forbidden.

✓ If children become too angry for sensible discussion, suggest they take a break and return to the issue later (and it might just blow over).

✓ Make it clear that it is fine to feel insulted, anxious, jealous, aggrieved but it's not fine to use hurtful language or to hit out physically. All children have rights not to be abused or assaulted by siblings as well as parents.

✓ If one child damages another's toy or book on purpose, ask the offender to propose three ways to make up for it; for example: give the following week's pocket money; take all their turns in the car's front seat for seven days; or do their household or pet chores for an agreed time.

> ✓ Have clear guidelines and review them regularly so
> they remain fresh; for example; 'possessions are never
> used or borrowed without the owner's agreement'; 'the
> TV remote control is in his care Tuesdays and
> Thursdays'.

Rights, possessions and territory can become fiercely
defended in reformed families, as considered in chapter ten.
However, if we try to create a coherent family identity yet respect
each child's space and autonomy, the inevitable rivalries should
be more easily contained. This is the issue that we turn to next.

Finding space: Increasing autonomy in the home

Tweenies' growing desire for autonomy cannot be completely
satisfied outside the home, for children of this age generally
don't, and indeed should not, spend that amount of time away
from their families. Home is the best, and certainly the safest,
place in which to extend tweenies' sense of themselves by putting
them increasingly in charge of selected aspects of their lives and
giving them a greater say in what happens there. After all, it is
their home too.

Here, we flag up only a few issues typical of family life that
reflect tweenies' greater desire for autonomy. We look at enabling
tweenies to have more personal space at home, particularly in
relation to bedrooms (and whether we should insist these remain
tidy), without encouraging them to cut off. We also look at passing over responsibility for personal care and at the need to balance
growing domestic rights with equivalent domestic responsibilities.

CREATING PERSONAL SPACE – A ROOM TO ONESELF

In this increasingly possession-conscious world, one commod-
ity that tweenies come to value very highly is something that,

in an immediate sense, comes free. It is space, and particularly private space that they can feel they 'own' and on to which they can stamp their identity. Typically, bedrooms become tweenies' preferred private territory. Where one has hitherto shared, around the age of eight the fun side of giggling in the dark or the comfort of company in the early morning may become less appealing.

During the five years that comprise the In-between years, children change radically and demand very different things from their personal space. Eight- to ten-year-olds will increasingly want space that's theirs: somewhere to take their friends, to store their personal possessions without the risk of younger siblings messing them up, and on which to stamp their personal taste and identity, so they may want to dump the cartoon character duvet covers and the cuddly bear wallpaper. In the later tweenie years, the demand is increasingly for privacy from siblings and particularly parents, brought on both by the physical changes that accompany puberty and the emotional developments of later childhood. Around ten to twelve, it is common for children to feel they don't want to share everything with parents; they will experience swings of emotion and unexpected feelings – towards friends, family, themselves, their life, their future – that make them feel uncertain and vulnerable. They need time on their own and time to sleep in while they make sense of all this, time sometimes spent actively thinking, but sometimes fiddling fairly mindlessly while their brain churns things over probably without them realising it is happening.

So now is the time to respond to any plea to go it alone in sleeping terms if it is raised and if, of course, there is a suitable spare room at home. It would be sensible, though, not to push the suggestion if they have not thought of it; children generally know what changes they are ready for and when. There are a few points to consider.

- New decors and new desks or other furniture can be expensive. If money is scarce, the bedroom improvements should be phased in – included as birthday or other special presents with the child saying which they'd like first.
- If sharing is unavoidable, apart from changing the bed cover, we might provide new shelves for sole personal use or offer exclusive use of a drawer or shelf in a room downstairs. If there is a garden, children of this age love to have their own little flower or veggie patch to tend and water.
- As computers become cheaper, games become more compelling and music systems more compact, more tweenies are asking for the ultimate multi-media bedroom. Though such a room might make homework more attractive, if bedrooms become an Aladdin's cave of distraction there is a real danger that children won't emerge, preventing the sharing, compromise, family play and conversation advocated earlier. Gradually and surreptitiously, the seclusion could make our tweenie feel isolated from us, even though this could be vehemently denied.
- A tucked-away child will feel far more spied upon if we feel the urge to find out whether homework has been started and need to check with questions. Better, then, to have them where you can see what they are doing and can talk to them about trivial or important things when they occur to you; and they can do the same.
- Around the age of puberty, many children ask for a lock on their bedroom (or the bathroom) door. First, address the possible reason – irritating younger siblings barging in, finding our presence intrusive, embarrassment over their physical changes or fear that private writings may be discovered – and deal with it: commit to impose strict entry rules on any siblings, always to knock before entering, and never to open drawers or to read their diary. If a lock is eventually fixed, for health and security reasons it should be one that can be opened from either side and not be an internal bolt. It might be sensible to agree

a special emergency knock that would indicate that the door must be opened immediately.

In summary, then, it is not appropriate for any eight-year-old to be encouraged to lead a separate life in a home-entertainment-style bedroom and probably neither for a twelve-year-old who will be coping with her new school and could be suffering without us realising it. While tweenies certainly need some *personal* space to assert their identity and gain peace and privacy, they should not have so much private space or private time that they become isolated and lose their sense of belonging. Isolation among pre-teens can encourage selfishness, a distorted view of themselves and their problems and very rusty relationship skills.

Messy bedrooms

The last word, or perhaps the first word and certainly the most heated word, on bedrooms must relate to tidiness. There can be few discussions between parents of tweenie-aged children that do not home in on this hot topic. It is a source of frequent and intense anguish to parents who fear the mess on the floor reflects a mess in the mind, which predicts a future strewn with failure. This is, of course, as much rubbish as may festoon the bedroom itself. Tension over bedroom bombsites should be kept in proportion and should certainly never be allowed to destroy a relationship or be the cause of putting a tweenie down. Phrases such as, 'It makes me feel dirty just to look at it!' will appear hugely offensive, as we appear to say they are dirty and disgusting to us by association. The issue is their room, not who they are. And we have to choose our battles carefully. If we fight on too many fronts at once we are likely to lose all of them. If the state of the bedroom is our biggest bugbear, we should drop some of the other gripes and select some more subtle or focused ways to get change. Danny, twelve, for example, began to put his dirty washing in the laundry basket only after he had chosen to buy three stylish pairs of underpants rather than five cheap ones. Conveniently, his laundry requirements became far more urgent! If another problem looms far larger, drop the bedroom skirmish and accept that if it is their space, they must be allowed to slob out in it if they so wish.

However, a measure of tidiness is a useful form of time and space management. We can encourage helpful bedroom routines if we approach the issue in a positive and practical way: 'Why do you prefer to have your stuff left out and about?' (perhaps this is their little bit of rebellion to feeling over-controlled); 'What do you think creates most mess?' (clothes, magazines or snack packs); 'When does it get too bad to sort out?' (when fifteen minutes' tidying will make no difference/I can't see my chair).

Taster tips on tidy bedrooms

✓ Tidy the bedroom with your tweenie as a shared project, to be followed by a nice reward for you both at the end; and, within reason, let her choose the moment to start and the target finish time to encourage a sense of commitment.

✓ Remember rooms generally get much messier as we relocate and sort items: they don't look better until close to finishing. Remain positive when dejection and boredom set in.

✓ Focus on the practical reasons for tidying up their room – too many lost or trodden-on items, not on your need to have it looking orderly. Whose problem, in truth, is the mess?

✓ When tidying, be sensitive to the fact that the room and the belongings are personal. Ask permission before you open a drawer, merely suggest alternative storage places, and *always* check before you chuck!

Sarah's story

Sarah, aged ten, was a dutiful daughter, the oldest of three. Her mum had high standards and ran an organised household to ensure everything worked smoothly, given the pressures of three children at school and two parents working full-time. Sarah had to share a bedroom with her younger sister, and their precise territories – in the room, the car and elsewhere – were agreed and jealously guarded. The domestic tasks were fairly apportioned and monitored: Saturday morning was bedroom inspection time and no one was allowed to do anything until its state had been passed as satisfactory. As a top year junior school pupil, Sarah then went away for five days on her first residential school trip. Mum saw this as a great opportunity to sort through and tidy her drawers, places that were not subject to the regular inspection. When Sarah returned, she was livid – her only bit of privacy had been intruded upon. Her mum realised her mistake, but said nothing. Sarah then harboured a grudge and began to get more secretive. Some months later she even managed the onset of her periods on her own, not telling her mum. This was the big wake-up call. Her mum said she deeply regretted the drawer-tidying incident, ended the weekly bedroom check and agreed to let Sarah spend more time at weekends with friends as her way to gain more space and autonomy in quite a crowded home.

NEW RIGHTS, NEW RESPONSIBILITIES: PERSONAL CARE AND KEEPING FAMILY SPACE TIDY

It is sensible to aim to balance any new freedoms – for example going to the shops with a friend, playing in the park in a group, going to bed later and choosing their own clothes – with extra responsibilities. Responsibilities mitigate the tendency of growing children to become totally self-focused; encourage them not to take us or anyone else for granted; teach them to think sequentially, about what comes before and what happens after (after I grab my snack, I have to put the packet away and tidy up); and develop time-management skills as they fit in chores and commitments. Making a contribution to the family's needs helps tweenies to keep one foot firmly in the family base camp while they go out and about, and having new responsibilities will even help our tweenie to define her sense of self. As Charles Handy, the well-known writer on organisations and management, has stated, it is through responsibility that we find out about ourselves. This is the essence of sound self-esteem: self-respect develops when we know we can be relied upon and trusted, as well as knowing we can achieve things and do well.

Of course, it is for each of us to decide which tasks to allocate and at what age during these five years and after. The first set of tasks can focus on personal care and self-management. Parents are often blind to the insult they cause when they check whether a tweenie has brushed her teeth, washed her face, changed her underwear, been to the toilet before bed, got everything needed packed in the school bag, and so on. This attention can come across not as caring and supportive but as intrusive and untrusting: infantilising a child who is trying to grow up. During the tweenie years we have to learn to back off and let children manage their personal care. Failure to do so may establish a hostility towards us that could result in blank refusals to co-operate. However, rather than stop everything at once, we can do it in stages: 'You are old enough to manage this on your own; after your tenth (or eight or ninth) birthday, or when the new school term starts, I'll no longer remind you. It's down to you now.'

A range of possible jobs a tweenie can be asked to take responsibility for is presented in the box below. Having given a tweenie responsibility for her personal care, we can then extend it to include tasks that help the whole family, so our tweenie becomes a team player.

46

Some suggested jobs suitable for tweenies to take on

	TAKING RESPONSIBILITY FOR SELF	TAKING RESPONSIBILITY FOR OTHERS
Household jobs	remove used plate to kitchen	lay tables for meals
	leave shoes neatly in hall	clear everyone's plate from table
	put used clothes in wash basket	empty drier and fold clothes
	put clean clothes away	load/empty dish-washer
	close inner bag of cereal packet	help with washing/drying up
	put tops back on bottles/jars etc.	take out the rubbish
	put muddy sports kit in to soak	put shopping away
	put any instrument in case after practice	wash car
	put away homework/pens in case	help with food preparation
	pack overnight bag for sleepovers	feed/play with/wash a younger sibling
	clean teeth without reminder	help with garden-ing/decorating
	tidy bedroom drawers/floor	some general vacuum cleaning
	run own bath	cleaning the bath/shower after use

Managing pets	daily feeding, clean out cage/tray, groom or wash, daily play/exercise/walk
School-related responsibilities	do homework without reminder, pack bag the night before, pack snacks, organise sports kit, soak muddy kit, bring the right books home, pass on notes and other information brought home from school

Care when we're not there

At some point during the five pre-teen years the big issue looms. When is it wise, safe or legal to reduce our use of childcare and leave a child in the house alone, or alone with a brother, sister or friend, and for how long? What can or should we do to prepare a child for being alone, after school or while we are out, so she feels comfortable and does not become over-anxious? And what rules and drill should we put in place to protect her if something does go wrong?

HOME ALONE

In the US, it has been estimated that half of all children aged between six and thirteen spend some of the day home alone. No equivalent estimates exist for the UK, but towards the upper end of this age range most of us will have left our tweenie for a short time at least – while we pop to local shops or the post box, for example, and some tweenies will already be managing alone after school until a working mum or dad returns. Does the law tell us when it might be safe or appropriate to leave a tweenie alone in the home?

Unfortunately, it does not. The law is not clear about when it might be considered suitable because it does not state an age when children can be left alone. However, parents can be prosecuted for wilful neglect if they leave a child unsupervised 'in a manner to cause unnecessary suffering or injury to health', as stated in the Children and Young People's Act 1933. 'Wilful neglect' has to be established in each circumstance, so there are no hard and fast rules. Parents have discretion to decide if a child or young person is mature enough to cope in an emergency, and feels happy about being left. However, people under sixteen cannot be held responsible for any accidental harm that may happen while they are alone. The National Society for the Prevention of Cruelty to Children considers that: 'Most children under the age of about thirteen are not mature enough to cope with an emergency and should not be left alone for more than a very few hours.'

But we can, and probably should, begin to leave an eight-, nine- or ten-year-old for the occasional ten minutes during the day, so they become used to being on their own gradually and comfortably. We should also avoid being so obsessive about safety and danger that we plant a fear that did not initially exist, especially as the likelihood that something awful will happen is minute. My own daughter was unconcerned about being left for short periods until I began to deliver the full safety drill in preparation for slightly longer absences. It freaked her enough that she opted for quite some time to join my supermarket trips rather than stay behind. From the age of eight, there should be little need for concern if we pop to a close neighbour to return or borrow something, provided we do not stand there gossiping for half an hour without warning or notice. The next stage might be to leave them while we walk to the nearest post box, if it is a little further away and takes only a little longer, or while we walk or drive a younger sibling to their friend or class or an older one to a bus or train station. Because our absence will be only short, there is no need to take them through the domestic equivalent of a full fire drill each time. Indeed, if we over-emphasise any danger at this stage, our tweenie could focus on fear instead of enjoying the freedom and responsibility offered. When we return, we should check how they felt. A simple, 'Was that okay for you or not?' is enough to encourage a reaction; but pointedly asking if they were scared, worried or felt unsafe could sow the seeds of anxiety rather than provide useful feedback. On a following occasion we can be more pointed: 'Did you feel happy about it last time? Would anything make it any more comfortable if it was not?'

If our child is anxious and can explain why, we should try to settle her anxiety in practical ways. If she cannot, it is best to defer further experiences until she feels ready. We should never ever, of course, leave the house, even for a few minutes, without saying where we are going or indicating for how long we will be out, or stay out significantly longer than we indicated without an explanatory phone call.

HOME ALONE AFTER SCHOOL – AND SAFE

If you are really confident your tweenie is ready for the responsibility of being home alone for a short while on a more regular basis, for example after school, and could manage any likely minor emergency, here are some suggestions that will maximise her confidence, her safety and her and your comfort.

Let her know she can change her mind if she wants to: if she has any worries at all, she should speak up. She should be clear we would be willing to revert back if it's not working.

Check her readiness: to check if she is ready, make sure she can answer yes to the following 'would you know how to . . .' questions:

- Deal with an emergency situation like a fire, a skin burn, a badly cut finger, an overflowing sink or other domestic flood.
- Respect the house rules without being monitored.
- Take care of her basic needs such as snacks, drink and homework, while still following the house rules.
- Take safe care of the house key so it does not get lost or find its way to another's hands.

Make sure the home is safe: here's a checklist. Are emergency telephone numbers accessible? Do you have a functioning smoke alarm? Can visitors to the front door be seen, for example, from a downstairs window or peep-hole? Does your telephone have an answering machine or caller ID display? The message should never mention any child's name. Is there good outdoor lighting? Is your mains water stopcock accessible, to be turned off in the event of flooding? Can all the downstairs windows and doors be locked securely? Do you have a fire blanket or extinguisher readily accessible in the kitchen?

Taster tips on house rules for home alone

✓ Don't open the door to anyone, and no friends round. Later, only open the door to familiar faces and only one friend round at a time.

✓ Always check call to report safe arrival. Stay indoors at all times; no visits to the corner shop, a friend or the park.

✓ Don't answer the phone – and certainly never tell a stranger your mum's out. Just say she can't come to the phone right now.

✓ At school, keep the house key safe in a purse or a zipped pocket in a coat or school bag, not round the neck. Don't delay or fumble at the front door – have the key out ready to use on arrival.

✓ Do make clear that problems are extremely unlikely, but it's sensible to be prepared.

Whatever system or rules are put in place to ensure safety during those toe dips into being left alone, they must be agreed with anyone else involved in providing permanent or temporary care for our children: au pairs, childminders, nannies and grannies.

CHANGING THE ROLE OF MINDERS, GRANNIES AND NANNIES

An eight-year-old has a very different view of how much care she needs compared with a twelve-year-old. The first may feel she knows exactly what she wants to wear, what activities she wants to try, what her favourite colour or food is, but most of them do not feel remotely competent to manage their own lives and keep themselves safe. They still feel very childlike and are happy to defer to the authority of an adult parent figure. The same is not true four years later. Typically from about the age of ten, our tweenie is likely to start to buck against the right of the carer to tell her what to do or to cramp her style, or the need to attend an after-school club or go to a minder every day. Toni, a twelve-year-old, is adamant that she is 'too old for a minder. I can look after myself!' She wants, she says, 'someone who never tells me off, who is young and funny and can drive me where I want to go!' She has clearly grown out of the mother-figure carer and would prefer a soul mate, someone with whom she can identify, discuss clothes and music, have some fun and, perhaps, negotiate a more equal relationship and gain more power. She would rather have an au pair than a nanny. Her sister, Petra, two years younger, is also resisting being 'policed' and treated 'like I was still two'. During these In-between years, then, if tweenies need their parents less, they will be bound to feel they need their 'minder', who is *in loco parentis*, even less. They may begin to feel insulted that they are not trusted to manage for two or three hours on their own at home, being keen to test out their more mature and acute sense of responsibility. A complaint typical of tweenies who go to relatives or activity clubs after school is that they now need private time and peace and quiet after a noisy school day.

Only the parents can judge what will work best for them and their child, based on factors such as the nature of the area, their child's personality, the proximity of the school or emergency support such as neighbours, the age of other siblings, their own finances and so on. Some children are ready for a big change before others, especially those used to spending some time alone. However, given that younger children need company and conversation to develop fully, it is less suitable for a primary school-aged child to spend hours on her own in an empty house. After the transfer to secondary school, it would be wise to wait until our tweenie is well settled before withdrawing her after-school support. If our tweenie has turned on the pressure, we could:

- Discuss any alternative changes that might satisfy her wish for more control over her life, such as going to the shops on the bus with friends at the weekend.
- Have a tactful word with the current carer to relax some of the rules.
- Ensure our tweenie gets a quiet half-hour in her room before tea or supper.
- Employ a student from a local college for after-school care instead of granny or a nanny.

It is certainly an issue that should be discussed fully, respectfully and constructively. If we dismiss a complaint simply because we can't face the upheaval, we could stir up their anger.

DRAWING THIS TOGETHER

Tweenies are like teenagers only more so: at times they feel very grown up but at others they need still to be 'babied', to rely on us and demand our total focus, care and attention. Their 'wish list' speeds ahead but their requirements remain basic. They need increasing personal physical and mental space, but alongside continued intimacy. They need our trust that they can manage more things on their own, but they need on-call support and guidance too: after all, we are still legally responsible for their welfare. In the home, we should create domains that can safely and appropriately be viewed increasingly as theirs: personal care, the basic care of pets and certain collective chores; homework, and how they fill leisure time; sibling tiffs, and staying home alone for short periods. Tweenies' new taste for self-determination also gives them power in the shops, and this is explored in the next chapter.

Ten top take-out tips

- Try to think one step ahead: be prepared for their requests for more self-determination and autonomy in relation to household rules and space.
- Step back, very gradually, to create specific domains over which they have an increasing measure of control.
- Do demonstrate – by phoning in or leaving notes – that out of sight does not mean out of mind, which an insecure tweenie might interpret as neglect.
- Always attend to safety issues as they spend more time out of our care.
- Understand that an older tweenie's need for privacy does not indicate she hates or rejects us.
- Avoid doing too much for them: respect their need to feel competent because this is the energy that will create opportunities in the future.
- Encourage any siblings to respect and value all landmark achievements.
- Provide lots of time for family fun, and time for quiet togetherness too.
- Rivalry between brothers and sisters is normal and can be healthy, but they should none the less be encouraged to respect each person's essential rights.
- Eating should be a social and family activity, not always solitary.

And Remember!

Every tweenie needs some private space within a warm, family-oriented structure.

Space should not equal distance, nor out of sight mean out of mind.

Show concern and be interested, but avoid being inquisitive or intrusive.

3
TROUBLE IN STORE:
Countering Pester Power

'THIS IS WHAT I WANT, and I want it now!' We have all heard something similar: a pressing, verging on the desperate, cry from a child. Children learn early that the more urgent their pleas the more they convey the strength of their desire; and if they can convince parents that they 'really' want or – even more convincing – 'need' it, they are more likely to get it. Tweenies have become the latest consumers. They are big business, and companies are piling in to exploit them. Conveniently for companies, peer pressure begins to bite in a serious way from the age of eight. The trends that friends set sweep through school playgrounds like a Mexican wave of wanting. Following on from fads in toys, tweenies become highly susceptible to fads in fashion, fads in friends and even fads in food. Our eight-year-olds are now more conscious of money, more conscious of what other children think of them and more conscious of body image than ever before. If we are not careful, we can spend our days reeling, trying to provide the 'right' clothing, footwear or school bag, the 'right' snacks, the 'right' videos, bankrupting ourselves in the process and never getting everything right because the ground shifts just when we think we have fulfilled the latest whim. If we begin to see the immediate delivery of these 'must have' wants as a way to stay in favour and 'buy' our children's affections and approval, we are bound to fail and feel miserable, as will they.

Many people are getting very angry about the commercialisation of childhood that seems to force tweenies, especially, to grow up too soon. The sexual side of these trends is discussed later in chapter nine. It is not quite war in the conventional sense – though it resembles biological warfare: insidious, silent and infectious – but it certainly involves a battle of wills and power. Big business has power; children are learning to exploit very effectively what power they have; and parents have power, though many have forgotten this and feel very exposed. Knowledge increases power. In any confrontation or negotiation, a sensible starting point is to assess the relative strengths and weaknesses of each of the parties and to understand what each of them wants and gets from the transaction. To maximise our power, we must be fully aware of the sophisticated nature of marketing and assess the possible longer-term consequences of that exploitation for our children.

This chapter assesses the power and tactics available to and used by business, tweenies and parents. It suggests that parents can gain strength if we understand children's pester power tactics, feel okay about saying no, manage choices more skilfully, give pocket money and explain how marketing works. It ends with a short section on what we might do and say if we suspect our tweenie has succumbed to temptation and been involved, even in a small way, in shoplifting.

The marketing power of companies

Let us be clear what we are up against. Tweenies are now very big business. The marketing industry has researched the growing amount of money tweenies have to spend individually as well as their influence on family spending on food and drink, toiletries, and even on cars, electrical and other goods. The UK research company Mintel reports that mothers admit their children influence three out of five of the brands they buy. The music industry is targeting tweenies by 'packaging' selected bands to appeal to younger fans. Marketing specialists assess the tweenie potential, to divine future trends and seek to influence or even create them. There are now tweenie versions of established teenage magazines and a contributor to the relatively new *International Journal of Advertising and Marketing to Children* has written: 'different age ranges and genders use current musical trends to shape their outward identity and satisfy their need to belong [so] music can be used to unlock the commercial potential of this market'. In-store environments, to use the industry jargon, are now being designed to encourage brand loyalty across the generations through the 'flashcard approach': pitch (or flash) early and pitch often, to inculcate brand awareness and impress their own.

So the power of marketing executives rests upon knowing our children uncomfortably well and openly exploiting their innocence and vulnerabilities. They know tweenies need to define their separate identity yet fit in and be liked by friends; they know what food they like, how they like to spend their time and what they like to look at, because psychologists tell them.

Taster tips on resisting the onslaught

- ✓ Get briefed about the manipulation involved.
- ✓ Teach our tweenies to be aware and sceptical.
- ✓ Understand the potentially negative consequences for children's physical and mental health if we allow them to be pawns in the bigger game.
- ✓ Use all this information to strengthen our resolve to resist fabricated and fleeting wants.

> ✓ Strengthen our child's identity and self-esteem, so he
> feels less need to use possessions to impress and is less
> susceptible to false promises and pretension.

Tweenies' power: perseverance and persistence

Children learn to read people long before they learn to read
words, and our children have been reading us all their lives. We
are told parents are the experts in relation to their child, but our
children are certainly A-star experts on us! By the time they
reach the age of eight, tweenies have perfected a variety of tactics
to win their way and over the next five years deploy yet more.
We need to realise exactly what these are.

THE PESTER POWER LADDER

Toddlers have tantrums. Six-year-olds often break something of
ours if they don't get their way. Tweenies, though, explore more
subtle and devious tactics. Their pester skills develop and we
can liken these advances to climbing a ladder.

By the age of eight, most children are beginning to use reasons
and arguments comfortably and skilfully, if not manipulatively,
lobbing them as seductive subtleties into the general barrage of
word power to catch parents off guard; but they are still young
enough to turn on nuclear emotional meltdown when it suits.
A horrible sense of *déjà vu* descends as we hear played back
familiar echoes of the arguments we have used to win advantage, as in, 'Give me one good reason why I can't have this!'
Especially after changing school, an eight-year-old will often be
less certain about what he wants, and more prone to be swayed
by prevailing fads. Sometimes, the possession itself is not what
they really want; instead they desire temporary advantage and
status over their peers, or their parent's attention and apparent
love when the item is bought following pressure.

Ten-year-olds have moved beyond this. They want something not because they believe they can't have it, and not just because someone else has got one, but because they are much more sure of themselves and clearer about what they want. Their arguments will be more personalised, less related to what others have or do; they may therefore feel more insulted if we reject their request. Any refusal must be framed very carefully. Having grown up a bit and found alternative freedoms, they could be less likely to demand things simply to test their power over their parent.

By the time tweenies reach twelve, the peer group-influenced, guilt-trip-wire tactic ('I can't believe you can be that mean. Raj's got one *and* he's got a . . .') is deployed with increasing effect. Twelve-year-olds' greater cognitive powers and understanding also enable them to see and select the best moment to ask for things (in front of friends, after supper or on pay day) and to assess and exploit the style and personality of each parent, to approach the softest target for each specific demand.

ASSESSING THEIR PLEAS AND PLOYS

Let's assess their power and their pleas and ploys in more detail. They occupy the red corner – the danger corner – of the ring. We sit opposite in the green corner, for they want the green light from us. Their power rests upon six main tactics, presented here in the general order in which they are brought into play as our tweenie becomes more devious:

1 The warm-up. Watch out for angelic behaviour, cuddles and declarations of love, a tweenie's version of flattery, all used to soften us up.
2 The strop. Children learn early that if they cause a scene, turn on the tears, sink into a sulk or become unco-operative, you are more likely to have second thoughts. This is a less sophisticated version of the guilt trip, because the aim is to make you feel guilty for having upset them so much.

3 The guilt trip. A guilty parent is a vulnerable parent, one who is far more open to persuasion. Even eight-year-olds can induce guilt by poking a soft spot, especially if they have learned it from us.

4 Timing. Catching us at our most distracted, weakest or most mellow moment, or when other people are present when we will not want to appear mean.

5 Divide and rule. Creating a dispute between parents encourages one side to give in to keep the peace.

6 Exploiting the left-hand, right-hand chasm. Trying to ensure the right hand does not know what the left hand is doing by, for example, asking one parent when the other is not around.

Typical pleas and ploys include:

The 'oh please' plea

This is the approach of a younger or 'good' child, one who has not yet sussed more subtle tactics. When we give in – but not until a child has grovelled and said 'please', really convincingly – 'please' becomes a kind of password, not mere politeness. The more times the word is repeated, the more our child is trying to meet our approval by being appealing and appropriate. But giving in only after the third degree, 'please' pressure teaches that nagging and being ingratiating work. Instead, we should ask them to frame reasons because these are the basis for all rational choice. We should not challenge them as if to a duel by saying, 'Give me one good reason why . . .'; we should comment, 'Thanks for asking so nicely but the real issue is, is it a good thing to spend either your or my money on? How important is it to you, and can you tell me why?'

The 'I really, really want it/need it' plea

Children learn quickly that the more they want something, the more it sounds justified and the more they're likely to get it.

'Needing' something sounds more powerful than merely wanting it. 'Need' implies that they'll fall apart without it, whereas a want can be passing and superficial. The greater a need or want, the more devastating will be the disappointment if they don't get it. Children know parents hate to disappoint them so their strongest suit is to claim an intense desire. In the face of this plea, we should, as above, ask our pre-teen to evaluate the genuine strength of that desire. We can also consider why most of us hate to disappoint, and why it might be beneficial for children to realise that doing without is not the end of the world. Ways to deflect a child's frustration are suggested in the section that follows.

The groupie 'I'm the only one in my class who hasn't . . .' plea

How gullible are we to this one! No one likes to think their child will be left out and, knowing that times change, we can all question whether we might have got completely out of step or worry that our thoughtlessness could lead to our child being ridiculed yet be wary of abandoning long-held views. When we judge whether to shift our position we should ponder how genuinely important the issue is, first, to us, second, to our child, and assess what is *really* at stake – is it his wider acceptability to his peer group or a merely temporary dent in his pride? Offering a compromise might help, but the most useful lesson to teach is that we should do things because they seem right, valuable or appropriate to us, not just because everybody else does. We are all individuals, and 'everybody' won't provide the best guidance in every situation.

The emotional blackmail as rejection ploy

The earliest version of emotional blackmail is '*I won't be your friend any more!*', then threatening to leave home or actually doing it and getting as far as the street corner. Some eight-year-olds, probably female, may still be using these tactics, but by now they are more likely to be going sullen, or running upstairs to shut themselves in their room if we say no. If we feel confident in our reasons, we just have to stand firm against the blackmail. With blackmail, of course, the payments get higher. Buying our way into continued peace and 'friendship' with our children is rarely a one-off; it gets increasingly expensive. It's not helpful to children, either. If they take these relationship tactics into the wider world, they will soon come a cropper with friends who are tougher and less emotionally committed to them.

The 'You've been trollied' ploy

Supermarkets and toy stores are, in the words of the old sweet advert, made to make your mouth water. There is enticement on every aisle, especially where non-food items, such as toys or stationery, are for sale among the groceries. Tweenies are tantalised constantly. And we can be astonished when the desired and denied item suddenly appears on the check-out conveyer belt, having been popped in the trolley when our back was turned. So what do we do when confronted by this *fait accompli*? Accept defeat to avoid the row? Reward them with the item because we admire their cunning? Definitely not! We should grab it before the assistant does and say no firmly. If we give in at this point because we are too hassled to argue it could become a regular wheeze. And if we get sucked into compromises, they may learn that the more items they sneak in, they'll get at least one.

The persuade me that I can't have it ploy

'Give me one good reason why I *can't* have it!' challenged Laura, aged eight. Adults frequently press their child to justify a request by demanding: 'Give me one good reason why you should have it'; here we have a child turning it round in a perfect example of a child not only copying adult phrases but also using them with equal manipulative effect. Although children usually deserve an explanation, they shouldn't learn to pin you down with bullying tactics and get away with it. So don't succumb, even if you realise you don't have an answer then and there.

The guilt trip ploy: for example, 'You're tight!'

Guilt-prone parents make themselves vulnerable to endless manipulation and pestering, and always end up fudging. In a television documentary on children's pester power, a nine-year-old girl sulked because she could not have the shoes she wanted. She gave her mum a withering look and exclaimed, 'God, *you're* tight!' It had more barbs than the usual 'You're so mean', a comment that smacks more of frustration than anything else. What we heard was a full guilt trip, and almost certainly not a child's own words but those of an adult laced with insult. But 'tightness' should not be the key issue; decisions should always be made on their merits, even with all the money in the world. If we want to avoid endless negotiation and argument, we need to develop a coherent and convincing position that states firmly: 'end of story', no more debate.

Taster tips on parrying pester power

✓ Try the response, 'If you want it that badly, you should be prepared to wait . . . until your birthday / you have saved something towards it / you have reconsidered whether it really is that important to you.'

✓ Say you will consider two reasons only, and invite them to pick the two that are closest to the truth. Any more, and you'll definitely say no because you won't be badgered.

✓ At the first hint of a pleading whine, ask for the request to be restated in a normal voice. Suggest they

---

include their reasons for wanting something and any relevant background information.

✓ This house isn't a toyshop / clothes shop / supermarket. I can't buy everything, even though you want me to.

✓ If it's a big request that needs a detailed assessment of finances or full thought, such as buying a cat or dog, give them a set time by which you will have made up your mind. Endless procrastination is infuriating, and endless nagging irritating. Everyone wins with a clear timeframe, provided further nagging is an absolute no-no in the meantime.

✓ Pestering should never be seen to win. If you have, in fact, simply caved in, disguise it or excuse it with a good cover story! And if you say, 'Just this once . . .' stick to it.

The more we give in, the more we encourage our children to become a 'high-maintenance' nightmare. We should register that their power in the cases above exploits our weakness – our guilt, our heavy time commitments that prevent us from communicating clearly with our partners, our unwillingness to face them down, especially in a public place. To 'win', we do not have to fight and beat them but to make ourselves stronger and then stand firm.

Parental power: tactics to stay ahead

So we have decided to be stronger from now on. Where does *our* power lie? Without doubt, the first advantage is simply being an adult. We have age, experience and knowledge on our side, and we are in charge. We have to believe this otherwise we might as well hand over the credit card – smart or otherwise – now. And we are the parent, which confers a natural authority. So we're on to a winner. We have the authority to say no, and we have to accept that this is what they really want to hear, at least some of the time. Children don't like to feel they are in charge; it makes them feel insecure. They need adults to set the limits. If the limits are fuzzy, children will push and push until they find them, so the more we give in, the more they push – there is no stopping point. Another fact about tweenies is that they are so desperate to find some way and somewhere to assert themselves that they will go for it big-time in the consumption game if they feel they have no power or autonomy in other bits of their life. If our tweenie is becoming seriously pushy and acquisitive, it may be time to reassess whether we should reduce our involvement and leave more decisions relating to self-care to him, as suggested in the previous chapter.

We also have the advantage of knowing from experience that:

- Most of the time they just try it on, crocodile tears included.
- Their current 'want' is most likely to be passing and will soon be forgotten.
- The money is in our purse, not in theirs.
- Grudges are not held for long, because they need our love and approval so much.
- We are better able to plan ahead and have our replies at the ready.

LEARN TO SAY NO: PREPARING FOR DISAPPOINTMENT

One of the reasons we give in to children is that we hate to see them disappointed. And one tactic tweenies perfect is the act that they will utterly collapse without the said item. To be forewarned is to be forearmed. We must prepare ourselves in order to hold firm against the emotional tornado that saying no can release, and the best way to do this is to understand both why we find it hard to disappoint and why it is absolutely okay to do so.

How to say no, convincingly and firmly, without getting wobbled by guilt

We send children messages through our tone of voice, our eyes, and through gestures, or 'body language'; so try to:

- Stop what you are doing, stand still and look them in the eye.
- Say no quietly. If there's a need to repeat it, say it more softly – shouting isn't needed to get a point across.
- Offer one reason, stated briefly, as an explanation: no more.
- Use clear, not floppy, language. Words like 'please', 'perhaps' or 'I think' suggest uncertainty and leave cracks that growing children spot and exploit.
- Avoid looking hostile. If you put a hand on their shoulder and acknowledge the possible disappointment, they can see you understand and love them.
- Demonstrate your conviction and authority by waiting quietly until they show they accept. Don't leave instantly to escape any backlash.
- Realise that it's your job to decide these things, not theirs. Giving in gives them more grief longer term than saying no will short term.
- You are not rejecting them just because you choose to reject their request.

Why we hate to disappoint – but why it's frequently okay to do so

We may want to protect him from the hurt and sadness that follow disappointment

Yet not getting what you want is a fact of life and contributes to resilience and a clearer view of what is important. Of course it hurts to upset a child, and it seems perverse to cause distress when our job is to 'make them feel better'. However, it is important that our tweenie realises we do not reject *him* just because we reject some of his demands, so stay friendly after saying no, offer a modest token of compensation or give a caring cuddle.

We may want to avoid a possible emotional upset or outright row

Paddies are a pain but to avoid them altogether is equally dangerous. What children thereby learn is the more disruption they can threaten, the more likely their wants will be satisfied. This is emotional blackmail; and if we deny them nothing and hand over authority when our tweenie is merely at the threshold of adolescence, he could find the imminent temptations far harder to resist.

We might fear his disapproval of us

However, a parent's most important job is to do the right thing, not to curry favour. Of course children flourish when a relationship with a parent is naturally friendly, but any parent who begins to rely on their child's approval for his or her own self-worth is being selfish and irresponsible. No child should carry the responsibility for delivering happiness to his parent, being on constant watch to avoid upset and if it occurs feeling punished by parental rejection. Children need a parent to be a central tethering point, to provide constancy and security, even if challenged. It is our job and responsibility to remain strong and ride the knocks.

When might a need be genuine?

How can we decide whether our child's demand reflects a real and appropriate need, a passing whim or an understandable wish to feel part of a group, even if the item is non-essential? Here are some check questions that will help you to decide.

- What is the item needed for? (School, a favourite sporting activity, to look good for a particular event, for fun or entertainment, to feel part of a gang or group he identifies with.)
- Is it likely to encourage a child to develop a particular interest further?
- What effect would waiting a couple of weeks make, if any?
- Would he still want it if he had to pay for it – if the cost is within his budget?
- Does he ask for it ten times a day over two days, or once every couple of days over two or three weeks; in the latter case the request is probably more measured and genuine, not born of superficial desperation for instant gratification.
- Was there a problem last time you agreed to something similar?
- Might your child be bullied and made miserable if he doesn't have the item he seeks?
- Does meeting the request put you out a lot, financially or in terms of time commitment?
- How often does he ask for things? Is it possible he's simply seeking attention or confirmation that you still care? Or does he often feel different from his friends?

Although in general things should be bought on the merit of the case, it is important to keep a balance. We should be firm but fair too, and it shouldn't always be 'no'. It might be appropriate to agree to something simply to redress the balance of recent denials just so our child feels he has some say about his life and doesn't feel totally put upon, especially if the current demand is not significant. Equally, if we see a pattern of continuous demands developing, it may be the time to say no even if the latest request is a small one and costs little; at least in that event we can be sure no great harm will be done by our refusal.

Two further weapons in an adult's armoury available to defuse pester power are the careful use of choice and pocket money.

MANAGING CHOICES

The choices that we have are multiplying and border on the bewildering. From beers to paint colours, from schools to mortgages, this is the age in which consumer choice rules supreme. Common sense tells us that children should have choices too, and most of us want that anyway. Choice is about freedom, and children need to learn to handle choice. But infinite choice is not good for them, nor a route to peace for us. Some degree of choice helps children to feel in charge and respected, to clarify their self-image, to tolerate restrictions elsewhere, and to take some responsibility for their behaviour – if they choose to have or do something, they must learn to accept and face the consequences of that decision. Too much choice, however, can undermine these benefits:

- Far from developing a healthy sense of autonomy, tweenies can feel they control us too, which is not healthy.
- Wall-to-wall choice pushes children to ask for things they don't necessarily want, thus obscuring their true preferences and priorities.
- The more we accede to choices, the more boundaries will become blurred.
- Children can use choices to wriggle free from, not face up to, responsibility: 'Whoops, sorry, wrong choice! I meant this one.'

To avoid open-ended choice but retain the essential advantages, we should manage and limit it. Managed choice means the adult decides which options a child can choose between, making sure that, whatever the choice, it can be followed through without a problem. Limited choice means we keep the opportunities for even managed choice to a practical scale, perhaps once a week in relation to buying things, or once a day if we include other choices such as food, clothes to wear, and so on. This may sound very controlling, but if our life is made miserable by constant demands, this strategy should rein things back, and once our tweenie realises he cannot push us about, his choices will become less contentious. We do our children few favours if we indulge every whim or provide no experience of budgeting. This is where pocket money can help.

Taster tips on offering manageable and appropriate choices

✓ Let them choose two or three things to go in the weekly shop (perhaps one sweet and one savoury, but exclude multiple packs!) rather than ask, 'What would you like bought this week?'

✓ Keep Friday as the treat day, giving fifty pence after school on that day only to spend on anything – edible or otherwise.

✓ Those who change from their uniform after school can wear what they want then, though not necessarily for special family events.

✓ Let them select their preferred flavour of snack, rather than have free choice about when it is eaten.

✓ Which magazine you buy for them each week should be their choice, but not more than one.

✓ When renting a video, offer a pre-selected choice of two or three, rather than asking an open-ended question that could become a fierce argument.

POCKET MONEY

Pocket money, given regularly once children are old enough to make sense of it, can defuse pester power and provide some peace. Instead of making constant requests, our tweenie can buy items independently. Pocket money has benefits that go beyond teaching tweenies the value of money and capping their consumption. Having a regular, weekly amount to spend or save can extend his autonomy, make him feel he's 'growing up', buy things that express his individuality and learn from any mistakes to spend wisely. Pocket money is proof that we accept his growing independence and think of him each week when we hand it over or leave it in an agreed place. As pocket money is, in an odd sense, both a gift and a right it is important that we remember to provide it. If we forget and produce it only when prompted, it appears as grudging. So, pocket money is a 'good thing'; but, like any household practice that involves children's commitment and co-operation, the guidelines must be made clear. If pocket money is genuinely to help tweenies to feel more organised and self-directed, the parameters must be consistent. Thinking through some or all of following issues will help.

When should it start?

When a child turns eight, for the developmental reasons rehearsed above. It's also a good time to review the rules if it is already paid. Any decisions should be taken with all other adults in the household, or at least clearly explained to them, to ensure consistency and to prevent a devious mind from trying to wriggle round the rules if you're not there. It keeps things simple if only one adult hands over the money, but we can all be caught short on change so some boxing and coxing may be inevitable.

How much should it be?

The box below offers a snapshot of average levels of pocket money nationwide as a starting point. When fixing the level, we need to take into account fairness between siblings, comparisons with friends and our own attitudes and values. It also helps to think ahead to future annual increases: a clear, logical basis for the payments and what they should cover will cut arguments and save time and stress in the long run. It should also be available on a set day each week – probably a Saturday to mark the weekend, make it feel special and offer the chance to go out and spend a bit straight away.

Information points: How much pocket money do most tweenies actually get?

A well-known UK ice-cream manufacturer undertakes an annual survey of pocket money received by children aged five to sixteen. In 2001, the survey showed:

- Eight- to ten-year-olds get an average of £4.30 a week, while eleven- to thirteen-year-olds get £7.16.
- Pocket money is often not a child's sole source of income: friends and relatives supply one-off handouts to the tune of £1.52 per week, and children earn a weekly average of £1.52 for doing odd household jobs.
- Boys and girls receive very similar amounts.

What should it cover?

The amounts in the box mean little without knowing what it has to cover. Younger tweenies will have fewer responsibilities than older ones, so eight-year-olds are likely to spend the bulk of their money on personal items such as snacks, magazines, single CDs, small toys or collecting fads – cards or stickers used for swapping or keeping. By the age of twelve, girls may want a clothes allowance, but beware: it can be too much too soon. My daughter gave up the requested modest allowance after a while because she realised she wasn't ready, that she still needed me to buy things so she felt treated and looked after.

Should they have total freedom to spend it at will?

Probably. After the age of eight tweenies need to have some

freedom from parental control, to face the consequence of their decisions and yet be safe from real harm. Pocket money fits these criteria well. Children under eight need help to spend their money with foresight because they are more self-focused and impetuous; but by the age of eight children should be clear about what is healthy or sensible and be left to confront their inclinations, reflect on our rules, experience the consequences and experience self-discipline determined by their own system of preferences. If our tweenie is inclined to 'blow it' and then regret it, we can consider paying pocket money fortnightly rather than weekly.

What about saving – should we force it?

Probably not, given the above, but having some savings enables children to contribute to family birthday presents (and spend on others, not just themselves) and to the cost of more expensive 'designer' items, to discover they enjoy working towards and achieving a goal, or to buy something more expensive without having to save from scratch. But how can savings grow if we don't make them do it? Birthday money or other one-off cash gifts from relatives can be used to start savings. We could put a modest amount into a savings account each birthday, add a 'savings bonus' component to their pocket money each week – so it feels like an extra – that has to be kept separately, or agree to match whatever they manage to save each month, if that's their preference. Teaching by example may encourage good habits, but given that most people now rely on credit rather than savings for special purchases putting money in a jar or box – though desirable – would be purely ritualistic.

Should pocket money be a right, or conditional on performing household jobs or being 'good'?

All, or most of it, should be given as of right. Once it becomes, in effect, a payment, it becomes a contract which can lead to numerous arguments about whether the job was, or was not, done or done well enough to merit the payment. Our decisions can seem arbitrary and cause resentment. In effect, the contract approach gives us too much power over an issue that is hugely personal and important to children.

Should we pay our tweenie to do household jobs, on top of pocket money?

Tweenies are old enough to be expected to undertake some domestic tasks without payment as their contribution to the effective functioning of a busy family that has to be a team effort. We can give some money as a gesture of thanks afterwards for the occasional job that we might pay someone else to do, such as cleaning the car or clearing the garden, or for a difficult job like cleaning the oven, but not for daily tasks such as washing up or clearing bedrooms. Avoid becoming ensnared in the 'I'll help if you pay me' negotiation trap, or paying them for jobs they ask to do but that don't really need doing as a way for them to 'get rich quick'. Although it's good to be helpful and flexible if they are trying to save, frequent extra payments will undermine one purpose of pocket money: to learn to manage a budget and to make choices.

What if we have little spare income and it's not very regular?

Most of us will buy our child a little treat during the week: it might be something on a Friday after school, a bun in the supermarket or a weekend ice cream in the park. We could offer the money spent on these treats as pocket money instead, leaving it to our tweenie to decide which he would prefer. If our income is irregular and comes in lumps, rather than give him a sizeable sum when we're in the money, we might put that sum in a box or children's account and allow him to draw down from it weekly to regularise his spending.

WHEN TEMPTATION TRIUMPHS: DEALING WITH SHOPLIFTING

Sometimes, children want something so badly, and believe they cannot cope with not having it, that they are tempted to steal. Most goods are so enticingly displayed and seem so accessible. Note the two separate issues: wanting it and thinking they cannot manage without it. It is fine for a child to want something intensely, but it is not healthy if he feels a lesser person for not having it. The more we give in, the less he will realise that, in fact, life does not collapse. But the tempting displays also encourage tweenies to take risks, which they are increasingly prone to do during the five tweenie years.

Although younger children steal for a variety of understandable and excusable developmental reasons, by eight years of age any theft at home or elsewhere should be taken far more seriously, even shoplifting which is known to be something quite a few children aged eight to twelve try for laughs then drop. As well as being overcome by temptation, our tweenie can be cajoled into shoplifting by friends too scared to do it themselves or simply be putting his new-found freedom to the test, albeit inappropriately, and enjoying the thrill of danger. By no means all those who offend at this age are destined for a career of crime. However, apart from the simple truth that stealing is wrong and an offence under the criminal law so must be stopped, shoplifting at this age can be a sign that all is not well at home or school, and it may whet the appetite longer term for illicit excitement that becomes hard to give up. Either way, we should act decisively to end it and get to the bottom of how and why it happened.

All instances of stealing from shops should be dealt with firmly and promptly, yet with kindness and tolerance. First offences should not be 'let off' but it will not help to be harsh and hurtful. A clear, relevant punishment, or consequence, such as not being allowed out to the shops for a weekend or two, imposed neutrally yet laced with expressions of disappointment, should be enough to send the right message. It also makes sense to discuss how it happened: how did the suggestion arise, why did you think it was an okay thing to do, what went through your head as you walked out with the item, have you felt any guilt since, what did your friends say, did anyone else do it too? This type of conversation will be more effective at ensuring our tweenie reflects on what he did than, for example, any harsh, physical punishment, which could make him push the whole episode out of mind immediately after. The shame a child feels when caught out is often enough to break any potential pattern before it becomes established and a tweenie gets blasé. It is reflection and engagement we want to encourage, not shoulder-shrugging indifference that frequently follows inflicted pain. Chapter eleven looks in more detail at dishonesty among tweenies and the next chapter on discipline considers appropriate responses.

Taster tips on responding to shoplifting or its possible evidence

✓ If you are not sure how something new has been acquired, it is better to ask about this first before posing a direct question or accusation. 'I see that you are still wearing that T-shirt / playing that new game you said you'd borrowed from Jonny. Can you tell me what the deal is with him? Shouldn't you have returned it by now? Did you really borrow it?'

✓ If theft is confirmed, consider returning the item to the shop, with him in tow: an experience he won't want to repeat.

✓ Encourage him to tell the story behind it, to understand why it happened, and who with.

✓ Make it clear that shoplifting is wrong and a serious offence however small the item, and that persisting could lead to deeper trouble.

✓ Discuss an appropriate consequence that will signify his responsibility and remorse and act as reparation for his wrongdoing, such as returning the item, a ban on shopping trips with those friends for a period and putting some of his pocket money in a shop or family charity box over two or so weeks.

DRAWING THIS TOGETHER

If it's hard being a parent at the moment, it is even harder being a tweenie. While tweenies are desperately trying to 'be', they have friends, magazines, shops and advertisers telling them how to look and how to be, making it harder. We, of course, want our children to be able to mix comfortably with friends but we should not be pressured into giving in and buying them everything they ask for to keep up. We should perhaps see the issue not as us against our child, as us – acting in the interests of our child – against some powerful and not always benign commercial forces. For it is in any child's long-term interest that we encourage him to question his own priorities, learn the value of things, understand how advertising works and to discriminate quality from presentation. Parents are children's whetstones: reasoning and communication skills get honed on us. But just because our tweenie has become sharper doesn't mean we collapse and concede. We have purchasing power too – the authority to decide when to spend as well as the power to resist and restrain, aspects of discipline and self-discipline. Our other job is to ensure a tweenie's confidence is not transitory and superficial because it relies on fads and whims, but is robust because he knows that what is inside him is far more reliable, lovable and precious than any possession. If we fail in this, there certainly is trouble in store.

Ten top take-out tips

- Be very clear when you go shopping what you're out to buy. 'This trip is for shoes, not for new tops, magazines or ice creams.' Then it is easier to stay firm.
- Put the waiting back into wanting. Say they should think again about their demand in two or three weeks. It's amazing how the '*must* have, *now*' soon fades in urgency.
- Keep a list of their 'wants' over two or three weeks, then ask them to prioritise and make choices. Writing down each request will prove they are not being ignored despite there being no immediate action.
- Where possible, buy on-line, then children can't get seduced by displays.
- As soon as possible give regular pocket money, and stick to it. This is their money to spend, they make real choices, they learn a sense of value and they can save towards some of the things they really want.
- For big ticket items that are hard to save for or cannot wait for a birthday, require a contribution towards it – appropriate to age and wealth of course!
- If they insist on labels, and not a substitute, ask them to help bridge the cost gap by contributing some of their own pocket money or savings.
- Avoid using presents to assuage guilt – love shouldn't be measured by price tags.
- Don't be frightened to say no. Children can learn that real friends don't judge by clothes or possessions.
- Teach them that 'you don't judge a book by looking at its cover', which goes for the packaging of goods as well as how people are dressed. We should always look *into* people (and packing boxes) to see who they are and value what they can do, not *on to* people to judge them by image.

And Remember!

Avoid treats becoming a proof of love.

Children prefer to be relationship rich and possession poor than vice versa.

Buying and demanding should not become their sole experience of autonomy.

4
DISCIPLINE, MORALS AND MANNERS:
Building a 'Me and You' Generation

GIVEN THE COMMERCIALISM DISCUSSED IN the previous chapter, it is hard not to agree that we are living in a society in which people have become more self-obsessed and selfish, not because we have become worse human beings but because many more of us have been able to have and do so much more of what we might want. It is only natural to take advantage of all that's available, but the 'me' generation could be said to be the result and is used by some people to justify their belief that morals, manners, values and standards of personal behaviour have declined. They claim that children, in particular, increasingly think only of themselves and seem less able to cope with discipline, disappointment and difficulty, whether this is due to being spoiled rotten or being neglected and left too much to their own devices.

Many of the strongest critics claim the fault lies with the promotion of self-esteem that they equate to self-indulgence; however, children are more, not less, likely to behave well if they have a clear sense of self and positive self-esteem. Both of these attributes help children to fit in, succeed, give to others and have happier relationships during childhood and later. The word 'polite' comes from 'polish', to make smooth or shiny. Knowing how to be polite helps to smooth our way in the world. But it is also important that tweenies learn to be caring, develop a moral framework and acquire a useful repertoire of manners – social habits or skills that encourage them to think about and show consideration for others. The earlier these attitudes are learned, of course, the more natural they become; none the less, the pre-teen years are a good moment to ensure they are in place. Parents are, generally, hugely tolerant of immature behaviour though friends are less so; as tweenies increasingly look to people beyond the family for acceptance their behaviour really begins to count. Developmentally, too, the time is right, as they are able to be less self-focused and to consider other ways of seeing and doing things. We can encourage this awareness by creating a set of 'kindness and consideration' codes – for everyone in the family to observe.

Discipline also involves consideration; poor behaviour is an irritant and an intrusion. Children cannot learn how to behave in a restrained way if we don't teach them how and it is this guidance and encouragement that constitutes 'positive discipline'. Punishment has little role here and should always be seen as separate from discipline; but during the tweenie years it is even more important to keep the two ideas distinct. The strong, negative messages conveyed by harsh punishment can do particular damage as tweenies check out who they are and what they can do and try to grow in confidence.

This chapter has three main sections. The first looks at the need to adapt our approach to discipline to ensure that it remains effective with tweenies by considering four levels of action: objectives, principles, strategies and tactics. It explores how our responses need to change and why girls and boys challenge in different ways at this age. The second section looks at helping our tweenie to become a full member of a 'me and you' generation through attending to morals and manners – why we should not reject all manners simply because some seem to be outmoded and how these can be enshrined in a range of social 'kindness and consideration' codes. It also discusses how our tweenie's moral awareness and sense of responsibility will be influenced by our style of discipline and how we can practise values such as honesty, fairness, justice and consideration at home. The third and final section reviews what the main discipline issues are likely to be and suggests useful approaches to two of these: rudeness and dishonesty.

Encouraging self-discipline through positive discipline

The most important objective for discipline in relation to tweenies is the encouragement of self-discipline, for we cannot remain 'in charge' of them for ever. Their maturing cognitive skills – the ability to think in more abstract ways, to think ahead and not to see everything through their own eyes – make these years suitable for passing more responsibility to them to anticipate and be considerate without being prompted. However, tweenies' growing self-awareness and objectivity also make them far more discerning; they begin to judge us, which marks a significant and uncomfortable watershed. It is not only that, as established little people, they need us slightly less; it is also that they have become wise to our ways, replay our tactics back at us and can see through our waffle. As a consequence, we have to stay on our toes, manage our moods better, be more consistent and argue more convincingly – in fact, be more self-disciplined ourselves! If we get it wrong and respond either clumsily or over-punitively to their challenges, tweenies can be more determinedly defiant. And if we get it consistently wrong and then refuse to listen to their complaints, they are of an age to begin to stay out late and intentionally thwart us. It is a critical time to get it right, but also a good time to establish habits and positive attitudes that will contribute to longer-term peace.

ENCOURAGING SELF-DISCIPLINE

Self-discipline is when individuals can limit and restrain their own behaviour. It is an extension of positive discipline because the behaviour we want to see has been internalised and sanctions and inducements are no longer so necessary. Eight-year-olds are becoming capable of deciding to do what they have been told is right without prompting, as well as anticipating the likely consequences if they choose not to; however, they are not yet ready to assume full responsibility. Even at ten, when the law assumes that most children know the difference between right and wrong and can be treated as criminally liable, some children remain confused about what is acceptable behaviour and what might happen as a result of doing certain things. Moral awareness does not develop at the same rate in all children, especially if they have experienced a number of traumatic difficulties at home or there are no clear boundaries.

Children find it easier to exercise self-control when they have followed clear family and personal routines; been used to delaying pleasure and rewards; and have been encouraged to consider the possible impact of their behaviour. It means, essentially, that tweenies should not always get their way and do their own thing. It is important that we can say no when appropriate and encourage them sometimes to save, wait for or work towards the thing they want to do, have or achieve, as discussed in the previous chapter. But these constraints must be offset by opportunities to make decisions and contribute to the discussion of rules so they feel respected and try out and learn to trust their judgement.

Taster tips on encouraging self-discipline

✓ Use routines to establish helpful habits, but be sensitive and flexible; for example, delay bedtime if a favourite aunt or uncle visits.

✓ Gradually involve them in discussions of rule changes,

new freedoms and possible 'consequences' if these are then ignored.

✓ Be certain to notice when they have done something without being prompted and thank them for it.

✓ Encourage them to think ahead and to reflect on the consequences of their actions and statements.

✓ Support them if they lose momentum so they don't give up before they have really tried.

✓ Respect their growing ability to form their own judgements.

✓ When they push for something we don't want to concede, invite them to guess at our answer. This will ensure they say the word 'no', not us, and will teach them to 'hear' and anticipate our likely view, a necessary step to achieve self-restraint.

✓ Encourage them, for example, to go off to bed, tidy their rooms after friends' visits, come back at the agreed time and clear their plates without prompting.

PROMOTING POSITIVE DISCIPLINE: THE UNDERLYING PRINCIPLES

Positive discipline is the approach that teaches self-discipline most effectively. With positive discipline, we give tweenies clear guidance about what they should do, instead of spelling out what it is they should not do. We notice and praise what they do right, instead of highlighting failure and punishing mistakes. Positive discipline nurtures self-esteem and leads to healthy social and emotional growth because it helps children to feel trusted, successful, relaxed and loved by and acceptable to the people they care most about. What we should avoid at all costs is implying that our child is a serial loser: someone who always gets things wrong, needs to be checked on and reprimanded constantly, is no good at anything and generally can't be trusted.

No tweenie will flourish if this is how she sees herself. In a news-paper discussion of discipline recently, a teenage boy wrote: 'If parents declare war on their children, they will maybe reject the whole idea of family and refuse to communicate because their friends are more important to them anyway. When you are labelled a thug, there's no reason not to live up to it.' We must always give our tweenie the benefit of the doubt and help her to feel hope in her capacity to do and behave well.

The importance of boundaries

One of the key principles of positive discipline is that all children need boundaries to help them manage and control their behaviour and to keep them safe. Boundaries are another name for family rules that help to balance and show consideration for everyone's needs and demands and to help the unit to run smoothly. Children also feel more secure when they know how far they can go and they feel loved when we demonstrate that we care what happens to them. Provided these guidelines are consistently applied and are not too numerous, rules can reduce conflict.

Taster tips on setting boundaries

✓ Write down the areas of your family life to which rules and routines apply; for example, bedtimes, first thing in the morning, food and mealtimes, television, use of the telephone or homework.

✓ Consider which of these, if any, cause the most friction.

✓ Select just one to start with – the aspect of domestic life that bugs you most – and state your objectives clearly.

✓ Place a list of the rules and expectations that apply where everyone concerned can read it.

> ✓ Too many rules and restraints can encourage challenge
> – better to have fewer and make sure they work.
> ✓ Be consistent by ensuring everyone does as they have
> been asked.

The positive discipline contract

Positive discipline is not a one-way process. It is an agreement, or contract, that enshrines the principle that both sides have to behave well for it to work. We cannot expect our tweenie to deliver if we do not fulfil our side of the contract, which means we should:

be fair	don't blame her for our mistakes, have unreal expectations or think that we should be exempt
be clear	check that the agreements and limits are understood
be positive	show you have noticed and be pleased when she does as asked
be consistent	remind everyone sharing in her care of what's important
be sensitive	to mood, other problems and tiredness
be creative	think ahead, compromise and use humour to laugh things off
give time	don't let disruption be the only route to attention
be the adult	don't try to win every battle; tweenies need little victories too

AVOIDING CONFLICT: INSIGHTS AND STRATEGIES

Tweenies need to challenge, for it is how they explore and assert their difference, learn about fairness and express self-respect. When they do so we must listen respectfully but not necessarily concede, for we also need sometimes to put our foot down, require respect and withstand the blast. However, families that are conflict-prone are rarely happy and rarely contain well-disciplined youngsters with a positive outlook or self-image either. We should strive, therefore, to select our battles carefully and otherwise settle things before they blow. Before suggesting some positive, preventative strategies, what are the special challenges we might expect from tweenies?

The gender differences

Boys and girls tend to have different discipline patterns from each other during the tweenie phase influenced by their gender and what they understand it means. For example, as boys identify more closely with their fathers and separate from mothers, they may initially display their awakening sense of 'maleness' through rudeness and acting up, resent any discipline and see how far they can go, equating masculinity with assertiveness. It is crucial that a father steps in to protect the mother and show his respect for her at this point. If a father has often insulted the mother, his language may be copied or the father's perceptions actively endorsed; or if a father has not been very present or nurturing, a boy may be more liable to reject the maternal warmth in order to prove his independence. Female teachers regularly experience the same 'bolshiness' and bravado from ten-year-olds, suggesting these patterns may take a couple of years to emerge.

Girls, on the other hand, are renowned for having a stronger desire to please and seem to need parental or adult approval for longer. In the early tweenie years girls are more likely to get 'lippy' rather than rude or offensive. One father of a twelve-year-old described his daughter as 'metaphorically hitting you in the face to get more freedom one minute, and curling up in your lap the next'. Some boys can manage to do both, but others find it hard. A girl may assert herself quietly and even deviously by pushing out the boundaries rather than by actively challenging parental or maternal control. Her 'gift of the gab' will incline her to argue more persistently and determinedly than most boys, but having had a vigorous verbal attempt to get her way, she is more likely to acquiesce calmly than to bear a grudge and become defiant, though this may come later. Age and stage battles are considered below in the final section.

Positive strategies to prevent unnecessary conflict

Treat them well
Behave towards them with courtesy and respect; listen to their point of view and be flexible, open and honest. Make our expectations clear and always warn when behaviour is getting close to unacceptable. Offer plenty of praise and approval. Accept that their needs will change and adjust accordingly. Above all be fair and reasonable. We should not need to act as heavy infantry and force a victory every time. Accumulated resentment can lead to a degree of havoc that is out of proportion to the immediate problem.

Don't be bamboozled
Avoid matters getting out of hand because we have agreed to something under pressure. We so often regret this later, get cross and make our children 'pay' by moaning and getting tetchy. Be confident about saying no – don't be afraid to say we need time to consider our answer if we get cornered unexpectedly. The more pressure is applied, the more we should stand fast: giving way under pressure simply teaches that nagging (or bullying or blackmail) works. If it works with us, they may be tempted to try this with others. We should be impressed by argument, not intimidation.

Say sorry if we get it wrong
It is important to apologise. An apology is a sign of strength, not weakness. It increases our authority because the respect we thereby show towards them is then reciprocated; it also demonstrates that we can admit to errors without losing face or

self-respect. An apology shows our willingness to reflect and accept responsibility for our actions and statements, something we should encourage in them. It is important that our tweenie realises that anyone can make a mistake and that the relationship will survive regardless.

Make a habit of monitoring and supervising

Children who are monitored effectively are known to be far less likely to 'get into trouble'. We need to start well before our tweenies begin to venture forth. Keep them fully informed of our movements, as a matter of courtesy and to model the behaviour we will expect later. It should be part of family sharing that we say when we are going out, to do what, and our likely return time. We should also apologise if we return late or telephone to let them know and later chat about what we did. With this pattern established, questions such as, 'How was it?' or 'Who else was there?' will not necessarily seem intrusive, just normal and friendly. When they first go out with friends we can ask what they plan to do, clarify when we want them back and ask again when they return what they did – not to spy but to show interest and get them used to accounting for themselves.

But if tweenies go too far . . . possible punishments

As children become older and bolder they explore and experiment, misjudge things, go too far and usually trip up. Just as we need to redraw the boundaries as they mature, so we also should review the nature and scope of any punishment we use. We can't, for example, send any tweenie to the 'naughty' chair, and it's hard to insist that an older one either miss a favourite TV programme if she can then go round to a friend or do without a favourite toy if these no longer exist. So what are the alternatives? Hitting children is never right, for reasons given later, but hitting out at a tweenie will more likely end in *our* tears at their barefaced defiance than in their genuine and tearful remorse.

Options that are more appropriate for tweenies include, for example:

- A serious 'talking-to' that should also include a 'two-way listening-to' and conclude with a verbal commitment not to repeat the event.
- Stopping, or reducing, pocket money for a week or so (any longer may generate resentment).
- Sending them to their room to cool down if they have been aggressive or rude.
- Preventing them from seeing a particular friend or from doing something they like to do at the weekend, such as going shopping or to a football match.
- Putting a set sum of money in a pot or jar that is then emptied and the contents sent to charity.

These options can be described as 'punitive consequences'; they can involve either a withdrawal of a pleasure or privilege, or a direct penalty. But if the objective is to encourage personal responsibility and self-discipline, we should consider an alternative type of 'consequence' known as restorative justice. This requires a child to do something to make amends, to face what she has done, try to balance out the damage or distress caused and thereby say sorry, often by doing something for the person affected directly. That person – a sibling, parent or perhaps a neighbour – should be involved to explain how they felt and to suggest something acceptable. For example, if our tweenie has thrown a stone at a neighbour's car and dented it, it will be more appropriate to insist on a personal apology, a contribution towards the cost of mending it or help with their garden than, for example, to wallop her one.

Punishment is relevant to any discussion of discipline because it makes children face the consequences of their actions and teaches responsibility. Used selectively as a constructive learning tool, punishments can also demonstrate that we mean what we say and that certain behaviour (bunking off school, hurting someone or an animal, or staying out late, for example) is absolutely unacceptable. However, to be effective, punishment must be used sparingly. Although it seems perverse, if we try to maintain control through a strong reliance on punishments, we undermine our authority. The more we use power, the more we lose it. We know that these In-between years are critical for crystallising a child's sense of self. When a child is punished frequently, especially if the problem is really one of misjudgement, or the punishment is harsh, humiliating, arbitrary or excessive, our tweenie will get the message that she is not worthy of respectful treatment. Just when she needs to feel more proud and confident, she will feel less so. To protect her self-respect, she may pretend to be untouched by the insult, cut herself off and become totally unco-operative in order to retaliate. Smacking, hitting, or any other form of physical punishment should not be in our repertoire. Surprisingly, studies show that 50 per cent of children aged eleven in both the UK and the USA continue to be punished physically, despite this constituting both a physical assault and an infringement of a child's human rights as agreed by the United Nations.

The lessons children draw from any punishment are not always constructive. It is vital that we respond to any challenge in a way that leads to positive results – reflection and responsibility – not shoulder-shrugging indifference or defiance. Research shows that children who are hit become more aggressive, short and long term. Naughty children become naughtier, and good children less good. Children who are hit are more likely to engage in antisocial, criminal and abusive behaviour as adults; and children who are heavily punished show a reduced capacity for empathy and gain a poorer grasp of the moral aspects of discipline, for the reasons outlined in the next section.

Taster tips on the effective use of punishment

✓ It is not wise to punish genuine mistakes.

✓ Respect honesty: go easy if they have owned up.

✓ An effective 'consequence' never needs to humiliate – leave their self-respect intact.

✓ Ensure that the punishment matches and relates to the crime.

✓ If a rule was not clear, let the error pass this time but then watch carefully for any repetition.

✓ Discuss suitable 'consequences' with your tweenie to encourage her personal commitment and responsibility.

✓ Behaviour talks: acts of open defiance or rudeness, while they need to be challenged, could mask a grievance that probably needs an airing.

✓ Always check if they consider the outcome 'fair', and if not, discuss why not.

✓ Use punishment sparingly. A caring 'talking to' can be very effective.

✓ Punish them for what they have done, not for who they are.

✓ Keep yourself separate: don't get mad because they have embarrassed you.

Morals and manners: Why good family relationships help

If 'charity begins at home', so do other virtues. The most effective way to 'teach' appropriate behaviour, manners and morals is to model them, and not to make too big a thing of it at the beginning, just as we read to our children for pleasure long before we start teaching them to read yet they learn certain essentials even as we turn the first page. It is not unusual for people to be in two minds about teaching children manners, because these are seen as customs that can become outdated and were used in the past to reinforce social divisions and protect advantage. Manners can even be considered a barrier to spontaneity and honesty, given that we now attach greater value to 'being ourselves'.

However, the downside of rejecting much of the formality of manners is that children could be in danger of growing up less sensitive to their impact on others and less thoughtful and respectful, which could impact adversely on their present and future relationships. Manners embody consideration and encourage moral awareness. Some manners are simply practical, and they certainly help children to be acceptable socially. It is therefore sensible to bring up our children with some know-ledge of manners and, from the age of about eight, to expect them to 'read' morals and manners for themselves, without too much prompting.

Manners, or 'kindness and consideration' codes, can be applied to many areas. Here, we look in some detail at meal-time manners, and at courtesy towards the elderly, kindness towards friends and consideration to others out in the street. Consideration is so important that it must be two-way. As well as seeking ideas from our tweenie about ways to show kindness to others, she will really appreciate being invited to list ways in which adults could be more considerate towards her.

TABLE MANNERS

In the family arguments league, feuds over table manners feature highly, along with sibling squabbles and untidy bedrooms. If we monitor every mouthful, criticise the use of cutlery and comment constantly on posture, we can be at our children relentlessly. Nagging about mealtime manners can certainly be taken too far, but table manners – maybe 'mealtime manners' is a better term

if our family does not always sit round a single table – are important for a variety of practical and other reasons. We should
encourage mealtime manners for our family because:

- *They're practical.* Sitting up straight deepens breathing,
  increases relaxation and aids digestion; sitting close to the
  table means falling food lands on the plate, not on laps or the
  floor; stretching for something instead of asking for it is likely
  to result in a messy sleeve; children who can stay put through
  a meal find it easier to be desk-bound at school.
- *They make eating more pleasant for everyone concerned.*
  Chewing with an open mouth turns it into a cement mixer: it
  looks as mucky and it's almost as noisy; someone who sits
  slouched over food, head down, can seem rude because fellow
  diners will feel ignored.
- *They teach children to think of others.* Waiting until everyone has finished eating before leaving the table shows the meal
  is a family affair, not a purely functional occasion; serving
  drinks or vegetables to others as well as yourself demonstrates
  thoughtfulness – and speeds things up; no one gets lumbered
  with all the cleaning up when each person clears their own
  plate.
- *They give children a skill that helps them to fit in.* It is a reality
  that people are judged according to such things as personal
  care and style, so children should not be disadvantaged through
  ignorance of common expectations about styles of eating.

Taster tips on encouraging mealtime manners

✓ Agree with any partner what mealtime behaviour you
  will expect from your children. Then ask your tweenie
  what issues she thinks are important and why. Tell her
  what you think, that you'll get off her back if she
  makes some effort.

✓ List the behaviour at table that you both want to see and pin it somewhere relevant and visible. Try two columns or sheets, one for top priority manners and the other the lesser ones. Or have one column for practical manners and one for those that demonstrate respect. Another possibility is to list the good manners under a smiley face and the 'no-no's under a sad face.

✓ Constant nagging delivers dollops of parental disapproval and can undermine talk and togetherness. To avoid it:
 – invite everyone to study the list before each meal
 – identify two or three practices to be that day's focus
 – ignore all other transgressions
 – tell your partner so everyone's in the know

RESPECTING OLDER MEMBERS OF THE FAMILY AND COMMUNITY

In a culture that highlights youth and beauty, it is easy for young people to feel that older relatives, neighbours and local citizens do not merit their attention. Of course, silly games such as knocking on an older person's door and then legging it, or otherwise taunting wrinkled and tetchy neighbours viewed as 'witches and weirdoes', have been around for centuries, but they are none the less inappropriate because they can upset and frighten the individual targeted. We can instil greater respect, compassion and understanding by helping older relatives and neighbours with specific tasks and involving our children in these.

Possible practices for inclusion in a tweenie's 'respect our elders' code

✓ Give up your seat to any elderly or disabled person when on public transport.

✓ Be helpful to elderly neighbours, especially the house-bound.

✓ Join parents regularly on visits to grandparents or other elderly relatives, even if it seems a chore.

✓ We can expect our tweenie to greet any elderly or other adult visitor who comes to our home. She can also be asked to offer to take the person's coat or any bags.

✓ Ensure that they open doors for all adults so they can walk through first.

COURTESY AND CONSIDERATION TO FRIENDS

Almost by definition, friends are people with whom we can let our hair down and drop the formalities, so why make an issue of manners with friends? However, eight- to twelve-year-olds spend time with a range of 'friends' of varying degrees of closeness and permanence, and their friendships won't yet be based on the same history, trust and intimacy as ours. In a sense, they are still learning to be friends, and through their passing friendships they learn how to be with others and to make relationships 'work'. This is why it is relevant for them to have a consideration code for friends. The list below is not exhaustive. You may wish to consider others.

Going to friends and having them round

✓ Always share drinks and snacks with friends, when out together, on arrival at the house, or when our tweenie digs into the fridge or cupboard.

✓ Always say 'thank you for the meal' when eating at a friend's house.

✓ Invitations, once accepted, should generally be stuck to, even if a seemingly better offer comes along.

✓ Saying 'thank you for having me' may not sound spontaneous, but it should none the less always be said, and passed on if the friend's parent isn't around.

✓ When taken on a special trip or holiday with another family, write a short thank you note after saying what was special fun.

✓ When a friend comes to visit, come to the front door both to greet and say goodbye at the end, stopping any play to do so.

BECOMING STREET-KIND AS WELL AS STREET-WISE

We cannot be with our tweenie every time she is out in public. We can't spy from street corners to check how she behaves towards others, even those who may be passing strangers. All we can do is to model the consideration we expect and make clear what we would like to see so at least she knows there is another way.

Taster tips on encouraging street-kindness

✓ Step aside to let someone pass, especially if they carry heavy shopping or have a buggy.

✓ When in a crowd, don't take up the whole pavement and expect others to move around you.

✓ Be helpful – pick up dropped items for other people.

✓ Don't drop litter; that spoils the look of a shared environment.

✓ Apologise if you accidentally bump into someone.

✓ Open a door for someone, especially if they are laden.

✓ Give your seat to a pregnant woman on public transport or at a bus stop.

Being encouraged to think about other people's, and animals', interests and feelings and to be kind and considerate will help our tweenie to develop her moral sense; but what is also valuable is the experience of respectful and caring relationships within the family.

MORALS AND VALUES: WHAT LOVING RELATIONSHIPS CONTRIBUTE

Like manners, moral development does not happen in a vacuum; children learn the sensitivities and capacities that they need for moral thinking from their closest relationships – or not, depending on how warm and understanding these relationships are. Teaching children about morals and values involves far more than simply helping children to recognise the difference between right and wrong which may, or may not, prevent them from breaking the law and getting into trouble. (Children, like adults, can know what is wrong yet still choose to do it.) Moral awareness also involves acknowledging, first our own and then other people's feelings, and understanding values such as honour, fairness, trust and commitment – that are manifest in every successful human relationship. We have to be able to imagine, comprehend and anticipate actions and the possible emotional and practical consequences of those actions. This is why positive discipline is important; but so is empathy.

Encouraging empathy

Research shows that children who find it easy to empathise when they are younger tend to be less aggressive, more helpful, more likely to join in and more willing to share as they grow older. Empathy is reacting to another's feelings with an emotional response similar to the other's feelings. Children learn the capacity for empathy in part from the emotional sensitivity close adults show towards them, yet parents often deny a child's feelings. Commonly heard phrases that trip off parental tongues include,

'Don't cry, that didn't hurt', 'Why are you getting so upset about that? It's no big deal', and 'I don't care if you don't want to do that, you just have to.' It can be hard to tap into children's immediate emotional experience when we are busy or preoccupied with our own problems, but we will need to be more responsive if our tweenie is to behave in ways that demonstrate moral awareness.

Empathy also involves being able to see something from another person's point of view, and it is this facility that changes as children mature. Initially, children imagine that somebody else feels the same as they do. From about the age of six they realise that people feel differently and each person's perspective is unique. Around the age of ten, children become capable of thinking beyond the individual to the general: they develop the potential for a social conscience because they can imagine the general conditions in which less fortunate people or animals must live.

Taster tips on encouraging empathy

✓ Talk about feelings and upsets. If someone's upset on TV, for example, we can ask our tweenie whether she might feel the same, whether it could or should have been avoided, and so on.

✓ Encourage the habit of anticipating people's reactions. 'But if you use your sister's coloured pencils, will that annoy her, or won't she mind?' 'If you leave Emma off your party list what might she say about it?'

✓ Make a habit of asking about our children's reactions to events by using phrases such as, 'Did that upset / disappoint / frustrate / sadden / excite / please you?' or 'What effect did that have on you?'

✓ Emotional literacy requires a vocabulary – if we speak of feelings, at least the language and phrases will be familiar.

Children will find it far harder to imagine what others might feel if they have not first been encouraged to reflect on their own emotional reactions. This is where fairness comes in.

It's not fair! Tweenies' growing sense of fairness

Avni, aged ten, told me, 'I don't think it's fair. I have to clean up my sister's bedroom even when mine's clean.' Her classmate, Rupal, complained: 'I wish they'd stop blaming me for things I didn't do. Sometimes I get told off when my brother hits me.' Mital, also aged ten, pinpointed adult hypocrisy: 'Adults are always going on about manners, but sometimes they forget to say "thank you", or "well done", or even "sorry" when they're wrong.'

One of the earliest 'moral' feelings young children experience is unfairness. Their sense of fairness is fierce and flowers early. It even lies at the root of sibling jealousy. It appears early possibly because it aids survival: it ensures they get looked after properly. Tweenies may have become less self-centred, but they will be better able to appreciate and evaluate the justice of things done to other people if their own need for fair and respectful treatment remains fulfilled by parents and other close adults. We need to be honest to our children, and respond fairly if we find they have been dishonest.

Developing moral awareness: the role of discipline in shaping shame and guilt

Once children reach their pre-teens, they become capable of behaving well to avoid feeling a sense of shame or guilt, not just to please and gain approval. Shame and guilt are vital components of any moral framework that emerges around this time to guide our tweenie as to how to behave. In combination, these two moral indicators act as internal and emotional, and there-fore essentially self-imposed, boundaries. However, shame and guilt can be misused and overused by adults, to the point where children can become either cowed and disempowered, or totally callous and disregarding of their relevance. What makes the difference? We can achieve the right balance and encourage a healthy degree of moral awareness in our tweenie by following the three fundamental elements of effective discipline: all children need boundaries; separate the behaviour from the child; and apply all rules and any punishments consistently. Morality has, in fact, very human and simple roots, as the following explanation shows.

Shame is something we feel when we fall short of expectations; it is a kind of embarrassment. If we operate a 'discipline-free' environment and fail to have clear expectations for our child's behaviour, there will be no marker against which to gauge 'falling short', and no opportunity for her to experience shame if it happens. However, children do feel much safer with boundaries and clear rules, so much so that they tend to behave outrageously in order to find them – located, usually, when we proclaim enough is enough. At that point, pushed to our limit, our reactions are more likely to be unpredictable and possibly punitive and hurtful, and directed more personally at our child not her behaviour. The shame she feels then will relate to herself, and could translate into a damaging self-doubt or self-hate rather than an appropriate check for managing self-discipline.

Guilt exists when we feel discomfort at another's distress that we believe we have caused. To feel a healthy sense of guilt, therefore, we have to be able to imagine the resulting distress, which is empathy, and to have an appropriate sense of personal power that we may have brought it about or been responsible for it. If a child does not generally feel able to control anything due to a life dominated by chaos, because no one listens and close adults fly off the handle unpredictably – or, indeed, if cause and effect never have to be tracked because the results of their behaviour are ignored – it will be near impossible for her to accept that she has caused someone's distress on any particular occasion.

And if she doesn't believe she caused or had some part to play in it, she cannot take responsibility for it. Consistent application of rules and punishments is important, not just to reinforce good behaviour but also to help a child to accept moral responsibility for that behaviour.

Where there is chaos, no consistency between cause and effect or no pattern to anything, it could make a tweenie feel either responsible for nothing or responsible for everything, a far more deeply confusing and disturbing state of affairs that may convince her that she is the central problem and must be *really* bad. And being actively blamed for something that she cannot possibly have caused (for example, our headache or if we break something) will make matters worse. Children who experience this deep and unrestrained guilt may find it too uncomfortable to bear and may retreat into a deep denial: refuse to entertain any guilt, shame or personal responsibility for anything, in effect losing touch with themselves in the process. As a further step, given the mayhem they believe they cause, they may choose to cut off totally from other people, a state close to autism.

To summarise, shame and guilt become effective, self-limiting experiences when each results from a focus on a child's behaviour, not on the person, keeping the two clearly separate. To achieve greater moral awareness and self-discipline among tweenies we should reject harsh, physical punishments such as beating and smacking that, in some people's eyes, 'teach what's right and wrong' but that generally fail to maintain that separation, and instead:

- Nurture a capable and positive sense of self.
- Model respect and consideration by showing it to our child and others.
- Maintain clear boundaries and consistent consequences.
- Encourage personal power and autonomy.
- Ensure that personal responsibility is tracked and acknowledged where appropriate.

- Absolve them totally of blame where they played no part.
- *Always* separate what they do from who they are.

Responding to challenge and dishonesty

Although tweenies have a reputation for being less challenging than toddlers or teenagers, they are by no means plain sailing. During these five years, as stated above, we can expect to have tiffs over such issues as how much freedom they should have to go places; how quickly they get the clothes, shoes or games they want, if at all; by how much their bedtime should be extended after each birthday; doing enough homework; the amount of time spent watching television or in front of the computer; territorial disputes with siblings; rudeness to us and whether they need to join family trips and outings. Most of these issues are considered in other chapters so won't be repeated here, though it is relevant to pull together some broad guidance to bear in mind in relation to rudeness, perceptions of challenge and dealing with dishonesty.

RESPONDING TO RUDENESS

When tweenies become freer with their tongues, which they will – especially to their mother – how much should this be tolerated? Should we explode at every mild insult because we expect to command respect; ignore it but try to discover what lay behind the apparent anger; demonstrate by example that we can be strong enough to ignore insults and avoid confrontations by so doing; defend ourselves forcefully on the particular issue; tell the other parent later and present a united, disapproving front; take it on the chin because we think we'll lose if we complain; forbid any rudeness because it is inappropriate for any child to be rude to any adult; or accept that everyone today needs to be able to stand up for themselves, so it's a good training ground?

The questions are not necessarily easy to answer. Each of us will want to draw the line somewhere different, though most parents seem to tolerate more rudeness now and there's certainly more of it about. 'I'd never dare to talk to my parents like that!' is a familiar comment. But in the next breath we might claim that our relationship with our parents was or is far cooler than our own with any older children we may have. The greater honesty and openness we now expect in relationships may well lead to some uncomfortable straight talking; nevertheless, close-ness never justifies abusiveness. A list of issues and principles follows that might clarify our position, help us to be consistent and, of course, help us to keep rudeness in reasonable check.

- If you are the only victim, your tweenie may understand the boundaries, feel safe enough with you to do it and value the honesty and opportunity to let off steam that you allow.
- If the rudeness goes further, it could be the time to enforce new rules.
- If the rudeness is recent, it may be developmental or a reac-tion to a particular difficulty that needs to be talked through.
- If it is longer-term and worsening, discard tolerance and put down some clear limits to terminate their inappropriately offensive behaviour.
- If they show warmth and affection at most other times, the 'disrespect' is not that serious.
- Consider if they show you respect in other ways, such as help-ing you put the groceries away after shopping, or fetching you a drink if you're tired.
- We can explode, ignore or concede. Ignoring a jibe is not the same as condoning it: this can be a neutral, blocking response, not one that justifies the behaviour.
- Remember to treat them with respect: if you don't want to be sworn at, don't swear at them.
- What is the difference for you between uncomfortable honesty, tactlessness, complaints and accusations, sounding off and

abusive language? Which of these do you find unacceptable, and which amounts to 'rudeness'?

• Are they prepared to say sorry after?
• Is your tweenie learning at the same time – on you, as it were – when to curb her tongue or how to be tactful?

Taster tips on possible ways to respond to rudeness

✓ Say that you found the manner of the comment unacceptable and explain how it felt to you.

✓ Acknowledge the strong feelings but ask her to rephrase the 'attack' in less accusatory or threatening language.

✓ Make light of it: 'Something's made you feel sore today!'

✓ Ignore it totally and walk away, though this could lead to a stronger outburst.

✓ Say nothing but shake your head gently, put your hand up or otherwise indicate the limit has been reached while saying nothing.

✓ 'Don't talk about/to your father/mother like that!' Arrange back-up. A strong, supportive, independent defence can work wonders.

✓ Swear words are lazy shortcuts to expression: ask for the underlying message to be spelled out properly.

✓ Become excessively polite and attentive to them for a while, to show how it can be done, that you have not taken umbrage and they have a chance to make amends.

Perceptions of challenge

All mammals are programmed to react to behaviour signals but these are not always clear. Some people see rudeness where others see straight talking; some see an insult where another sees a joke; one will bridle at a 'look' or a swagger while another will simply see an upstart who's trying it on, or see nothing. Most of us react more defensively than ever we need and see challenge or rejection when none is intended. This vulnerability, together with over-aggressive reactions, explains much conflict. Pre-teen children will rant and rail, experiment with put-downs to seem powerful and use language whose impact they cannot fully appreciate. Their vocabulary is generally more confrontational, as in 'talk to the hand, the face isn't listening', influenced by popular entertainment television programmes that encourage wars of words. Children will often do more damage than they intend, though some do strike to hurt. The following may help to keep a sense of perspective and minimise overt conflict with our tweenie.

- Just because you felt something personally does not mean it was meant personally.
- A child can feel the same about what we say and do, and defend with aggression.
- If a child feels something strongly inside, she may reflect that in her reaction, which is not, therefore, an 'over-reaction'.
- Carrying out our wishes, but not quite, could be our child's way of demonstrating independence, not a devious or spiteful further challenge.
- Young children, and some adults, see things in black and white; if a child is not 'good' (and what child is, 100 per cent?) then she must be bad. Consider which descriptions may prevail in our household and the impact they may have on conflict.

DEALING WITH DISHONESTY: LYING, CHEATING AND STEALING

We can feel particularly let down and threatened if our child lies, cheats or steals. Developmentally, we can distinguish between 'innocent', 'fantasy' and 'problematic' dishonesty. Children under five or so lie and steal innocently because they don't understand what it means or that it's wrong. They are also very prone to indulge in fantasy and wishful thinking. Most eight-year-olds, though, will have grasped the basics, be clear about reality and be strong enough inside not to have to engage in pretence or fanciful thinking. If they continue to be dishonest when they know they are doing wrong, even if it is akin to wishful thinking, it should by now be considered potentially 'problematic' and demands sensitive action. We should not forget either that in times of stress tweenies do revert to more child-like behaviour, or that this is the age at which children will take risks and might lie as part of that or to conceal any consequential mistakes (see chapter eleven). Though these are generally passing phases, we should not ignore any dishonesty; we should be firm, perhaps puzzled, but always kind and understanding. Any child who feels unsafe with us could seek consolation elsewhere.

Andy's story

Andy, aged eight, had been taking some small change from the shelf where his dad emptied his pockets, using it over a few weeks to buy a stock of cheap sweets that he had secretly hoarded in his bedroom. One day his mum found them, and confronted him after school. She asked him to turn off the TV because she had something important to say. She told him of her find and asked where the sweets had come from. She knew he had recently spent most of his pocket money, so was puzzled. Andy quickly owned up to his theft but claimed he thought his dad didn't want it as the money sat there unused. He said he wanted the sweets for his class outing the next week and needed to buy them himself because she never bought him any and he always had to cadge, which he hated. His mum was a bit taken aback at his reason and could see his point. She also realised the recent arrival of a baby sister might have made him feel left out. However, taking the money was wrong and she made Andy forgo his pocket money for two weeks to pay it back and she removed the sweets. But she also made sure he had something to share out on his trip the following week and nothing like that happened again.

Taster tips on dealing with dishonesty

✓ Make it absolutely clear that what she did was wrong, whatever the form or possible cause.

✓ Don't punish her harshly once she has owned up and told the truth: it may make her more deceitful next time. Ask her to suggest an appropriate 'consequence' so she judges her error for herself.

✓ Don't call her a cheat, a liar or a thief as the label could stick. She must retain sufficient self-respect to amend her behaviour.

✓ Act to boost her self-esteem if you judge a poor self-image explains the cheating or lies.

✓ Point out that cheating is self-defeating. Even if it raises results, these won't reflect true ability so cannot possibly deepen genuine self-belief or self-respect.

✓ Try to be more honest yourself. Don't lie to her, or cheat or steal.

✓ Be as worried about lies told to others as those spun to us.

✓ Increase her autonomy if a lack of influence could explain any deception that appears to seek to assert control or to manipulate.

✓ Make her return any stolen item, for embarrassment is a deterrent.

✓ Once she has admitted her wrongdoing, allow her to raise any gripes. It might clear the air and help in understanding why it happened.

✓ Be understanding, but unrelenting in confirming the behaviour as unacceptable.

DRAWING THIS TOGETHER

Although it is important that we teach our tweenie to develop a moral code and behave appropriately, we must be careful not to go overboard. Home should be a haven, a place to relax, not a torture chamber characterised by nagging and criticism. Telling our tweenie like a stuck record that she has fallen short, has done what she ought not to have done and not done what she ought to have done, will make her feel crestfallen, shameful and unable to please or get anything right. Given that a child will always find it easier to change a behaviour than who she senses she is, we should always direct our concerns specifically to her actions, not to her personality and being. This is not only practical but also fair; and fairness, kindness, consideration, self-respect, honesty and tolerance are the foundation for effective discipline, self-discipline and moral development, as well as for making and keeping friends, the subject of the next chapter.

Ten top take-out tips

- If your tweenie can 'turn on' her manners at friends' houses, even if she doesn't behave impeccably at home, then she knows what to do and you're winning.
- Don't expect too much too soon. Children make progress via small steps in every area of development.

- 'Walk the talk'. Children need models more than they need critics. Teach consideration towards others by first considering them.
- Don't take their challenges personally. Be sensitive to their age and stage, and what this means they need to strive for – to be different and to feel independent and capable.
- Keep criticism to a minimum and focus any such comments on their behaviour, not on them as people, for they are trying to flower.
- Stay positive: make all expectations very clear, notice the good and ignore the bad, and offset every criticism with at least four affirmations and plenty of praise. Accept them unconditionally and attend to them frequently.
- Their self-belief is their most precious possession. Do not undermine it with humiliation or sarcasm, or criticism and over-control. Tweenies will show respect for others more readily if they are able to respect themselves.
- Minimise resentment. Listen to their complaints: perhaps pin up a safe 'gripe sheet' on which they can record their grievances. Discuss these weekly, or more often if the sheet fills quickly!
- Monitor and supervise, quietly and from a distance. They may not like this, but deep down it makes them feel significant and cared for.
- Don't dismiss any developing thoughts, views, feelings, judgements or desires as unimportant, misguided, foolish, childish or stupid. Take each one seriously, and simply explain and present some alternative approaches if you disagree or are worried.

And Remember!

Always separate what they do from who they are.

Discipline is about learning, not dictatorship.

Warm relationships flow from talking, having fun, spending time together and lots of unconditional love.

5

THE SEARCH FOR SOUL MATES:

Learning from Friendship

ONE OF THE MOST NOTICEABLE changes that takes place in the lives of eight- to twelve-year-olds is their growing focus on friends. Over the five years, children spend increasing amounts of leisure time with friends and use them to explore what they can do, how to enjoy their new physical strength, what it means to be a boy or a girl and different ways to have fun. Friends also introduce variety; different friends like to do different things and these additional activities can be sampled, alongside different cultures, food and ways of living as they visit different homes. Friends give tweenies that all-important sense of belonging and the activities they choose to do together sharpen each child's personal and gender identity, even if it is just relaxing together at home, at the park or on the street. Of course, parents continue to be a vital source of warmth, comfort and security but tweenies look increasingly outside the family to their friends for the personal affirmation that keeps their confidence afloat.

For tweenies, the important thing about friends is choice and autonomy. Precisely because they begin to use friends to strengthen their sense of self they must choose their own. They are no longer happy to be forced to play with the children of our best friends or those of close neighbours. Neither are they so content to hang around with their desk partners from the classroom, just because a teacher sat them together. They are now able, and want, to be far more discriminating, having first whizzed through quite a few.

This chapter has two sections. In the first, we look at the benefits and patterns of tweenie friendships: how the joys and pitfalls of friendship contribute to our child's social, emotional and physical growth; how boys' and girls' friendship patterns differ; the power of peer pressure and its link to threesome difficulties; and how to preserve our child's individuality and self-respect while fitting in. The second section considers a range of typical tweenie friendship problems, including being bullied and getting into 'the wrong crowd'. Unfortunately, friends can be satisfying and growth producing, yet they can cause deep distress and be growth destroying.

The benefits and patterns of friendship

Friends are vitally important to all children, because friends encourage children to share, understand, use their imagination, argue, discuss, be creative and offer emotional support. Tweenies begin to use friends to try themselves out. Adults usually retain vivid memories of particular childhood friendships because they involved going to the edge in the safety of numbers – experimenting with daring and discovery, risk and disappointment. Friends become, in a very important way, a combined expression of freedom and individuality: 'I enjoy doing what this person likes to do', 'I work well with that person because . . .', 'This person is like me', 'With this person I feel safe.' And when someone chooses to become their friend, they know they are likeable and acceptable. Like loving families, good friends deliver fun, stability, hope and comfort and give useful feedback. Children are famously blunt, to the point of brutality on occasions, and friends often can pass direct criticism in a way many parents find uncomfortable. Straight talking can be effective; within a loyal friendship more honest comment and playful teasing can be heard and tolerated because it is balanced by plenty of kindness and acceptance. It is not surprising, then, that around the age of eight, the majority of children develop a great hunger for friends. If children can develop good, stable, supportive and respectful friendships during the tweenie years then the teens are likely to be far less rocky.

CHANGING FRIENDSHIP PATTERNS

Infant school children can be famously fickle in their friendships, being 'best' friends with one child one day and another the next. This is partly because they invest less in the relationship and partly because these are based far more on coincidence – who is around and available. Eight-year-olds may still move from friend to friend as they explore different aspects of their personality and gravitate to whoever lives close, but some of these relationships will become more significant. Tweenies begin to seek like-minded soul mates – one or several – with whom to forge a more enduring bond. Typically, tweenie relationships become more settled over the five years because they are increasingly based on shared and recognisable interests and attitudes and fulfil deeper social emotional needs. It has been written: 'One does not make friends, one recognises them'; however, it may take time for any child to become clear about who he is, what he likes to do, who else he is like – or wants to be like – and who could be trusted as a close friend. Different children will reach this point at different times, and in the meantime many may be entirely happy being self-absorbed in a particular passion, reading or being alone, and may therefore end up with a deeper sense of self than another individual who has been more 'popular' and socially active. Provided our child seems happy, anything is okay. No parent can or should prescribe exactly what pattern of friendships their pre-teen son or daughter will establish.

Taster tips on encouraging friendships if he seems sad without any

✓ Help him to be clear about his personal strengths: the qualities he has to offer.

✓ Let him know you like him and enjoy his company.

✓ Invite friends round when possible. Be warm and welcoming but then leave them be.

✓ Try to accept your tweenie's choice of friends and don't criticise or compare.

✓ Have clear rules, discussed in advance, so there's less likelihood of visitors going too far when you could lose your temper.

✓ Trying too hard to get a friend can be counter-productive, so don't collude with bribery.

✓ Discourage bossy and selfish behaviour; teach him to compromise and give way.

✓ Model the behaviour that helps to sustain friendships: listen attentively, show tolerance and demonstrate care and concern when others are in difficulty.

✓ Present the view that friends are not possessions: they should be allowed to spend time with others without the threat of rejection.

THE QUALITY OF FRIENDSHIP

Regardless of how many friends our child has, the important thing about any valued friendship is its quality. Good friends help our child to have fun, will have a similar sense of humour, have a shared rapport, can keep secrets, can be relied upon to play fair, will care if things go wrong and won't exploit any weakness. A good relationship is a balanced relationship, not a doormat relationship. Any friendship that requires one person to be walked over, or where one child seems content to be walked over, is unhealthy and sets bad patterns for the future. In either case, offer more opportunities for autonomy in case it is a reaction to being put upon at home.

Popularity is different from friendship. Although great status attaches to being 'popular', popularity may not rest in a genuine openness and accepting personality that appeals to and accepts all. It may attach more to material or physical advantage – being able to have bigger, more 'grown-up' parties or have 'cool' possessions or clothes. A child who is popular, or who seeks friendship with a popular person in the area or class, may get a short-term fillip but may not develop the more reliable relationship support and experience that helps us with our adult, more gender-focused, relationships.

THE GENDER PATTERNS: HOW BOYS' AND GIRLS' FRIENDSHIPS DIFFER

Girls and boys tend to have different kinds of friendships. Girls will usually pair off or join small intimate groups while boys tend to gather in a larger, looser group that shares a common focus and interest. Despite these differing styles, friends are equally important to both sexes for delivering affirmation and identity. Jordan, eight, said, 'It's miserable having no friends, with no one to care for you.' The one feature most tweenies display is having same-sex best friends. Girls may join the 'lads' in the park for a general kick about or join in a playground game of power rangers, taking on one of the female roles; some boys may enjoy playing sports such as tennis with girls or sharing music in a band or orchestra, but it rarely goes further. In one survey, boys aged eleven to fourteen ridiculed girls for even wanting to play football with boys, calling them 'geezer birds', though when interviewed in private they were more tolerant and valued girls' greater emotional insights. Adult friendships may ignore gender but it's a rare tweenie that finds a best friend among 'the other lot'.

Although tweenies' friendships can be very caring and supportive, they are by no means all plain sailing, largely because so much hangs on them. Children who are trying themselves out inevitably pull rank, which means that tweenie friendships can be marred by power struggles. Those boys who are interested in gaining advantage may use physical size or sporting prowess to compete to become top of the pile during these five years, but others may deploy their wit or humour to gain attention. Girls, on the other hand, may resort to their tongues, and increasingly their looks, for both status and attention. Girls express their competitive drive through friends: asserting that they have more, or are friends with the most popular or prettiest girls in the class or neighbourhood. They can include or exclude others seemingly on a whim, on the basis of superficial things related to clothing, body shape or facial features. One eleven-year-old reported being mercilessly taunted because one day she was spotted wearing red underpants, and a dark-haired twelve-year-old was ostracised for having 'sideboards like Elvis and eyebrows like a gorilla', so she shaved them off.

Garrulous girls: hitches, witches and bitches

Girls talk a lot; they see themselves as groupies and seek reassurance through intimacy. It usually matters deeply to them whether they are 'in' or 'out' and whether they have a 'best' friend to signify approval. Girls can be wonderful friends, showing great caring and consideration, insight and understanding, chatting at length and offering real emotional support during personally distressing situations. Indeed, girls may select a best friend who has had or is going through a similar experience – parental separation, loneliness or an alcoholic parent, for example – which means they can speak freely and learn from each other.

If they become particularly worried about a friend, an older tweenie may decide to confide in an adult as a way to get help.

The darker side of girls' relationships, however, is that girls can be queens of gossip and spite and may abuse that intimacy and trust. Their friendships can be fraught. The years of accumulated advantage in language and vocabulary have shined and sharpened their tongues, which are then used to either flatter or batter. The more girls seek superiority and judge themselves by comparison with others, the more they will keep an ear open for usable stories, plot and do others down to preserve their edge. Though traditionally thought of as 'sugar and spice and all things nice' – probably based on their wish to please and their penchant for pretty dresses – the female of the tweenie species is also quite capable of being witch-like and bitchy, becoming more prone, potentially, as the self-doubting teens approach.

Boisterous boys: bluster and bravado

Boys' friendships at this age are usually less complicated. Intimate talk with best friends is simply not most boys' style; indeed, a study has shown they are dismissive of girls whom they consider 'waste' time chatting, doing nothing. The basis of boys' friendships tends to be focused activity, whether in groups or in pairs. Encouraging friendships as the parent of a boy can be daunting because of the sheer number. We have to get used to five or more turning up at the house at once, so we need to be very clear about where and what they are allowed to play – and eat. Their appetites can be scary, though at least twelve-year-olds are not yet full size! Akin to pack animals, some boys can be easily led and others will jostle for leadership. Boys often seek significance through reputation, rather than intimacy. Many relish notoriety and enjoy playing up to it. If they cannot make their mark legitimately, some will seek it illegitimately through daring and disruption. This is the age and stage when many will court attention and a personal following through playing the class clown or displaying macho-style behaviour on the streets. This is discussed further in chapter eleven on risk and danger.

But not every boy feels the need to throw his weight about and boast on a grand scale. Many eight- to twelve-year-olds just knock about innocently doing 'stuff', having a laugh, jostling playfully, getting up to a bit of – mostly harmless – mischief, so having a sense of humour that sparks off others is a clear plus. Boys can be very loyal and interpret this as keeping things they know about a friend very private. If they are worried about a friend, they are far less likely to tell an adult because they see both this, and 'telling' if they've done wrong, as 'grassing'. But even good friends can compete, and enjoy it when they beat others for the team or get a higher mark in a test. If their gang contains younger or smaller boys, these will often be exploited to run errands or act as the fall guy if there's trouble.

The rough and the smooth: how parents can help

Both girls and boys can be acutely sensitive to the nuances of what were possibly offhand comments not intended to hurt, as well as to well-targeted, barbed ones. Girls can go up and down like a yo-yo according to who said what when, while boys may try to hide their distress. Supporting a tweenie who is the victim of friends' sharper manipulative skills or even clumsy social skills is very important and we should never belittle the hurt thus caused. We can try to offer a sense of perspective because it will probably all be forgotten the next day and explain how people often say things that, in the heat of the moment, they do not mean. We could suggest that our tweenie explain in a matter-of-fact way how much it hurt and that he or she felt surprised and let down by the incident, or even consider asking if there was a reason behind it. Other possible approaches are given in the section 'Three's a Crowd' below.

What if the boot is on the other foot and we don't like how our son or daughter behaves or talks to others? Should we step in and police their friendships, or define friends as personal territory and not interfere even if it seems to condone nastiness? As a general rule it is better to stay clear, unless we feel the verbal attacks or behaviour verge on bullying. If we criticise, our tweenie may feel put down. Both girls and boys have to work through the common ebbs and flows of their friendships, learning how far they can go before they really upset someone, just as children explore the limits as they play fight. But the occasional comment from us such as, 'That sounds a bit harsh', 'I wouldn't like to be on the receiving end of that', or 'Wouldn't that have really upset him / her?' is hardly intrusive and may be a helpful prod.

To sum up, through managing longer-lasting friendships without adult interference, tweenies develop vital social and emotional skills, learning to:

- Listen and compromise.
- Understand how other people think and behave.
- Solve disputes and differences.
- Be tolerant as they accept different ways and views.
- Care, as they hear problems and offer support.
- Appreciate the value and limits of loyalty and commitment.
- Function as a member of a group or team and not be wholly self-focused.

PEER PRESSURE AND THE PRESSURE TO IMPRESS

Peer pressure is another feature of friendship dynamics during the tweenie years. A peer group is usually broader than a friendship group and is influenced by a far wider set of local and national or distinct cultural trends, but it is none the less powerful and hard to resist because of growing children's general desire to be accepted and fit in. Children hate to stand out or look different in case they are jeered at or teased. Peer pressure is particularly potent among tweenies because they are so keen to conform, as we saw when discussing pester power. When children are not sure of who they are or what they should do, they feel more comfortable when they keep up. This also explains why spiteful comments can cut particularly deep. As Molly, eleven, said to me about her earlier experiences, 'At that age you're very, very sensitive.'

Peer pressure encourages children to follow trends, but when children enter the tweenie years they also try to be trendsetters in their desire to impress and gain advantage in the popularity and friendship stakes. Younger tweenies are prone to tell exaggerated stories about what they or their family have or have done and may pester to have the most glamorous birthday party or family holiday, for example. They may also nag to watch a 12-, 15- or even 18-rated video or to have a bigger and better sleepover. Older tweenies may tell fibs about what they have done to sound more daring and mature. If we feel our child is becoming competitive to stay ahead, reassure him that he is great as he is and does not need to show off. If we collude and give in it can deepen, not dispel, his insecurity because it suggests we agree that these things matter.

When our children want things others have and do – things we don't want them to have, it can be hard to judge whether our reluctance to give in represents an outdated position, over-control or justified protection of their best interests and our values. Each of us must reflect on this dilemma. Perhaps the healthiest response is to set out the issues, explain our view, invite our child to present his and then to stay true to himself as he weighs up the options and we review ours. Don't forget that particular peer groups can also be a force for good, for example when they encourage good eating, leisure and study habits. A good, longer-term protective strategy is to nurture our child's personal values and sense of self so he is better able to identify and resist inappropriate pressures when they arise.

Taster tips on managing peer pressure

✓ Make it clear that no one should have to sell his soul to be popular. It's okay to want to be liked, but not okay to give way on everything in the process.

✓ Discuss the difference between popularity and friendship; with friends they should not have to pretend, but to be popular people often have to adopt different personas, which obscures their core identity.

✓ Discuss the meaning of friendship and how it differs from 'peer relationships'. What behaviour can he reasonably expect from a friend that might determine how genuine the friendship is? For example, friends should respect his point of view and not force him to do anything unwillingly.

✓ Offer choices if the pressure seems overwhelming. 'I'll say yes to the issue that matters most to you but to nothing else. Which is it to be?'

✓ The easiest answer a child can give a pushy friend is, 'My mum or dad won't let me.' Don't be scared to be firm, if that's your genuine view, and realise many children like to feel 'looked after' and protected from pressures.

✓ Avoid giving in to requests for ever-fancier birthday parties. Having a good time doesn't necessarily mean paying a packet, and home-devised, themed parties that tweenies have helped to plan are often the most memorable.

✓ If our tweenie pesters to see a film certified as suitable for older children to impress his friends and feel 'cool', hold firm. It is valuable to wait until close to

---

the advised age in order to retain some personal authority and to demonstrate respect for public guidance and the law.

✓ Always check with other parents if their child is to watch a video recommended for older children at your house.

✓ Sleepovers symbolise growing up but eight-year-olds can get very homesick. To avoid returning the unhappy ones who could not cope, start with two or three who know each other and live close by. Make sure their favourite cuddly toy is invited too, and any other comforter, pillow or duvet.

✓ Best to reserve sleepovers for Friday nights, half terms or school holidays, as any child who stays the course will be in a foul mood the next day! If our tweenie is to stay over somewhere else, let him decline if his confidence collapses.

Friendships can become strained where one friend is more susceptible to the pull of the peer group than the other, or one set of parents is more resistant than another. They can also suffer when children try to impress and pull rank within the relationship, which can explain temporary hitches and some of the problems inherent in threesomes, discussed next.

THREE'S A CROWD – AND TEMPORARY HITCHES

Tricky threesomes are a particular feature of the tweenie years and are a minefield. They cause no end of problems. Lucy, aged nine, said, 'It's really hard having three friends together as there's always someone in the middle. If the other two have had a fight, each one wants you to take sides. They then say, if you don't I won't be your best friend any more.' Girls, for it is usually girls who form threesomes as boys tend to play together in larger groups, fall out over a range of issues. In the early tweenie years, the problem can be simple such as who likes whom best or what to play. Later, the dynamic can become quite complex and destructive as children become more manipulative in their search for power and status. Emma, eight, said, 'I didn't want to play Sarah's game so she started to ignore me. Sometimes someone thinks I've left them out and I really haven't.' Lucy went on to explain, 'I had a friend called Stephanie. She doesn't talk much so I wanted to help her. But I'm friends with Bethany too and I got caught in the middle. Bethany told me not to play with Stephanie. I tried to get them to be friends, and when I did get Bethany to like Stephanie they went off together.'

The closer, more possessive friendship that can emerge as children come close to adolescence are sometimes seen as the stage before a more adult model of commitment. Intimacy, loyalty, dependency, couple identity and even power are all being explored in these tiffs. Individuals can be very demanding of best friends on whom they begin to rely for so much and can test the relationship to its limits. Molly, eleven, said, 'If I didn't agree with Amy she'd go mad and turn other people against me. She was a complete stirrer.' It is not surprising that threesomes provoke such jealousies and tensions, for it is almost like sharing one's partner with another.

Alice's story

Alice, now fifteen, described what happened to her during her first year or two at her new school. 'I chose to go to a school that none of my previous friends were going to. I wanted a fresh start. But there is pressure to find a friend before everyone gets hitched and everyone's so eager to fit in. Quite soon I became best friends with Georgie. She then made friends with Sally and we went around together. Me and Georgie were quite similar and Sally was put out that she wasn't as close to either of us. She tried to start arguments between us about what seemed like nothing. She got upset if I talked to someone else or if I spent too much time with Georgie. She'd try to get between me and Georgie; she'd instantly report stuff back after she'd been with either one of us and you'd never know whether what she passed back was true. Sometimes she'd be really nice and you'd relax and then she'd do something really awful. She was a rebel and if we didn't want to join in she'd tease us. She'd say, 'You're such a weakling,' and then not talk to me for the rest of the day. She made you feel like you'd done something awful. If this person is always arguing with you, you think it's something wrong with you. But I didn't want to drop her in it in case I got left alone. The one thing you want is friends. In the end, it made Georgie and me better friends because she went so far and we shared that experience. Eventually she left. I feel more confident and a better judge of character, having been through all that rubbish. I'd say to all new Year 7s, don't commit yourself to one person straight away because they might not be as they seem.'

What can parents do to help?

Eight- to ten-year-olds can be enormously relieved to learn from us that threesome difficulties are common and are nothing to do with them individually; they are then better able to ride the bumps without taking personal insult. However, we should tread carefully: children can't be taught how to have friends; they must learn it first-hand. Alice, now fifteen, thought parents 'Shouldn't try too much to get involved (unless it's something serious like physical abuse) because it is important that you learn to deal with these kinds of people and parents can make things worse.' We should, therefore:

- Be there to listen and explain; only offer advice when it is specifically sought.
- Allow them to hold their own at home so they can do it elsewhere.
- Help them to feel confident; show that their views matter.

Finders keepers: friendship problems

Lucy, nine, admitted, 'You get into far more arguments when you're older. You have more things to fall out over and you always do. When you're younger, you just do stuff together. My friends have just fallen out over fancying the same boy.' Troubles with friends can loom large and hang heavy and we should try to support our pre-teen son or daughter through them. Friendship problems can range from not having a best friend, friends being 'stolen', having undesirable friends and bullying. This section looks at how to support our tweenie through some typical friendship troubles, including, first, having few or no friends.

'NO ONE LIKES ME, I'VE GOT NO FRIENDS!'

Friendship patterns vary considerably. Some children have one close friend and few others, while others have plenty of loose friendships but no special one. Both types might reasonably wail that they have no friends, if that's how they see it. One study estimated that one in seven children, about 13 per cent, have few or no friends. There is nothing 'wrong' with a child who has few close friends. Sometimes home and school moves disrupt friendships and it's hard to forge new ones when everyone else is 'fixed up'. Some children are evidently more, or less, sociable by nature so some are entirely happy on their own. Sometimes, children simply feel insecure and uncomfortable and don't have the confidence or style to rub easily along with others. Added to which, the more a child strives for friendship and curries favour, the less successful he is likely to be, either because potential friends withdraw through irritation or because they turn nasty, having spotted the weakness.

Children are prone to exaggerate, especially when things really matter to them, so when they wail that they have no friends, they probably mean something less dramatic; for example, it can mean they wish they had a best friend, they wish they had more friends, they wish they belonged to a clearly identified group rather than were friends with other 'floaters' or they wish they were invited to more parties. Being specific can encourage a more positive outlook and define clearer solutions. It's important to query the value so often attached to having a 'best' friend: adults invariably appreciate being able to socialise widely rather than focus exclusively on one person, and our best friends generally emerge and show their qualities over time. For children who have real difficulty making friends, books are available for teens and pre-teens that offer sound advice. One, listed in the resources section at the back, contains a four-point plan for making friends: 'learn to communicate, learn to listen, learn to be yourself, learn not to judge'. If we model all these skills at home, draw attention to them and encourage our tweenie to follow them too, we shall be helping him to fit in with and be acceptable to others.

Taster tips on supporting a child who has few friends

✓ Get to the bottom of the problem – you are no one's *best* friend, you weren't invited to the last two parties, you get teased about things, or what? Get specifics and work from there.

✓ Help him realise that, however lovely he is, not everyone's going to like him; and however awful he thinks he is, there are plenty of kids who won't remotely see

him that way and think he's great to be with, because
he is.

✓ Help him to be clear about his personal strengths and
the qualities he has to offer.

✓ Encourage leisure activities that engage him fully, so
he does not feel so alone.

✓ Help him to see himself in a positive light: let him
know you like him and enjoy his company and don't
shout or criticise.

✓ Invite other children round whenever it feels natural.

✓ If he has befriended someone younger because he
needs a 'best' friend but is chary of his peers, don't be
concerned. Provided there is no intimidation, it will
help him to feel okay while he grows in self-assurance.

✓ Encourage him to join a kids club that involves fun
activities so getting to know other people his age is
child's play.

✓ Discourage selfishness; teach him to give and take.

IN WITH THE WRONG CROWD

When our tweenie's friends 'fit' our family and complement our
values it gives us a warm, comfortable feeling. He is happy
because his loyalties are not compromised and we enjoy having
the friends around. It is a very different story if his friends challenge our values, have too many freedoms or seem to be leading him astray.

As we see in chapter eleven, the tweenie years can mark the
start of later trouble. Some eight- to twelve-year-olds are beginning to bunk off school, smoke tobacco or dope, indulge in
petty shoplifting, self-harm, cause minor damage to property
and cars and daub walls, setting a pattern of deviant behaviour
that could then upset their progress. Very occasionally, an individual child will wander off alone but it is more usual for there

to be others who egg each other on. It is, of course, natural for children to get up to mischief, so it is important that we try to judge whether any trouble is just high spirits and natural curiosity that will fade or the start of a more worrying and intensifying trend. If we invite the friends home, we can get to know them better and review the situation. If we remain concerned, we should try to understand why this has happened, why our child could find these particular individuals good company, and consider how to separate, carefully, our tweenie from his current crowd.

But what can we do?

Issuing decrees that forbid contact may be ignored and even backfire, so we need to work more subtly. We can, for example, try to arrange other activities for the times when the friends usually meet to make that difficult: we might, for example, change our after-school care plans, weekday or weekend work commitments or arrange for our child to stay for some days of the school holidays with a relative, to break the pattern. Quite often, children who seem comfortable with challenge feel they have failed in some way or believe they're not worth much. They might have been bullied, for example. We might suggest that he attend an after-school club that develops new skills and interests or we might spend more time with him and ensure he gets plenty of positive feedback.

We might try to reduce the amount of criticism or unfavourable comparison he receives by changing our ways or priming any siblings or other adult carers. Some children respond well to being given appropriate responsibilities so another option is to consider tasks he could be given. It might be useful to refer to the suggestions for monitoring and supervision offered on pages 90 and 298.

We can discuss the nature of friendship and why some kids seek to manipulate others to join them in doing wrong. And we can ask our child why he enjoys his time with this particular group of friends and what he gains from their friendship. If the children involved attend the same school, we could explain the position to and seek more advice from the school.

NEW SCHOOL: NEW FRIENDS OR NO FRIENDS?

It is perfectly natural for a child to be worried about losing or making friends when starting a new school. Lucy, aged nine, who was not even changing schools, said just before going back in September, 'It's funny, not being sure who your friends are until school starts again.' It could be an eleven-year-old's biggest concern. They will fret over whether anyone will like them; worry about any informal 'house' or style rules they might infringe unknowingly; and may be unsure which of their interests or which aspect of their personality to draw attention to. Those who move with familiar faces are sometimes felt to have a big advantage. If our child feels like a fish out of water when he starts, we can reassure him that he won't be the only one; and those who transfer with good friends frequently make new ones after a short while, as he undoubtedly will.

Taster tips on handling the secondary transfer friendship void

✓ Make sure they carry on seeing their old friends who have gone to other schools as much as possible in the first few months so they feel less stranded and desperate.

✓ Reassure them that most other children will be feeling the same. Be understanding of their strong desire to fit in and be accepted, and especially of their fear of being bullied that will be particularly intense if they are without the protection of a friendship group.

✓ Caution care in becoming over-committed to one particular person too soon. It takes time to suss what someone is like under the surface.

✓ Explain, too, that friendships based on personal things such as interests and views take more time to find and get right, so it's worth exploring and waiting.

✓ Make it clear that we enjoy his company, so he feels confident when approaching others.

✓ Suggest attending any relevant break-time clubs or activities to meet others with similar interests.

✓ Oil the wheels of friendship. Welcome new friends at home, and be happy to drive him to a new friend's house if it is difficult to reach.

BULLYING

Bullying can take many different forms and can be devastating whatever form it takes. It can seriously undermine a child's confidence and security and for a while obliterate any sense of self-worth. In the worst cases, bullying can lead to depression and attempted suicide. The scars can last well into adulthood, as many people who suffered as children have later openly admitted. Bullying is also known to spread, because victims quite often become bullies when they get the chance, to overcome the humiliation experienced and to regain the power, control and sense of status lost during their trials. It is very important to break the cycle. We should care deeply about bullying, and act quickly if we suspect that our child is embroiled at either end of what is, in truth, an abusive relationship. But harshness does not help and bullies and victims should both be viewed as in need of support, troubled rather than 'trouble'.

Bullying is deliberate, sustained, negative or aggressive behaviour by one or more people who intend to frighten or hurt. It always involves an imbalance of power, for control is exercised over the victim by exploiting a weak spot. Insensitive behaviour is not bullying, even though it can be hurtful, and children who are too shy to ask to join in ongoing games in a crowded and noisy playground and feel excluded are not being bullied either; it takes a lot of guts, and complex social skills, to manage playtime. Teasing between friends, where each side is confident the other doesn't mean it and can speak out if it goes too far, is more like verbal rough and tumble and teaches children to handle the playground. Bullying, by contrast, usually involves persistent verbal and emotional cruelty (hurtful teasing, taunting, exclusion); repeated physical aggression (hitting, kicking, punching); sustained extortion and intimidation or theft of money, snacks, school books or possessions. Some children are picked on for racist or homophobic reasons or because they have a noticeable physical characteristic. One boy suffered homophobic taunts on arrival at secondary school simply because his name was Simon. Bullies may be unhappy at home, trying to block out academic failures, dishing out to others what has been done to them or be seeking status because they are lonely. Victims may in some way welcome the attention of the notorious, be timid and crumple easily, or they may simply not have learned to defend themselves verbally.

Information points: Tweenies and bullying

- About one in five primary pupils say they have been bullied. In one survey of seven- to thirteen-year-olds, 27 per cent said that they had been bullied sometimes or more often that term.
- The most common type of bullying is name-calling, followed by being hit, threatened or spreading false rumours.
- Children often keep it to themselves. Some 30 per cent of victims of bullies in the UK never tell and suffer alone.

- Fear of bullying is greatest at the age of ten, linked to the uncertainty of secondary school and walking out alone more, though most bullying happens later.
- Smacking children does not toughen them up. The chance of being severely bullied increases significantly for children (especially boys) who are smacked or who witness violence between adults at home.

Source: *Bullying in Britain*

The rise of 'relationship bullying'

The most common form of bullying among tweenies is what might be dubbed 'relationship bullying': name-calling and being excluded. As this is the time when having friends *really* matters, these five years mark the moment when relationship bullies grow full-length fangs. Relationship bullies aim to hurt other children where it hurts most, by implying someone is not good enough to be a friend. They target a child's very being by using not only cruel words but also cruelly withheld words, creating a silence that will isolate the victim and makes him feel he does not exist, which is devastating. Caitlin, at the age of nine, lost all her friends when a lonely girl, jealous of her popularity, started a series of false rumours at her expense. It worked. She became totally isolated and so miserable that her parents moved her to another school, where she resettled well.

For many girls, failing in the friendship stakes can seem far more serious than failing academically: the former is absolute (you either have friends or you don't), it feels outside your control (you can't make someone like you), and it seems permanent (there's no obvious escape route), whereas academic failure is relative, temporary (because it is correctible) and in one's control. Boys who want to hurt at this age will also name-call, and frequently use homophobic insults to dismiss someone who appears, for example, too committed to school work or who mixes with girls as friends; but they also focus on boys' common fear of failing in the football stakes. They may pick on classmates who are either physically cumbersome, swots or 'weedy'; however, as sport is a common route to male friendship, it may be received as an equivalent insult.

Taster tips on how to support a child caught up in bullying

✓ Try to be understanding if he is upset – don't reject him for being 'weak'.

✓ Avoid direct questions that convey anxiety – gently ask what he does at break time, whether it's his best time or if it drags.

✓ If we learn our child has bullied don't punish or beat – think if anything at home or at school could explain a need to feel 'in charge'.

✓ Discuss making a friend with someone else who is alone.

✓ Suggest taking turns at what to play so there are fewer arguments.

✓ Discuss phrases that will help him to join in with others: *That looks fun. Will you teach it to me?* is a stronger approach than *Can I play too?*

✓ Suggest that he hide any hurt or say something appropriate when teased or excluded.

✓ Help him to appreciate the difference between accidents, playful teasing and good-humoured rough and tumble, and fighting or intentionally hostile acts – and react accordingly.

✓ Spend more time with your child, so he feels loved and accepted.

✓ Encourage a caring masculinity – being strong doesn't mean hitting or bullying.

✓ Recommend joining a club outside school to lose the 'victim' label and gain new skills, confidence and friendships.

BUT WE CAN'T HELP IF THEY WON'T TELL – HOW TO ENCOURAGE THEM TO OPEN UP

Tweenies begin to clam up and keep more things to themselves for a mixture of reasons. Feeling more separate, some prefer privacy and think they should now cope on their own. Some will feel personal shame at having failed to stand strong so they cover up the truth. Some children, particularly boys and in relation to their fathers, pretend everything is fine in order to preserve parental pride and expectation. And some don't tell because they don't want to add to any existing health or family problems. By the age of eight, most children will be sensitive to these matters.

The important thing is to keep the lines of communication open. There are statements and questions that encourage openness, and those more likely to switch children off. We should avoid questions such as, 'Why don't you seem to have any friends at school at the moment?' or 'Why are you so quiet at the moment? You've turned into a mouse.' They send a clear message about what we want and expect – what is important to us – and seem to accuse them. Questions that are too open-ended, such as 'How was school today?' allow children to walk right through them and leave us none the wiser.

Taster tips on encouraging tweenies to open up

✓ Deflect the spotlight from them and start with you: share your information and tell them about your day. Include things that didn't go so well so they know it's

136

okay to admit this. Then wait for them to volunteer their information, which may not happen straight away but is likely in time.

✓ Narrow the question down: ask, 'Did anything really good happen today, or anything tough?' so they know we are ready to hear about either.

✓ Show concern for any behaviour changes rather than ask directly about events. 'You seem to have lost some of your spark / had trouble sleeping recently. That's not like you. Is there something on your mind you can tell me about?' If the last question is answered, 'Yes there is but no I don't want to talk,' at least we have got somewhere.

✓ Don't force anything. Any reticence to talk should be respected. Simply say we're there if needed. We might gently probe with questions about timing and location. 'Is it about lesson time or break time?' 'Is it something that's happening every day or only some days?' Or we may try to reassure them at the beginning: 'When people get picked on, if that's what's happening, kids usually feel it's their fault. But it's the ones who do the picking who have the problem, you know.'

✓ Once we get close to the truth, try to get details about who, when and what and discuss possible responses. It won't help to go storming into school or to the offender's parents without either the facts or our child's agreement to a course of action. His support is important. The more embarrassed he feels about our reaction, the less likely he is to open up thereafter. (For suggestions on contacting schools, see the next chapter.)

And if they don't tell, what are the tell-tale signs?

Children are often either unable or unwilling to put into words what's troubling them so they show it in their behaviour instead. Every parent should be alert to any changes in their child's mood or behaviour. Signs that our tweenie could be being bullied or is troubled by friendship problems include:

• Becoming withdrawn, depressed and appearing lonely.
• Becoming more anxious or clingy.
• Loss of appetite, talking in very self-deprecating ways about looks and abilities.
• Wanting to give lots of things away to friends.
• Unwilling to go to school, dawdling, finding endless excuses or even truanting.
• Wanting to get away from school fast, be driven there and back, not walk.
• A sudden drop in the quality of schoolwork.
• Wanting to undress or bath alone to hide bruising or scratching.
• Having disturbed nights: crying, wakefulness or frightening dreams.
• Very hungry after school or suddenly wanting new things in packed lunches.
• Losing possessions or money frequently.

Other more general signs of stress that need to be borne in mind at all times with our pre-teens when trying to read between the lines of their behaviour include:

• A sad, unhappy mood that lasts for several days.
• Showing little pleasure in ordinary, everyday activities.
• Being unusually tired, or unusually aggressive.
• Bed-wetting, nail-biting, renewed thumb or finger sucking.
• Phantom aches and pains in limbs or head and neck aches caused by tension.

- Finding concentration difficult, becoming easily distracted and inattentive.
- Retreating into fantasy and make-believe, to a world where they regain control.
- Easily reduced to tears.

DRAWING THIS TOGETHER

Friends are absolutely vital to tweenies, socially, emotionally and developmentally. Without friends, they will often feel a failure; with plenty of them, they feel lovable and successful, and when friends are hurtful they can feel devastated. But friendships deliver very practical benefits too, as we have seen. It is very important that we respect and encourage friendships and offer support, reassurance and a measure of adult wisdom when things go wrong, for they almost certainly will. If we see our tweenie behaving in a less than perfect way towards his friends, we must understand and accept that it is entirely natural that he may to try to pull rank and explore how much influence he can assert before his friends and peers bring him back into line. Perhaps most important, friends make school worth while for the vast majority of children. School is where most friendships begin, continue and end; and it is our own relationship with school that is considered next.

Ten top take-out tips

- Don't knock the friends he chooses, for a tweenie can take this as a personal criticism.
- Avoid jumping in too soon to solve distress within friendships. Many problems disappear overnight and they need to learn how to solve things on their own.
- Never compare them to their friends in their hearing – it's too judgemental of either.
- Encourage friendships and be as welcoming as possible when they visit your child at home.

- Avoid chiding a tweenie in front of friends: take him out of the room first or wait until he's alone.
- Respect their privacy when they're busy with friends: knock before you enter or otherwise let them know you are approaching and certainly don't spy.
- If any friendship problem persists, tell the school and keep cool. Confrontations will embarrass our child and make it unlikely that he'll be so open again.
- 'Relationship' bullying that makes children feel unloved and unwanted can be devastating. Just because the weapons are words, it does not mean the wounds are not real. Show understanding and never blame them for being 'weak'.
- Encourage each child to seek and value the qualities of real friendship – loyalty, discretion, tolerance, understanding, trust and shared laughs and passions – and to be discriminating about 'popularity'.
- Friends are comfort zones: if they seem happy with the nature of their current friendships, don't imply they should have more, or fewer or change anything.

And Remember!

Friends indicate something about who a child is: let them choose their own.

Teasing among friends and falling out with them is normal; bullying is not and needs quick action.

Of course be friendly but your tweenie needs the real thing, not you as a substitute.

6

ON YOUR MARKS ... GET SET FOR SCHOOL:
Positive Ways to Support

MOST OF US REMEMBER OUR school days vividly. We don't recall every day in detail but certain incidents and events are etched on our memory – almost embedded in our being. And that's the point: both good and bad things can happen to us in school that can have a profound influence. School forms a big portion of any child's life and parents need to understand children's good and bad experiences there to be able to offer constructive, relevant and sensitive support. School is about a great deal more than academic work, a topic for the next chapter, and this explains why the tweenie years mark a notable change in a child's relationship with school. The time spent there becomes increasingly personal and important. Tweenie's friendships are mostly forged, explored and lost at school; independence is often fostered more at school than home; and school is increasingly viewed as a private and separate space – territory in which they can experiment with challenge and get up to mischief without constant parental monitoring and disapproval. School also offers stability and security if home life becomes uncertain for whatever reason. School time is their time, and they can push at the boundaries safely because that is what schools expect – in moderation, of course.

This is the good news. The downside is that things can go wrong in school perhaps as much as they go right. When friendships fail and children become isolated or picked on it can be devastating. When families falter and children become vulnerable, they lose the confidence required to flourish in what can be a demanding environment. Being expected to listen to and learn from a teacher whom they feel does not like them can be difficult and dispiriting. And when they change school they have to start all over again.

Different children mature at different rates and have more or less robust personalities; and some will pretend they are more self-sufficient than they really are. Just because we are not at our tweenie's side during the school day, and even though we may sense we are being pushed away, it does not mean our love and experience is not needed to help cope with the demanding social, emotional and academic challenges that arise daily. This chapter sets out to help us understand how to support our tweenie during these school years and find the appropriate balance between support for our child and for her school, especially if there is an apparent clash. The first section focuses on the value of working in tandem with the school in the interests of our child: how to show interest and stay involved, the importance of attending events and staying abreast of her progress without becoming intrusive. The second section offers advice about choosing a secondary school and how best to prepare for the change and to get settled in once term starts. The third looks at some common problems that arise within school and how we might respond.

Staying in touch: support and involvement

After four or more years developing an intimate relationship with soggy paintings, class outings and endless assemblies during the years our child has attended nursery and infant school, it is very tempting when our tweenie reaches the junior phase of schooling to grab the moment, breathe a huge sigh of relief, reclaim some time for us and leave our child to manage more on her own. We are all busy; but our tweenies still need us, and so does the school. When we support the school's rules (though we may query some), try to reinforce its values, attend school events and share in our child's experiences, she is more likely to attend and learn happily.

THE ADVANTAGES OF STAYING INVOLVED

Children enjoy their time in school better when we follow our child's work and progress and stay involved. How involved we get depends typically on the time we have available as well as our confidence level and interest; and being a fully committed activist is not everyone's idea of fun. At the very least, our tweenie needs to know that we respect and enjoy her efforts in all spheres and that she can rely on our support if there are problems.

Our involvement can range from a simple focus on our child and her experiences to a more substantial commitment to the school itself. We show our active support and involvement when we do any of the following, starting with the simplest level:

- Enquire regularly what our tweenie has found exciting or enjoyable during her school day.
- Show interest in the social side of her school life.
- Ask about her work.
- Attend the parent-teacher consultation sessions.
- Watch our child perform in plays, concerts, PE displays or assemblies open to parents.
- Encourage, though not force, participation in extra-curricular activities.
- Show interest in curriculum plans that cover what is to be learned.

- Read letters sent from school and return any reply slips by the due date.
- Attend school events such as fun days and sports days, plays and concerts (even if our child is not performing).
- Accompany class outings.
- Hear other pupils read.
- Offer to share any personal specialist knowledge or activity with the class.
- Become an active fund-raiser or member of the parents' committee.

Going into school helps us to find out what our tweenie is learning and doing across the broad academic and non-academic curriculum. We get a feel for the standards expected and will be better able to evaluate our tweenie's personal development and progress and discern any emerging problems. But these occasions are also important opportunities to share in her wider experiences, enabling home and school to dovetail comfortably and her to feel relaxed in either place. When we know most of her teachers, meet more of her friends and become familiar with the geography, we can visualise the people and places she includes in her stories and share in her fun. Confusing teachers' names or getting mixed up over lunchtime or assembly arrangements can feel as insulting to our tweenie as forgetting where her best friend lives or serving her most hated food. School absorbs 17 per cent of her life and feels central. If we fail to listen to or take the trouble to remember key details, she can feel a real disappointment.

It is also very useful to understand the culture, ethos and organisation of the school. Like everything else, schools are changing rapidly and each is now encouraged to develop its own policies and character, especially at secondary level. This should help us feel more at ease when on site, more comfortable about raising any concerns and more informed about whom, specifically, to approach: the class or subject teacher, head of year, the head teacher, pastoral head or special needs co-ordinator.

There is one caveat to our continued involvement with school. At this stage of development, tweenies begin to value the autonomy and privacy school offers. It is the only part of their life parents don't directly control, and this becomes highly prized. Tweenies therefore begin to prefer some separation between the two domains. Added to this, their growing sensitivity to the views of others leads some to worry about how teachers will judge their parents and others to protect their mum or dad from potential discomfort. Sam, aged nine, said, 'If it's like a parents' meeting [my mum] wouldn't go, she doesn't like it. She doesn't like anyone knowing all about her feelings. It's up to her, really, isn't it?' These perspectives show a far more sophisticated way of thinking, and it means that tweenies are becoming active players in the home-school game. They watch it, intervene in it and help or hinder it, for clearly stated reasons.

Information points: What children think about parental involvement

A study led by a team at South Bank University in London interviewed nine- and fourteen-year-olds about their views of parental involvement. Overall, the team found that:

- Children have a strong sense of privacy about the details of their family lives, and want control over how much the school knows about this.
- Children in middle-class circumstances were more likely to encourage their parents' involvement, and children from ethnic minority and working-class backgrounds to resist it.

- Children see home and school as very different, with home being about relaxing and doing what you want, while school is about rules and timetables – its main upside being meeting friends.
- Girls tend to feel more comfortable about parental involvement and more likely actively to encourage it than boys.
- Both boys and girls were often happier to involve parents in school issues at home, via conversation and homework, than on the school premises.
- Some children spoke about actively blocking and evading their parents' getting involved in their education, sometimes to avoid 'stressing' their parents.
- Only rarely did children or young people speak of wishing that their parents were able to be more involved in their education, or described lack of involvement as holding them back educationally. More often, the separation between their home and school lives suited them.

So while most tweenies accept it is important for parents to attend formal events such as parents' evenings, many of them feel uncomfortable if they believe personal stories are shared with teachers that signify intimacy or collusion, possibly implicating them. We need to respect their view in our communications with school yet stay sufficiently in touch to remain abreast of progress.

Taster tips on showing interest without interfering

✓ Ask open-ended questions that allow a child to withhold detail. 'Did anything good happen today?' 'Did you learn anything interesting?' rather than a more direct 'Who did you talk to at playtime?' or 'What happened?'

✓ Enquire casually about marks gained. 'That tricky homework, how did it go down?' rather than 'What marks did you get for that homework? Was it good enough?'

✓ If you overhear a conversation about a playground problem, offer to discuss it if they'd like but don't immediately demand details.

✓ Enquire what the homework topic was and invite them to describe what they did but don't ask to see it and then pile on the criticism.

✓ Make sure questions are genuine and straightforward, rather than designed to collect information to discover something else.

✓ Before you help in the classroom or help to organise a school event, discuss any possible qualms or fears your tweenie may have.

CONSULTATION EVENINGS

The regular consultation session that schools arrange once or twice a year is an important occasion, for our child and for us to liase with school. Attendance is crucial to receive professional feedback on our child's welfare and progress and to present any alternative view or any particular concern direct to her teacher. Sometimes the event is the only opportunity to visit the classroom to enjoy the artistic and academic work on display and appreciate the class's and teacher's collective efforts; and in particular to see the fruits of work our child has described. However, the main focus should be on our child: her efforts and achievements as well as where she might be falling short.

Preparing for the session

Both parents should attend if possible. If one cannot, a debriefing session for the absent party with our child present will make sure she feels fully supported and appreciates that responsibility for her learning is taken seriously and shared. If the other parent is no longer around and you have an involved, live-in partner, check with our tweenie that she is comfortable for him or her to attend.

To use the event to our best advantage, identify beforehand any points we wish to raise. The allocated time slots are always limited: if there is something significant, write an advance note so the teacher can respond more adequately; if you wait until the session to raise it, suggest a follow-up meeting if the time is tight. Add to this list anything our child might want us to raise. Even if she is not present, it is in effect her night and being offered a say will help her to feel more included and respected.

If there is an issue that needs to be addressed urgently or separated from the regular consultation, refer to the suggestions in the problems section that completes this chapter.

Handling the session

Be clear about the purpose of the session: to help our child do well, not to criticise our child or blame the teacher. Any frustrations should be channelled through questions such as, 'I am worried she is finding things too easy. Do you feel she's in the best group?' Any itemised queries can be placed on the table, though the teacher should speak first. It is natural for parents to feel anxious at the prospect of this event. Even parents who are teachers say they get nervous. It helps to realise that any criticism of our child's work or behaviour is intended to help her to improve and is therefore well meant and necessary. And though our children feel part of us they are separate. If we take any implied criticism of our child's work or behaviour personally and react defensively we're less likely to identify solutions. An unspecific complaint, such as, 'She can be lazy', is better answered with a request for details – 'Can you tell me when you find her lazy?' – than flatly denied. If we still disagree, it's less confrontational to reply, 'I don't find her so.'

Teachers often comment voluntarily on emotional development – on friendships, how well a child co-operates, her overall disposition and attentiveness – because this can affect her work and is therefore important. We should check whether our child fits in well and seems happy where the discussion has focused on work alone. And don't forget that teachers like to be appreciated. Simple comments such as, 'She really enjoyed that last project. Thanks for making it so interesting', and 'Her maths has really come on. I appreciate what you've achieved', help to maintain teachers' enthusiasm.

Children of this age do not often attend the session, but if our tweenie is expected to, realise that she would prefer us to be seen but not heard. Be businesslike and brief, avoid telling jokes or treating the teacher as our best friend and never criticise our child in front of the teacher.

After the session

When we feed back what took place, we can pass on what we noticed about her school environment – the class displays, for example, some redecoration, any new playground equipment or even mention the teacher's lovely smile or manner. Before we tackle any specific problem, we should continue in this positive vein and endorse her overall commitment. Avoid being critical of anything you saw that the teacher did not mention – the standard of drawing or tidiness issues, for example. The teacher is a better judge of age-appropriate standards than we can be. Pass on, too, any compliments concerning friendliness or calming classmates down, for this report back should extend beyond work. If we have been disappointed with the report, any temptation to reprimand should be resisted. Better to ask, first, what kind of report our child expected. If she thought it might be poor, ask for her explanation of this setback and focus on how to get back on track, not on your frustration.

Changing school

Children's progress often stalls during the first year in a new school. This reflects the effort entailed to adjust. Most tweenies will experience two school changes during the five 'In-between' years because they turn eight during their first year at junior school and will move to secondary school aged eleven. The prospect of change can be nearly as worrying – and sometimes more so – as when it actually arrives, so our tweenie will need plenty of reassurance and confidence-boosting support during the last few months of the familiar school as well as encouragement during the first year of the new one. This section suggests ways to involve our tweenie in selecting a short list of possible secondary schools, to prepare for the change and how to help ease the transition when it takes place so it is managed as comfortably, confidently and successfully as possible.

MOVING TO SECONDARY SCHOOL: SHOULD OUR TWEENIE CHOOSE WHICH ONE?

The first issue that arises about the transfer to secondary school is, of course, which one. In some areas the choice is very wide. It takes time to assess the options thoroughly and it is important to involve our tweenie at every stage.

But should she be given full responsibility for the choice? Only you can decide this, having taken into account the maturity of your child, the range of options available, any particular academic strengths, the likely influence of friends, or any guidance from the current school. But remember that this decision is important and could have long-term repercussions. An eleven-year-old is still our full responsibility and it may not be appropriate to pass that over completely. Whatever your decision, make her role clear from the beginning. The worst situation for her would be to be told she will have the choice and then for it to be refused. Having an influence in the choice is different from being the sole arbiter in the matter. A child can be involved in the choice of her school at different levels, as the following suggestions indicate.

Molly's story

When my dad told me he wanted me to go to the same school as my older sister, I was so angry at him. I felt he was deciding my future, which seemed totally unfair. But then Mum disagreed and said as it was my future it should be up to me. I was so relieved that I had a choice. I didn't want to go with my friends or be influenced by them. I wanted a fresh start. I wanted to meet new people. But actually, when I went to see the schools and thought about it, I chose my sister's school so now everyone's happy. If I hadn't got in I would have felt very disappointed.

Taster tips on involving your child in the choice of a secondary school

Your tweenie can be invited to:

✓ Contribute to a list of general considerations that might influence the choice (single sex or mixed, somewhere different from or same as a sibling, academic achievement or travel implications, for example).
✓ Visit possible schools with you and offer her views and reactions to each one.
✓ Compile a list of particular features to observe at each

---

school – the facilities that relate to her favourite
subject or sport, for example.

✓ Visit the website of each possible school, then show
you any interesting discoveries.

✓ Help you to compile a short list prior to or after visits
and represent each institution's advantages and short-
comings to reach a clearer assessment.

✓ Reflect on whether the reasons for the friend's choice
are relevant to her, should she be inclined to follow
her friend against your wishes.

If we decide to make the final decision, it is crucial to respect
her input and explain our conclusions in relation to her particular concerns. We can offer an opt-out after one or two years
should any early unhappiness persist. Whoever has chosen, we
need to be fully supportive during those initial terms.

Although parents are allowed in law to nominate their
preferred school, we don't always get our first choice. Waiting
to hear can unsettle the whole family. During this time, it may
be useful to reflect on the following:

- If your child is reluctant to lose friends, point out she can
benefit by gaining two sets and in any case, original friends
are often substituted in time.

- Remember that the biggest influence on how well children
achieve academically is still their family, though schools can
add value.

- No school is tailor-made for a particular child. We have to go
for 'best fit' and accept compromise. Any shortfall can usually
be made good in other ways.

- Each school will have strong points independent of exam
results. Keep these in mind to reduce any disappointment if a
first choice based on academic criteria is unavailable.

- If you are tempted to reject the place offered and appeal, consider the impact of further uncertainty and the implication that the offered school is below par.

HELPING TWEENIES TO PREPARE IN ADVANCE OF THE CHANGE

To appreciate what kind of support will be most useful as our tweenie approaches the change, it helps to know what children typically worry about during their last weeks at primary school.

Tuning in to tweenies . . . on changing schools

'We're used to being the cats, and now we'll have to be the mice.' Andy, eleven

'It feels like we're having to jump off a cliff.' Gemma, eleven

'I pray at night I'm not going to get Mr . . . I've been told he shouts at you if you get the slightest thing wrong.' Brian, ten

'I'm worried about getting the wrong bus, because I'll be so tired from getting up early after all those late nights during the holidays.' Jubayed, eleven

'I've heard the big boys nick your pokemon cards.' Mital, eleven

'I'm not really looking forward to it. I'm sad, because this school's just got better and now we're leaving.' Zakaria, ten

'In a way I'm looking forward to it, in a way I'm not. I'm looking forward to the homework, the clubs and

---

learning new things, but I'm worried about not being liked and being late and getting a detention. You might get lost. I'm sad to leave, especially as one of my friends is not coming to my new school.' Rachel, eleven

'It feels like I'm moving city again.' Craig, eleven (who had recently moved house)

So our tweenie will need lots of positive reassurance: about the likelihood of finding new friends and still finding time for old ones; that it is natural to feel uncertain because it is a big step to take; about our willingness to help them initially to become organised and manage the journey and thereafter be available to discuss any possible problems.

Taster tips for parents on preparing children for their new school over the summer

- ✓ Understand how they might be feeling – probably both excited and anxious. Ask questions that will encourage them to open up, such as, 'Going to the new school in September probably feels scary. What's your biggest worry?' This shows you appreciate their doubts.
- ✓ Encourage self-organisation; for example let her put her own clean clothes away from now on.
- ✓ Boost her confidence. Praise and notice things she does well, and minimise criticism.
- ✓ Attend the open day and induction opportunities with her, and encourage any non-resident parent to get similarly involved.
- ✓ Familiarise her before she starts: walk or drive by the school occasionally; do the journey together with a

map to hand so she understands the route and
journey time.
- ✓ Keep the school brochure handy so it can be reread at
  any time and try to get an advance plan of the school.
- ✓ Advise a sceptical attitude to any negative stories –
  frequently exaggerated – until she can check these out
  and judge for herself.
- ✓ The last days of the holidays should be left free for
  some reflection – and a bit of boredom may help to
  get her more in the mood!

EASING THE EXPERIENCE WHEN THE NEW TERM STARTS

When the new term actually starts, there are several things we
can do to help them adjust to the new rules, new teachers, new
subjects and new expectations and to buoy up their confidence.
First of all, treat their first day as an important right of passage;
mark it with a special breakfast or tea, for example. Realise
they're likely to be tetchy for a while. The sheer variety of new
experiences would take the stuffing out of anyone so push for
sensible bedtimes and lots of sleep, and delay any new after-
school commitments until the initial tiredness subsides. We
should certainly make time to listen to what they've been learning and doing and reassure them if they're finding any lessons
hard to follow initially. Family mealtimes may need to be re-
scheduled around new homework commitments. Poor personal
organisation can hold children back academically, especially
boys: once we have contributed some practical suggestions about
managing kit and homework we should then step back – otherwise they'll never learn. Finally, children need to believe in their
school. Being critical now will make it harder for them to fit in
and do their best.

What can we do if our child clearly hates the new school? It might be reassuring to learn that it takes most adults a good six weeks to feel comfortable with new people, routines and places, so recommend patience. In the meantime, it is worth trying to locate the source of the feelings: do the teachers seem unfriendly, is it fear of older pupils, about friendship problems and feeling isolated or have bullies threatened her? Don't forget that, in general, boys like school less than girls. In Ben's words, 'Girls are more into school than boys. Not many boys like school at all, but girls do.' And many boys are simply not interested in study. A group of them aged eleven and twelve said, 'I like break time and dinners', 'The best thing about school is the social side, being with your mates and stuff', 'I like it when you do stuff with your hands and PE, when there's not much writing', 'I like playing football, IT and PE lessons.' There's not much point in reprimanding them for being half-hearted. It's a boy thing and they're more likely to find enthusiasm if we understand, show interest, stay involved and constantly tell them they can achieve. Most schools invite the parents of new pupils to attend a social or feedback event early in the first term so these issues can be raised and then addressed. If any distress becomes sufficiently serious that she wants to stay home or cannot sleep, approach the school for an individual meeting. If her unhappiness continues, it might be appropriate to consider a move elsewhere.

Possible problems and how to respond

By their very nature, problems at school are likely to damage a child's sense of self – how likeable she feels, how competent she believes she is, how effective she is at protecting herself. These are powerful worries that cannot be parcelled up and left locked behind the gate. Any difficulty must be taken seriously and addressed before it does long-term damage. For tweenies, common problems that relate specifically to the experience of school include inappropriate behaviour, not wanting to attend school, clashing with a teacher and a reluctance to join school trips (work is to be addressed in the next chapter). How do these problems emerge, when might we become aware of them and what support can we offer our child or should we expect from school?

BEHAVIOUR THAT CAUSES CONCERN

Schools are right to worry about how tweenies in their care behave. Children who are unnaturally quiet and withdrawn are as troubling to them as those who are noisy and disruptive. Of course, disruptive children make it hard for others to learn and can make some feel unsafe, but challenging behaviour can indicate deeper unhappiness or learning difficulties and schools care about that aspect too. They try to do their best for any child who struggles with learning, for whatever reason, and detailed, staged procedures exist to ensure continued progress, set out in the Special Needs Code of Practice.

Why do some children behave differently and what might influence whether our child becomes withdrawn or aggressive at school? As we see in chapters eight and ten, which discuss events that can interfere with children's development, children are easily upset to the point that it shows in changed behaviour. When girls have their confidence dented, they frequently become less assertive and more retiring. Boys, on the other hand, are more likely to cover any insecurity or fear of failure with a veneer of bravado and become noisier. But boys can become withdrawn and girls can certainly be challenging. Boys often become more lively and disruptive nearer their teens as their confidence grows, but some children have by then become accustomed to behaving badly and challenging adults. It is vital that we respond to our own or the school's worries and trust them to help our child. We know that isolated or withdrawn children who do not receive help can become depressed when they are older, and children who are more than normally disruptive are more likely to truant and get into bigger trouble, so it is important to act and ensure that our tweenie receives the appropriate support as early as possible. It is worth raising with teachers any change in behaviour that we notice at home – such as increased aggression with siblings, rudeness to us, crying or destroying homework that is felt to be substandard – to see if it may be related to a difficulty associated with school and to discuss possible responses.

Bullying behaviour

Schools are particularly keen to curb bullying behaviour – a subject that has already been discussed in the chapter on friendships. We can reinforce their efforts at home by reacting with disapproval if we see or hear of our child acting aggressively or threatening any animal or person. It is never clever to hurt or upset any other person. We should teach that to resolve a dispute without resorting to spite or intimidation is a sign of strength, not weakness.

If we learn that our tweenie has been involved in bullying via mobile phones, e-mail or through physical or emotional intimidation we should remain calm. Neither abuse nor accusations help, though we should state clearly that the behaviour is wrong and unacceptable. We should try to understand that a child who seeks to gain advantage might have been treated badly by others, for it can be a rather twisted response to having felt powerless or exploited previously. Consider strategies that will reinstate or increase the sense of autonomy and control. Talk to the school to agree a joint response and a date ahead to confirm progress. Taking quick supportive action can help to avoid a variety of longer-term problems that include attendance.

NOT WANTING TO GO: SCHOOL REFUSAL AND TRUANTING

The tweenie years are critical for establishing the habit and expectation of regular school attendance. We know that those who enjoy junior school settle better into secondary school and those who truant at a young age are more likely to become seriously disaffected. Most children moan about getting up in the mornings and prefer school holidays to term time but some have a real problem and become genuinely panic-stricken about school. Anxious school refusal, or school phobia in its extreme form, is not only increasing but is thought by some to be more common than truanting. It is certainly different either from an occasional bunking off by a pupil who wants some excitement or from more established truanting. Tweenies are particularly likely to use school refusal as a response to anxiety because school changes can intensify any deeper insecurity and become the problem; but they may also experience the same events that will unsettle any child.

What might explain a reluctance to attend school?

The source of a child's reluctance to attend school can be found either at home or at school. Where there are difficulties at home, a child may prefer to remain there:

- To protect someone she loves who may be in distress (related to rows, a serious illness or a recent bereavement, divorce or separation).
- To offer company to a parent or carer who has few friends and feels lonely.
- To meet a parent's need to keep the last child close by after an older one has left for good, leaving the parent bereft – the 'empty nest' syndrome.
- To experience stability and security after having moved between relatives, carers or separated parents; having returned from hospital or from a long period abroad.

School-based problems that may lead a child to prefer the safety of home include:

- A difficulty coping with a particular teacher, the journey, noisy corridors or break times.
- Arguments with friends.
- A genuine fear of crowds or open spaces, bullying or violence.
- An undiagnosed learning difficulty, such as dyslexia, that leads to repeated failure and confusion.
- Academic pressure. (As one mother said of her daughter, 'The environment of the new school was wrong for her, and she took it out on her family. They put this incredible pressure on the girls to achieve. No one spoke to her on a personal level. I shall never forget that time. I felt like I was drowning. I didn't know how to cope. Eventually, she moved to a more relaxed school and all's now well.')

What are the early signs? What can be done?

Children who can find school attendance difficult are often quiet, non-communicative, without friends and may be unhappy or unusually anxious. They may drag out an illness to delay returning to school, ask for Mondays off, complain of stomach cramps or become unusually bad-tempered. Victims of bullying can show similar symptoms. Indeed, girls frequently identify relationship problems – being teased and excluded – as the reason they begin to bunk off. But it is dangerous to give in to pressure to have yet another day off, for this could become a comfortable habit that becomes very hard to break. Better to raise any worries early with an appropriate teacher than to allow home to become her only comfort zone. Many schools have strategies to help a pupil manage any anxiety. Very occasionally, children use school refusal to get parental attention if they feel neglected, so we should ensure each child receives the time and attention she needs. If there have been family rows, let her know they don't continue during the day. A reassuring text message sent via mobile phone – on an exceptional basis – to affirm that all's well could put her mind at rest. Try to uncover the real problem, always careful to avoid blaming her for her difficult experiences and feelings. If possible, welcome at home any school friend with whom our child feels comfortable.

Taster tips on helping children to return to school after a long absence

✓ Their fears and feelings are real; try to imagine what it is actually like to feel such panic.

✓ Be clear about the longer-term objective: a full return to school.

✓ If the absence has been prolonged, accept that reintegration will have to be gradual and could take up to a year or more.

✓ Encourage attendance wherever possible. Beware collusion through being too sympathetic and easily manipulated.

✓ Ensure a united approach between parents; splits tend to lead to failure.

✓ Help your child to stay feeling connected to school by attending school events and encouraging visits from school friends.

Peter's story

Peter found it hard to go to school from the age of eight and it lasted until he was thirteen. He suddenly began to be afraid of being left at school, forgotten and uncollected, though it had never happened to him. He would hide under the covers, refusing to get up, resulting in some heated arguments. At the school gate, if he got there, he would become pale, start shaking and become unable to move; his voice seemed to disappear inside him matching his crumbling confidence. 'His anxiety was so physical,' explained his mother. During that school year, his anxiety became so intense that it had to be accepted and he spent the final term at home with a home tutor, at the end of which he was required by his school to return gradually. Every day for three weeks, the school nurse met Peter at the entrance and helped him through. It was made very clear from the beginning of the period he spent out of school that this would be the plan, so he was not able to duck it. Though he then settled, a couple of years later he became anxious about being bullied, despite never having been a victim, and going on his first residential trip with school was a real struggle. With continued understanding from his parents and teachers, Peter's anxieties finally disappeared. He is now living happily away at university and enjoying his studies.

'MY TEACHER HATES ME!' CONFLICT IN THE CLASSROOM

Children can become negative about school when they clash with a particular teacher. Either there is instant mutual dislike – a personality clash – or, more likely, they firmly believe a teacher has a 'downer' on them and they feel 'picked on'. The two are usually linked. We warm to people who seem to like us, and recoil from those we imagine do not. Where children have the same teacher for most of the day, any clash becomes significant for there are few alternatives. At secondary school, however, the existence of subject teachers and multiple sets within subjects lessens the difficulty and offers the possibility of change.

Sometimes conflict between pupil and teacher is a genuine personality clash. Sometimes a vulnerable child will misinterpret a passing show of impatience as generalised dislike, and take it too much to heart. Sometimes, the problem is a mismatch between a teacher's preferred teaching style and a child's natural learning style, leading to the frustration and boredom that so often fuel trouble. For example, an extrovert child who thrives on discussion can switch off from a teacher who sets clear tasks within a tight lesson plan – the teacher may get snappy if diverted. And then there's stress; this affects teachers too and inclines both sides to feel 'got at'.

If our child complains about being picked on, listen; for she could be right. Try not to deny her view, but don't jump immediately to the phone to complain either. We all have to learn to get on with others. Suggest our child reports to us daily for a week or two. Keep a detailed record. If the pattern is confirmed, approach the head, or head of year, and ask for it to be investigated. Heads do, occasionally, agree to move a child if the problem is verified although some prefer to leave arrangements in place, believing tolerance of tension to be a useful lesson. If we feel our child could have a point, we should then consider the degree of possible harm. For example, the situation may be more serious where a child has struggled with maths for some time and is on the edge of abandoning all effort than where a child has enjoyed the subject, is competent but is no longer doing her best due to the unfavourable relationship. Provided the school knows a child well, we can take their advice and suggestions unless this runs counter to our strong instincts. Supplementary lessons outside school may help to maintain our tweenie's enthusiasm, although school-based solutions are usually preferable.

SCHOOL TRIPS AND RESIDENTIAL ADVENTURE WEEKS

Day trips and residential holidays organised by school often take place either in the term before, or the term after, secondary school transfer, to help forge fresh friendships in Year 7 or to boost tweenies' confidence in readiness for the big change. Year

6 teachers also see a holiday as a reward for hard work done for the tests – a fun time when the pressure can come off, but the experience also signifies tweenies' growing maturity and enables them to socialise with people in a new way. Many ten- and eleven-year-olds love these trips; however, some are less ready than others and it is not uncommon for a child to be extremely nervous at the thought of spending time away from home. These trips are never compulsory, so faced with a tearful child, should we argue strongly in favour because we know how much she will learn or allow her to opt out?

Gaby, aged eleven, didn't want to join her Year 6 residential holiday but was very grateful after that she had been made to. She explained her problem. 'I didn't want to be stuck with a whole load of people I didn't know very well, especially teachers. You don't know if you want to live with them for a whole week and not see your mum and sister for that long. I felt happier about going when I knew it was too far away to pull out. If you're close enough to go back home then it's worse. The daytime's fine. It's at night you miss your family, but you realise you're not the only one who's scared. And if you don't go, you'll always wonder if you would have liked it and you can't talk about it after. You get to know your friends a lot better than you did.'

As Gaby discovered, children who face their fear benefit. Teachers are keen to allay pupils' natural anxiety and will review all arrangements at length, with parents too. We might worry more about dangers and accidents but the chance of a child suffering a fatal accident on a school trip has been estimated as one in 8 million. Seven of the eleven deaths in the last two years took place abroad and the vast majority of eight- to twelve-year-olds stay in the UK. All schools now have an Educational Visits Co-ordinator who must agree a comprehensive risk assessment before any trip, confirm the appropriateness of any residential staff's credentials and abide by comprehensive government guidelines. We should therefore encourage our reluctant tweenie to participate. If cost is a problem, many schools can help.

COMING INTO SCHOOL WHEN THERE'S AN ISSUE OR PROBLEM

When there is a problem or issue that relates to our tweenies' welfare in school, it is important that we acknowledge it as quickly and as constructively as possible with the relevant staff both to restore our child's happiness and to prevent any long-term damage. Sometimes the first we hear of a difficulty is an invitation to attend school to discuss it. At other times, we may initiate the approach as it relates to a family matter or school has not spotted the problem. There are some sensible 'dos and don'ts' to bear in mind in either of these situations.

When school initiates the approach

- Do respect the school's view of the scale of the problem so try to be available to attend any meeting at the time suggested, even if this means leaving work immediately.
- Don't imagine the worst and get distressed: ask for as much detail on the telephone to enable you to remain calm and rational.
- Don't view the event as an attack on you or your family but do consider the range of possible explanations offered.
- Do take pen and paper with you to record details and decisions. Ask for clarification if terms are used that you cannot understand – we cannot be expected to be familiar with every scheme, initiative or approach.
- If we feel we only get approached when things go wrong, do ask to be kept informed of our child's successful efforts to behave and work well.

When parents need to initiate contact

Many parents are deterred from contacting school to raise any issue or problem for fear of being labelled a nuisance or 'pushy'. However, we are the experts on our children and our tweenie's academic and emotional welfare is our key responsibility. We should therefore trust our judgement and speak out if we're worried, not delay it so the problem worsens or we become frustrated or short-tempered. Children sense these feelings and then can worry that their school is no good. It is best to:

- Wait until we feel calm.
- Ask for a meeting in advance; we shouldn't just turn up and expect to be heard when we demand it. The teacher may be attending to other children and not be able to listen properly. If the issue relates to our child's welfare, we should prefer a considered, well-prepared response.
- Make a list of the issues we wish to raise, and use it.
- Raise the most important issue first to ensure it is addressed, even though it may be tempting to start with something less controversial.
- Keep the list in full view: it's easy to forget what we meant to say when we get a bit nervous or cross, and far better to have that prop than to come away dissatisfied, having left out something important.

Taster tips on useful principles to consider when there are problems

✓ Always consider a child's feelings when we contact school to request a meeting or inform them of something – there are times to tell our child of our actions and times when it is better to keep quiet about it. If we are worried about what *might* happen (following

---

family problems, for example) keep this quiet. If it's about what *has* happened to our child (bullying, illness, falling standards), be open.

✓ If our child knows about a planned meeting and will not be directly involved, tell her in simple terms beforehand what we plan to say and debrief her after. This will remove some of the mystery, reduce her anxiety and show respect for her right to know.

✓ Arrange to have any other children looked after; it is not suitable to have any sibling attend and overhear.

✓ Be sensitive to the potential embarrassment children feel when disagreements between home and school become heated, so don't start a war.

✓ Ask for a meeting in advance; don't just turn up and demand one.

✓ Difficulties at home may feel very private but should be shared with school as they can then observe and support our child.

✓ Don't be shy to ask even the most simple of questions, and always check at the end of any meeting what is to happen as a result of the discussion.

✓ Avoid seeing a complaint about our child as a personal attack. Keep all meetings controlled and respectful.

DRAWING THIS TOGETHER

Tweenies do best when parents and schools trust each other and act as partners. Teachers may be the professionals, but parents always make a vital contribution to their children's learning through showing interest in what they do, being personally committed to reading and learning, and engaging with the school. Although some tweenies may prefer parents to be seen rather than heard, we should be prepared to ask questions if in doubt about anything, be helpful if approached and let the school know of any event that might affect our child's state of mind and ability to work. School can provide a vital stable base if things become tense or uncertain at home. We should never forget that our child takes her whole self into school, not a separate part used only for studying: her overall welfare is our business, not just her academic progress. Yet if we become too intrusive and allow no personal, private space for our tweenie in school, she may create the space she needs elsewhere. We need to achieve a balance, just as we need to ensure our tweenie achieves a sensible balance between work and play, the subject of the next chapter.

Ten top take-out tips

- When tweenies change school, help them to feel secure: be around more, minimise other changes, maintain familiar routines, assist them with organisation and show faith and love, not doubt and disappointment.
- Trust they'll do well. Saying 'I hope you will / will not . . .' suggests you really expect the opposite.
- Tweenies should have a say in what school they move to. If you intend to take the final decision, specify which issues will carry weight.
- Show interest in the day's events and work but don't be intrusive. She'll want to feel trusted and will want some privacy in relation to school.
- Criticising her school or teacher may inhibit her ability to work well and feel part of the new community.
- If we can't make a parent-teacher consultation, another time should be arranged so it's clear we care.
- Let school know of major problems at home. Most offer extra support during difficult times that can disrupt work and friendships.
- Don't take any criticism of our child as a personal attack. If

we get defensive the real issue may get lost. Teachers try to help, not challenge.

- A problem at school can seem small to us but will be full-sized to our child. Listen fully and give it serious attention.
- Studies show that as little as two weeks' absence during term time (and that includes being distracted or 'absent in mind'), can set a child back long-term.

And Remember!

Show interest but don't be over-intrusive: it's their space, not yours.

Starting a new school is exciting, but it's terrifying and tiring too.

Don't put your child down in front of her teacher, or criticise a teacher in front of a child.

7

DON'T FORGET FUN:

Balancing Work and Play

TWEENIES ARE LEARNING AND MATURING almost every moment of every day, through schoolwork and in the course of their play. Play, it has been said, is young children's work, and with older children, too, it remains hard to draw a clear line between work and play. Work is the serious bit of their life, but it should also be fun given that friends are usually involved and needs to be so to cultivate commitment and motivation. The social co-operation entailed in much play and work is central to healthy development; and tweenies learn a huge amount from play, just as they learn far more than mere facts and procedures from lessons and homework. Both work and play encourage self-management, position children in a wider world and deepen their sense of personal strengths and abilities.

It is not surprising that the key physical and mental changes that take place in children during their pre-teens impact on their inclinations and preferences. Heightened self-awareness enables tweenies to be more confident and comfortable with their own ideas and approaches but also, less helpfully, more inclined to match and measure themselves against others. Lucy, nine, explained that her classmates often fish for compliments. 'They say, "Oh, your picture's better than mine, but what they really want is the attention and for the compliment to be returned because they do think theirs is better."' This greater tendency to rank and compare means tweenies may also begin to take academic failure and peer rejection much more to heart. By the age of ten or twelve, children can think more independently and understand and manipulate more abstract, and then more conceptual, ideas and arguments and accept other children's views. Teachers expect tweenies to need less handholding, both individually and collaboratively (something for parents to note) and children are rightly proud of their growing capacity to manage. Tweenies may also want their play to be more challenging and exciting, which can have educational benefits, for independent learning entails taking risks, and children who are risk-averse make far less progress.

This chapter looks at work first, then at play. In relation to work, it considers how we can best help our child's learning and development. It then reflects on the pressure children currently face and suggests strategies to manage and reduce this, identifying how we often make things worse, unintentionally. Play is introduced with a review of the changes we might expect in children's choices of what to play over the five years. It addresses the need to keep a balance between work and play and between different playful activities. The chapter ends by urging caution that our tweenie's leisure really is for his pleasure and not directed by us for our own purposes.

Learning and development: what we can do to help

These five years are crucial for reinforcing confidence and competence in literacy and numeracy and a range of other social, emotional and study skills that develop alongside learning. The launch into secondary school will be more successful if good working habits and a positive commitment to study are well established, helping them to strive and stay on task. Encouraging these attributes is far more valuable than taking on the role of teacher, becoming immersed in the work itself or pushing our child to achieve a particular standard at a particular point in time, all of which can generate a potentially counter-productive friction.

As learning involves mastering the unknown, it is natural that every child will experience moments of dejection, frustration and boredom. During these dips, rather than harangue or cajole we should offer plenty of support and encouragement.

SUPPORT AND ENCOURAGEMENT

Children need us to be patient as they try to grasp a concept, not critical. The purpose of support and encouragement is to share our tweenie's problem, help him to be courageous in the face of difficulty and bolster self-belief so he can eventually help himself. (Note that when we control and push we achieve the opposite: by implying he needs a shove we foster self-doubt and add to his burdens. He may also become more anxious while attempting to meet our expectations. The difference is stark.) He will want to be helped towards the answer, not to have us provide it either because we can't bear to wait for the penny to drop or because we want school to believe he can get it right. The box below shows how to keep support and encouragement constructive.

Taster tips on support and encouragement

✓ *Show interest*: watch him doing his favourite activity; ask how something went when he's made extra effort or been somewhere special.

✓ *Offer help*: discuss his difficulty, suggest where to find answers, take him where he needs to go and help him through when he's stuck.

✓ *Listen*: to his problems, disappointments and excitements when he does well.

✓ *Understand*: his concentration patterns and preferred ways of working.

✓ *Notice and show enthusiasm*: praise, appreciate and celebrate achievement.

✓ *Share his excitements and dreams*: and don't knock anything he enjoys doing.

✓ *Show faith*: in what he can achieve and give him chances to prove himself.

✓ *Value a range of skills*: so he can feel effective in many ways.

Children need to be noticed: but keep praise constructive

Praise, of course, is affirming and encouraging and is therefore a crucial supportive tactic. All young children love praise, but as they reach their pre-teens they may become more suspicious of it or simply get bored with trying to please. They would prefer to get on with life and not be on constant watch for an adult's pleasure or disappointment. None the less, they do need their efforts across a broad range of activities to be noticed and appreciated. Useful phrases include, 'Well done, you took a lot of care over that,' or 'That's terrific. If I were you, I'd be really pleased with that grade.' From now on, our main goal should be to encourage our tweenie to assess his work and trust his own judgement as part of the shift towards self-direction and self-discipline. If we say, 'That looks great. Are you pleased with it?' we reaffirm that he no longer needs to rely on us for his sense of achievement. Parents of older tweenies especially need to become much more savvy and sensitive about how, when and how often to praise, their sons especially. Teachers find that boys, typically, become more reserved about and embarrassed by public praise than girls.

The ten principles of constructive praise below will ensure that our praise is acceptable to and effective with both sexes.

Ten steps to effective praise

1 *Let him impress you*
   Children love it when someone they admire is clearly and freely impressed by something they have done, with no qualifying ifs or buts or measured judgement.

2 *Keep praise private*
   Not in front of friends or siblings unless it's a success the family should share.

3 *Praise the achievement rather than the person*
   Children prefer to be *appreciated* when they manage to achieve something and *approved of* unconditionally for who they are. So keep the two clearly separate and distinct.

4 *Praise the effort rather than the result*
   Trying is important; no child can go further than a certain point without it.

5 *Make it mean something – be specific*
   Don't just say it's 'good'. Describe in detail what we've found pleasing, so our tweenie knows what he has done right and can repeat it.

6 *Say it straight*
   Don't qualify it or undermine it with sarcasm or reminders of past failures or other put-downs that dilute or negate its effect. 'This report's really good . . . have they got the right child?!'

7 *Be truthful, not gushing*
   False praise is offensive, insulting and eventually ineffective. It distorts self-evaluation and makes children sceptical.

8 *Don't forget physical responses*
   Spontaneous hugs, kisses, smiles and warm touches also say 'well done'.

9 *Let a child take all of the credit*
Comments such as, 'Great, you passed! I told you my revision method would work,' diminish the achievement and force it to be shared.

10 *Apply the 4:1 formula*
It takes four 'praises' to undo the damage caused by one harsh criticism. Children lose motivation if they feel they can do nothing right

KEEP ALL EXPECTATIONS APPROPRIATE

In relation to most activities, including schoolwork, high expectations get good results and low expectations poor ones. Children live up to – or down to – their reputations and our expectations. Most children prefer to be stretched because this is when they give of their best and experience pride in their progress. But just how much should we expect, and can we go too far? Although easy targets neither excite nor reward children, impossible ones can lead to distress and despair. How can we ensure we don't ask for too much?

The safest way to judge this is to ask our child what he believes he can manage. When a group of tweenies were asked about school pressure, they said they didn't mind being asked to aim high but any goals should be reachable within a manageable time scale. Teachers and parents who set unrealistic goals were seen as 'pushy', and not, in fact, helpful. Don't be sceptical. Encouraged by government, schools are increasingly trusting children to help set their own targets, evaluate and mark their own work as they work towards them and assess when these have been met. Most computer games prepare children for this, allowing them to select the level of challenge and move themselves on when it becomes too easy.

Understand their developmental stage

Parents sometimes don't account for a child's developmental stage when they intervene or suggest targets. Although during these five years children's capacity to think and understand improves dramatically, we can still either expect too much of them at any particular time or become concerned if they seem to slip backwards, which is not uncommon especially before a surge in progress. Until the age of about eight, children learn most comfortably when they can relate things to their personal and practical experience. From aged eight onwards, their thinking becomes freer, less locked on to themselves, more sensitive to other approaches and more flexible. They begin to make sense of abstract ideas and enjoy asking reflective questions about these. They can accept that other people see things differently and can apply rules to problems, though as yet in an all-or-nothing way. These new perceptions are a consequence of their sharpening identity, burgeoning confidence and brain development. We must allow them the freedom to explore their ideas, even if these appear far-fetched, and interfere as little as possible as they decide how to approach their work so they learn, gradually, to trust and rely on themselves. If we have a suggestion, we should ask if they wish to consider it, and not assume they could grasp it, for many children cannot relate adeptly to more advanced conceptual ideas until they are twelve or thirteen.

Understand our tweenies' individual learning style

To keep our expectations appropriate, we should also be sensitive to our tweenie's individual learning style, the way he understands things best that reflects the natural bent of his mind. It is pointless trying to get a child to learn something our way if he feels more at ease with another. For example, he may prefer to make sense of or remember information through drawing pictures, through recitation or through singing and being active. He may prefer precise instructions or learn more effectively through trial and error or discussion. Each child has unique qualities, strengths and preferences and this is where we need to start. We need to work with, not against, the grain of our tweenie's preferred style; in other words, we need to be patient and allow him to work at his pace, in his way, to his targets and within a time-scale of his choosing, provided he delivers.

Make it okay to make mistakes

Whatever the particular learning style, all tweenies need to be able to take risks and make mistakes, for learning is risky. A child who cannot accept, live with or learn from mistakes cannot progress and therefore maximise his potential. When we criticise or, worse, punish a child for making a genuine mistake in his work and make him feel ashamed of it, we imply the mistake was unacceptable. This may make him reluctant to risk error again to avoid censure. To demonstrate by example, we need to admit to and remain upbeat about our own mistakes. For further advice on responding to mistakes, see the section on success and failure later in this chapter.

Tuning in to Tweenies: The views of ten- to twelve-year-old boys on why girls do better

'Girls mature quicker so they work better.'

'Boys try to work as hard as girls but they don't push themselves as hard as girls do.'

'Boys try to impress the girls. They say, "Oh, this is easy" so they don't study it, whereas girls go over it over and over again.'

'After school, girls may read a book taken home from school. Boys go out and play football.'

'Boys get bored more quickly. We can't be bothered to finish things so we mess about.'

'Girls talk and work at the same time, and they don't talk as much as boys do.'

'Girls take up offers of help. Girls are more likely to come to teacher to ask for more work or seek help at dinner time if they don't understand it.'

Be sensitive to gender differences

Although, of course, every child is different, teachers agree that certain skills, attitudes and working styles are associated with gender. Girls' strength lies in their greater verbal skills; they generally talk earlier than boys, an advantage that seems to help them read, write and speak more fluently. Boys' strong points are their mathematical and mechanical skill and spatial sense and a confidence that later helps them to perform in exams. Teachers experience girls as more dutiful and able to apply themselves despite having a low level of interest, but this can make them reliant on others for approval and direction. Boys tend to be more fidgety and physical and find concentration difficult, but if they become fully engaged with a subject or issue they can become highly motivated and focused. They tend to learn better in shorter bursts, with plenty of positive feedback, and when they understand the practical point of learning something.

When we appreciate our child's individual capabilities, inclinations, strengths and limitations, we are more likely to interact in a manner that reduces the pressure.

Taster tips on helping children to learn

✓ Success is catching. Encourage success in non-academic areas so they feel more capable.

✓ Start from their strengths, but acknowledge and work on their weaknesses.

✓ Make learning fun: chanting multiplication tables on journeys beats sitting in a bedroom when you're desperate to be out with friends.

✓ Ensure boys understand their mistakes and are clear what they need to do differently.

✓ Ensure all children have times when they let off steam and times when they sit still and focus, to help them concentrate on their studies when they have to.

✓ Ensure girls know why they did something well and are convinced it was their doing so they know they can repeat it.

✓ If they get stuck, show faith that they'll crack it. 'New work's always muddling, and frustrating. Take your time, because I know you'll get there.'

✓ Let children do things their way and at their pace. Don't interfere, get impatient at the time taken or hover expecting something to be or go wrong.

Testing times: reducing the pressure

Today's tweenies face a significant degree of pressure. Rarely have they been so monitored and tested, formally and informally, or had so much expected of them. According to one teacher, eleven-year-olds arrive at his comprehensive secondary school already obsessed with scores, success and failure. Of course, children enjoy success when it happens; what they do not enjoy is feeling anxious about their grade or whom they will disappoint if they don't fulfil that person's hopes.

The current pressure to do well in tests may make tweenies more inclined to compare. Sam, nine, told me, 'There's lots of competition, lots of it, over tests. People compare marks all the time and snoop at how other people did. We always did it a bit in infant school but it's far worse now. A girl in my class bragged about getting only thirteen out of fifty-four in one test, but I think she did that to hide her shame. We're all in maths groups at different levels and the teacher tries to hide it, but we all know. The top group brags about being top.'

A middle school teacher told me of a ten-year-old pupil whose behaviour was always exceptionally trying. One particular day he created havoc, moving desks around and rocking them noisily mid-lesson. Finding himself ignored by everyone, he approached her, stood silently for a while then asked if she understood why he was doing all this. Invited then to explain, he said he felt a complete failure and had messed up his life – aged ten! To relieve this pressure, it is vital that we involve ourselves in a practical and useful way.

HELPING WITH HOMEWORK

Most of us are happy to help with homework but, despite the best of intentions, we know that careless and critical comments can start arguments, undermine our child's confidence and deter him from seeking help again. There are, though, some tried and tested principles of good practice that ensure the experience is relatively hassle-free and constructive.

Taster tips on helping tweenies with homework

✓ Homework teaches children to work on their own. If parents manage it too closely, this important skill is not learned.

✓ Offer some choice about where, when and how they do it. Even sprawling on the floor is fine.

✓ Set up a routine, or agree a time when it will be done by so it's never left too late.

✓ Homework is for the teacher to mark, not us. Avoid imposing our standards on our child's work and being critical.

✓ If you see any mistakes, ask if your child wants to know. If he does, identify the sentence or area on the page and suggest he tries to spot it first. If he can then explain his error, it becomes a constructive learning experience, not a telling off.

✓ Find something to commend – frequently.

✓ If he seems stuck, be patient. Don't pelt him with ideas to get him started: children prefer first to decide what they want to do and then receive help to achieve it. Your ideas will stop him from feeling the work's his and he won't learn to generate his own with confidence.

✓ Be there to talk about it or look at it if he wants but to check it habitually will seem untrusting.

✓ Be sensitive to any tiredness.

✓ Show interest by asking about what they had to do and whether they enjoyed it.

✓ Ask them to turn off the TV because it usually impairs concentration.

✓ Accept that they may need to wind down, eat something and relax with friends, siblings or the TV before settling down to work.

✓ Be understanding if they show reluctance. Few adults relish evening work after a full day's effort elsewhere.

✓ Don't compare the work to that of a sibling, either favourably or unfavourably.

> ✓ If he finds something difficult to understand, explain it in different ways. Avoid merely repeating a single explanation and getting cross, implying he is stupid not to grasp it more quickly.

The common mistakes we make that cause upset and create crises include:

- Being too bossy and telling them what to do and when to do it.
- Trying to take it over, injecting our ideas, methods and solutions.
- Chiding them for being slow.
- Berating them for doing it quickly and assuming it is therefore sloppy.
- Making them consider or explore a related issue that fascinates us.
- Asking them to attempt a more advanced, or just different, way of working for which they're neither ready nor prepared.
- Expecting a higher standard and thereby being too negative and critical when or if we check it.
- Complaining that the task is too easy and the school should know better.

The time taken is a common bone of contention. Children benefit from doing a range of things after school, so it is not advisable to let homework take hours, because it doesn't need to be perfect. Schools normally indicate the time they expect homework to take. A child who regularly takes more than the recommended time may have concentration problems, be working to an unnecessarily high standard, not be listening in lessons so not know what to do, have a genuine difficulty with understanding or execution or be diverted by a personal problem. A child who regularly takes less than the expected time could be working very efficiently, be bored with repeating tasks he has mastered and give up, doing a minimum and copying the rest from someone later, or be disillusioned with persistent low marks despite trying hard so losing commitment. If we hear no complaints concerning quality, we should assume all's well. Should the work seem easy, encourage other interests to stretch ability rather than suggest more homework, or speak to the teacher concerned.

Don't control and push

It can be hard to recognise when support and encouragement merge into control and pushiness but we need to be alert to the difference if we are to minimise pressure. Those with a tendency to control will do things like finish tasks for a child because he is too slow or not doing them well enough, make lists of things he has to complete, get physically involved in homework (rubbing out poor work, improving the handwriting, tearing out pages or insisting work is redone), see carelessness as a sign of future failure, feel competitive with other parents, set a new goal as soon as the current one has been reached or 'go cold' when disappointed by a result or report or a poor performance – as in a swimming or football match. The great danger if we carry on in this vein is not just the pressure it produces but the anxiety and resentment it can generate. The more we fear our tweenie might not be good enough, the more he might opt out to express his anger or to prevent further pressure, criticism and shame.

It doesn't need to be perfect

Another pressure we can put upon children is perfection. No child develops consistently – each one will coast or even roll backwards at times between periods of rapid progress. And when children make real gains, they are operating at the limit of their ability so it is inevitable they won't get things right first time.

PREPARING FOR EXAMS AND TESTS

Tests and exams, even end-of-year exams, are momentary snapshots of a child's learning and state of mind. They are not, at this stage, signposts to the future and should not be seen that way. They are a tactic to encourage consolidation: to bed in the knowledge gained and identify any gaps that need to be filled to prepare children for the next stage. Tests and exams function, in the words of one teacher at a high-flying school, as diagnostic tools. 'The results give us a range of information about the strengths and weaknesses of any class or child and about what might be happening if the results are either better or worse than the year's work might have indicated. If children experience pressure from an early age and see parents ranking them against others, they'll be a basket case by the time they get to the real things. For any individual child, we see exams results as just one dot on a large landscape,' this teacher explained. We should try to see them that way too. Exams are not a beauty contest, either between children or, worse, between parents as they feed off the glory.

Entrance exams to selective schools take place to identify children who will fit in comfortably, in their best interests.

> ### Taster tips on keeping pressure at bay while preparing for tests or exams
>
> ✓ Keep it low-key. If school seems to be piling on the pressure, say clearly the tests are for the school's benefit and we don't see the result as make or break.
> ✓ A few early nights beforehand will help a child give of his best, but don't make this obvious.
> ✓ On the day, behave as normally as possible, be calm and don't refer to the event constantly. Reassure him by saying we know he'll do his best and we'll love him

whatever the result. If it goes wrong, he can do better next time.

✓ Offer some tips if he seems panicky: take several deep breaths; if stuck on a question, leave it and move on and return to it later.

✓ For entrance exams to selective secondary schools, make it clear we simply want to ensure their new school suits them and there could be several possibilities, including non-selective ones. Any rejection will then be less humiliating or disappointing.

✓ Have a special tea ready after to show we appreciate their effort.

. . . and when the results appear

✓ Let them tell you the result in their own time.

✓ Let them open any letter if it arrives in the post.

✓ Accept the importance of 'good enough' success. If they have done their best or near best, that is good enough.

✓ Don't belittle their success: 'Okay, but half the class got that mark, so what was so special?'

✓ Encourage self-appraisal. 'Were you pleased or disappointed with that result?' and then respect their viewpoint.

✓ Where a particular selective school turns a child down, we can suggest that it was merely an option and was not, in the event, a good match. No child wants to equate rejection with being 'second rate' or 'not clever enough'.

RESPONDING TO ANY RESULTS: HELPING TWEENIES TO BENEFIT FROM SUCCESS AND FAILURE

Success and failure are frequently loaded with moral significance, because we see success as something desirable to be celebrated and failure as shameful to be ignored or even punished. However, success and failure are neutral, factual outcomes that tell a child what was done right or to work out what has been going wrong. To go beyond this can be dangerous: success is not always an unqualified joy for a child and failure often shows the way forward. If we respond unthinkingly, we can turn success into a burden that can lead to failure, and failure into a humiliation that blocks learning rather than aids it.

Success may be soured for our child either when *we* appear to take the credit for it or when we react so effusively that he feels we feed off it and our approval rests upon it. If he believes he can't keep it up, he may give up. If he tries to do so obsessively, he may burn out. If he feels we steal his success, he may become disenchanted. The constructive way to acknowledge success is to:

- Separate the success from the person: love them for who they are, not for what they can do. Being a talented dancer, tennis player or musician does not make any child more lovable.
- Don't ration approval through continued success. Tweenies like to enjoy their skills, but if they feel approval is conditional, they could become self-doubting perfectionists.
- Let each success be 'good enough', at least for a while. Tweenies need time and space to breathe, relax, savour the achievement and absorb it as part of their identity before being asked to move on. If they could have done better, the achievement should still be 'good enough' if the effort was serious.
- Check he knows what it was he did right so he can repeat it and the success benefits his self-belief.
- Treat the success as his – to have and enjoy. Ask his permission

to let Grandma or someone else important know, or if he would like to pass on his news.
- Encourage healthier, self-referenced competition against the last personal best performance. No one can be certain of 'beating' fellow competitors who are also trying hard. Competing against others can be dispiriting, because competition often stiffens as a child improves.

We should also be careful how we respond to failure. No child should be told he is a 'failure' – on a certain road to an empty future, a no-hoper, 'thick', or 'useless' – otherwise he will develop a no-hope self-image. These are unyielding labels that shame and humiliate, deny any possibility of change and ignore any endearing personal qualities. Shame makes children want to hide under the bedclothes. Humiliation makes them want to disappear through a hole in the ground and become nothing. Shame and humiliation directed at a child rarely kick him into action and can be a disaster for someone who is vulnerable, making him tense, withdrawn and self-doubting, the opposite of what learning requires. Mistakes are useful in that they tell a story, about what was not understood or poor preparation for example, and it is this story our child and we need to understand.

Failure can, then, be seen as a problem to be solved, a challenge to be met. The constructive way to respond to failure is to:

- Separate the failure from the person and attach it clearly to the event.
- Respond constructively. Discuss what went wrong, identify what needs to be done and jointly agree a detailed and staged action plan.
- Respond sensitively. Failure is usually upsetting even if he declares he doesn't care; go easy on him for a while, make him

feel useful to you in practical ways and make it clear you love him none the less.

- Respond genuinely. Weasel words won't help so be straightforward and honest. Though it is hard to sound positive while highlighting errors, if we fudge and he knows it he could reject our judgement thereafter.
- Make him take responsibility. Don't claim it was the teacher's fault or down to his wayward friends. Minimising the failure or blaming others may protect him (and us) but it clouds the responsibility and prevents lessons being learned.
- Put him back in charge. Once the joint action plan is agreed, see it as his responsibility to follow it up, with our help, not ours.

Remember, too, that the process of getting something wrong or right often contributes more to progress than the grade alone. 'I now know what I was doing wrong,' is a far healthier attitude than, 'I did well though I've no idea why. I'll probably fail next time.'

'ALL WORK AND NO PLAY . . .': BALANCING THE TWO

With all the stress that can surround schoolwork and achievement, it is extremely important that children have plenty of time off to relax and have fun out of school to pursue a range of interests and sometimes to do nothing much, fiddling about in their bedrooms, a garden or at a friend's house. Children are usually tired after a day or week at school so evenings and weekends should be as unpressured as possible. While extra studying packed into 'free' time may help us to feel confident that our tweenie is progressing well academically, we also should want him to be well-rounded, self-motivated but not hooked on success. Plenty of self-directed play helps to deliver that balance.

example. By the age of twelve, they will probably go to the cinema en masse, and be collected after by an adult. They can also be expected to organise more of their own play with friends.

Another strand of development in play is the growth of physical strength and competence. Tweenies can develop real skill in pursuits that test their physical co-ordination and strength. They will enjoy developing their talents, going beyond the basics of tennis, ice-skating, gymnastics, athletics, swimming, skateboarding, martial arts, cycling or football to master more complex manoeuvres. And craft-based hobbies become increasingly popular, largely because tweenies are more deft and dextrous. Whether a hobby is bird watching, constructing simple plastic or wooden models, playing in a brass band, drama, threading small beads, working with clay or drawing, the activity selected will add variety and self-insight. Younger tweenies, though, still enjoy rushing about wildly. Emma, eight, described her school playground: 'We play games like horses – galloping around with a skipping rope tied around one of us like reins. We play power rangers too, or we act out books or other TV programmes.' Lucy, nine, said, 'We play Harry Potter. We each take a character and add new ones if more people want to join in and we make up new stories. The older girls just hang about and talk.' This description highlights another change that occurs: as tweenies mature, they are able to adapt and develop themes and use their growing imagination to create more elaborate plots.

Risk-taking is a further important facet of tweenies' play. From nine or ten, risk-taking is an expression of independence, having fun, showing off and finding out how far they can go. A little bit of living dangerously is what every child craves – and needs – because it contributes significantly to the growth of confidence, judgement and development as he begins to master things that previously scared him, learn about safety and find out when to stop. In a study of nine- to sixteen-year-olds, more than three-quarters of them preferred being out and about than being in. Tactics to ensure that risk-taking remains within safe limits are discussed in chapter eleven.

GIRLS AND BOYS COME OUT TO PLAY

We saw in chapter one how girls and boys often play separately around the age of eight and can become quite dismissive of each other. Girls, and some boys too, go through a phase of playing with make-up, styling and applying extraordinary coloured hair mascara to their friend's and their own hair and donning their mum or sister's outfits, for a laugh and to experience what it means to be female. Boys have a harder time exploring their masculinity because there are no obvious roles or images to copy. Though few will become soldiers, boys still play military-style games with cap guns, water pistols and model tanks and aircraft, as well as combat-based, fantasy computer games. Their fascination with fighting must reflect an association of masculinity with strength and power. Of course, girls enjoy fighting with swords too and both girls and boys will enjoy a range of activities not all of which will have gender associations.

Maintain balance and variety: the six 'Cs'

Many activities, like some friends, will develop only certain facets of any child. Children grow in a more balanced way and gain a fuller sense of self when they follow a variety of interests. Tweenies' free time can include physical play, social play, playing alone, imaginative play, 'free' play, playing outside as well as in, and play that has rules, winners and losers such as card and board games.

To gauge whether our tweenie is developing a healthy range of experiences, we can refer to the idea of 'quality play'. Regardless of age, quality play is play that:

• Shows, or builds on, a child's inner resources for coping.

- Develops powers of understanding, therefore empathy and insight.
- Extends his range of experience.
- Offers scope for experimentation and personal development.
- Develops social skills.

Quality play therefore encourages the six 'Cs': creativity, curiosity, confidence, concentration, physical co-ordination and co-operation. It involves choices and decisions, imagination, other people (real or made up), a degree of risk (in the form of challenge and experiment), self-management and self-expression. We don't need to apply a checklist and tick off everything our child does that is 'valuable', but it is no bad thing to assess every so often whether he may be becoming over-focused and what he might be missing out on as a result.

WHAT CAN TWEENIES PLAY AND DO?

Some ideas for games and activities often enjoyed by tweenies are included in the table below. It is not exhaustive but suggests possibilities across different categories. Some will be more suitable for younger tweenies, and some for the near-teens.

'Free' play

CREATIVE	IMAGINATIVE	PHYSICAL
Sewing/knitting	Dressing up/cosmetics	Tree climbing/houses
Artwork (collage, painting, charcoal)	Indoor/outdoor tents	Skipping/football
Designing clothes	Construction kits	Bike riding
Woodwork	Mini micros/soldiers	Swimming
Cooking/gardening	Drama – creating a play	Ice-skating
Clay sculpture/modelling	Dungeons and dragons	
Drawing rockets/dragons	Barbies or similar	

Structured play

TASK-FOCUSED GAMES OR ACTIVITIES	GAMES WITH CLEAR RULES	SPORTS/GAMES WITH SKILLS AND RULES
Jigsaws	Board games (ludo, Scrabble)	French cricket
Crosswords	Card games (patience, snap)	Tennis
Craft activities (beads, models, paper-folding)	Paper games (noughts and crosses, boxes, hangman	Football
Painting by numbers	Video/computer games	Ten-pin bowling
	Dominos etc.	

And don't forget 'pootle' time. Every child needs private time in which they do nothing very much, time that is theirs to idle away if that is their current mood.

MANAGING THE PULL OF COMPUTERS AND TV

Most of us have mixed feelings about computers, which we see as both a bonus (potentially educational) and a bogey (addictive, time-wasting and encouraging a taste for violence). We worry about the time spent on them, but how much time is too much depends on what else our child does, whether he plays alone or with friends, whether he is generally a good mixer, and whether the equipment is tucked away in a bedroom, thus isolating him further. The main issue is that time spent in front of a screen is time not spent exploring wider talents, having real-life experiences and confronting real-life challenges – learning more about himself. A secondary issue is that our lack of involvement in it could make him feel neglected, so he should certainly not eat his meals there too. Computers and televisions are great provided they don't take over to the exclusion of anything else.

These machines should not allow him to escape from other people, reality or, indeed, himself.

We also worry about a possible obsession with violence and copying specific acts. However, research on the link between watching violence and actual violent behaviour has generally been interpreted as inconclusive. Most eight-year-olds can and do separate cartoon violence from the real thing and one study found that the young offenders began watching unpleasant video material only after they had begun to offend, having decided this is what bad boys did. The best way to protect our tweenie from being tempted to copy screen violence is to remain close and loving, to supervise gently and to foster a range of talents so he invests in his future and steers clear of trouble. (For guidance on safety in Internet chat rooms, see the reference section at the end of the book.)

Taster tips on keeping a balance

✓ Discuss a new regime to reduce the time spent in front of screens or make up for what's been missing.

✓ Encourage talking, sharing and being together – watch TV with them, talk about what they've watched or played, ask what happened and what they liked.

✓ Stimulate their ideas and imagination: 'How would you have liked it to end?' 'What would your ideal game be like?'

✓ Give them time with you – preferably talking or doing something, not watching.

✓ Make sure they take physical exercise.

✓ Encourage other activities that involve concentration and to introduce variety.

✓ Limit the hours. Late-night viewing or playing make children tired for school the next day.

> ✓ Check how much they have understood about a TV programme or use it to initiate discussion.
> ✓ Suggest they could learn more about something they have found interesting by using the Internet and the local library.

LEISURE IS FOR PLEASURE: THE ACTIVITY DRIVE

During the 'In-between' years, as children develop a clearer identity, they come to realise what it is they really enjoy doing and what they're especially good at, or not. Until then, parents tend to choose their children's activities and drive themselves almost crazy finding things for each of them to do and fitting it all in. We can also drive our child crazy. A child's talent can become a parent's passion, and a parent's passion can become a child's nightmare as all possibilities for excellence are exploited. Once that much time and effort has been invested, it can be a real blow to learn that our child wants to drop this to try something else.

If he wants to give up, ask him or yourself any of the following: has he given it his best shot; whose idea was it to start with, his or yours; is there something he wants to do instead; might a different teacher or different group give him a fresh impetus; might he like to take a break and start again after a breather; is his waning interest due to feeling untalented, and does this really matter (around the age of eleven, children become able, developmentally, to appreciate that some have a natural talent and will always be better, regardless of the effort they apply); does he feel he's doing too much; is starting and giving up an emerging pattern that he needs to challenge; does he want more free time; will giving up be like a snake shedding its skin but leaving the old self still there? Remember that praise and encouragement often help to sustain interest, so perhaps more appreciation of the achievement and commitment involved would help. But it is very likely that he simply wants more time to himself. Pushing a child to attend activities when he has had enough is pointless. Children do not need to uncover every potential talent by the end of primary school, and new interests can emerge from reading, playing or thinking.

Just because a child could achieve excellence does not mean he has to. Leisure should be for pleasure, not pain, and developing a talent involves hard work though the process can still be enjoyable. If our child wants to find out how far he can take his talent we should of course encourage him, but striving for stardom can involve painful setbacks and social and emotional costs are common. The safe route that avoids both burn-out and serious disappointment is to keep the child at the centre: never make him do anything he does not want to and put his future in his hands. He should pursue his talent because he enjoys it, not to impress us, please us or as his sole way to feel happy with himself.

As tweenies need to be treated as a source of authority about themselves, we should allow them to choose how they spend their leisure time, be prepared to compromise, accept that they need time to relax and appreciate they have a lifetime ahead to pursue a rich range of talents.

Keeping boredom at bay

Parents can fill their child's time with commitments to stave off boredom, but boredom is not such a bad thing. It is a kind of pain barrier, the other side of which – once children find the way through – is creativity and self-discovery. Boredom sets in when life feels dull, but it enables a child to confront himself and discover untapped interests and resources. Toddlers and young children need to be spoon-fed entertainment. Tweenies, however, should begin to sort themselves out. They cannot experience autonomy, explore their personal limits or develop their initiative and creativity if we fill their time to the brim and arrange everything for them. Although the excruciating whine,

'I'm bored, what can I do?' can tempt us to fix almost anything as a shortcut to peace, it's for our benefit, not theirs. The more we fix, the more they become fixed. Tweenies must gradually learn that a solution will emerge, one that will reflect and deepen their character. They need not fear empty time. Initially, we may need to help them to brainstorm and list various things they might do either with friends or by themselves, something to refer to when boredom looms. Even then, rather than direct them to the list it is better to say, 'Yes, being bored is dreary but I know something will come to you. Didn't you think through some possibilities once?' and pass the responsibility back to them.

DRAWING THIS TOGETHER

During play, tweenies explore their limits, develop their character, deepen their creative potential and develop self-confidence. It is hard work. 'Achievement is not about the number of facts you are able to absorb but about how effective you are as an individual.' This sound piece of advice from a former leading school governor should be widely supported. We should never forget, as we pore over targets and tables, that children's other 'work' – time spent playing with friends, imagining, creating or enjoying greater physical prowess – aids learning and can have a far more significant impact on future success, health and happiness than schoolwork. But schoolwork is important too and the support we offer to help them achieve and do well should be positive and enabling, not create anxiety and become effectively disabling. Our children should be able to relax and have fun at home and be trusted. We need to take the pressure off, not add to it, which means we must love them for who they are and not for what they can do; and *never* imply that they are not *quite* good enough.

'*Everyone gets scars on the way to the stars*' is the title line to a jazz number composed by Fran Landesman. She meant that sometimes we have to suffer to reach our dreams. But it can be read another way: that no child should get scarred in the quest for more stars. Healthy confidence grows from feeling that we are good enough yet have more to give, and it is to children's mental and physical health that we turn next.

Ten top take-out tips

- Make it clear we love them for who they are, not for their achievements.
- Leisure is for pleasure. No skill or activity should be pursued for our glory at the expense of their enjoyment.
- Never punish mistakes in work or play: focus on the learning – what needs to be done differently next time and to improve on their last personal best.
- Help them to develop a sensible attitude to exploration and risk-taking and the confidence to try new things through accepting mistakes and encouraging adventurous play.
- Encourage balanced variety. Wide interests are associated with emotional stability.
- Encourage self-motivation and self-direction in work and play. Let them determine their own plans and preferences and develop approaches that suit them.
- Growing up is a serious business; and socialising is as serious as studying.
- Give them time to do nothing and the space to be bored, to encourage self-discovery and deepen self-knowledge.
- Don't fret if much of their play conforms to sexual stereotypes – or if they have fun donning the clothes of the other sex. But do provide opportunities to explore hobbies or sports that are less gender-specific.
- Parents are models. Make fun and entertainment, reading, discussion and an interest in learning part of normal family life.

And Remember!

Don't judge yourself by how well they do. Help out, but don't do it for them.

Self-belief is the engine of opportunity, so beware pressure, criticism and showing disappointment.

Foster initiative and ideas: let them decide what to do, how and when to do it, and who to do it with – provided it gets done.

8

AN APPLE A DAY?

Keeping Tweenies Healthy

CHILDREN'S HEALTH AND WELL-BEING HAS become a big issue – a major concern of teachers, doctors, politicians and parents. Although life-threatening infectious diseases such as polio, measles and tuberculosis that used to debilitate children are now rare, other health problems have arisen to take their place that also threaten our tweenie's future. We still need to aim to keep the doctor away. There is concern about children being overweight to the point of obesity, but also about them becoming life-threateningly thin. Tweenies are very image-conscious, so they are especially vulnerable to the toxic environment of fast, high-calorie junk food. Yet many also care about how they look, which poses a dilemma. It is far harder to have the figure of their dreams while they play out less and, when housebound, snack constantly and sit tight apparently glued to screens and chairs.

It is clear that some of them are taking the desire to be fit and slim – countering this trend – too far in the other direction, with the result that eating disorders and exercise fanaticism among both girls and boys aged eight to twelve are on the rise. The fully equipped, professional, child-sized mini-gyms being imported from the United States are not merely innocent, growing-up versions of tumble tots for bigger children: they can seduce young boys and girls to care more about how they look than who they are and to develop an obsessive dissatisfaction with their efforts and bodies. It is unhealthy, emotionally and physically, for growing, highly impressionable children to be on the margins of an acceptable weight and fixated on looking and being perfect human specimens.

From a straightforward medical perspective, eight-to twelve-year-olds are just about as healthy as they'll ever be. They now have greater immunity to the endless coughs and colds that bedevil infant school children; from seven or eight, the rate of ear and tonsil infection falls significantly; they resist other infections more effectively because they are bigger and more robust; most learning and behaviour disorders (for example, autism, Asperger's Syndrome and Attention Deficit and Hyperactivity Disorder) have already emerged; and by the age of twelve most asthmatics are symptom-free. The most common reason for a tweenie to visit the doctor is physical injury.

However, before we breathe a sigh of relief, mental and emotional health matters as much as physical health. We have a clear responsibility to try to keep our tweenie on an even emotional keel. This is a serious issue. There is plenty of evidence to suggest that children's mental and emotional well-being is taking a tumble, like adults', as they cope with the stresses of modern living. More children are finding it hard to go to school, more are quiet and withdrawn, being disruptive, seem unhappy within themselves and are more prone to tears as well as anxiety and eating disorders. Stress affects children as well as adults; in fact it is now accepted that children and even babies can be depressed. We know that even mild unhappiness can undermine a child's confidence, weaken her ties of friendship, affect her concentration and school performance and increase the chances of later teenage risky behaviour that can threaten health and happiness further. There are, though, strategies available to help children cope and even to emerge from any difficulty feeling stronger. And there are plenty of ways to boost their emotional strength to help them remain stable and happy throughout the challenges of normal daily living, even if there are no expected problems on the horizon.

This chapter focuses on how to encourage and 'normalise' healthy behaviour in relation to eating; how to keep our child fit and active without turning her into a perfectionist fitness fanatic; and how to support her through any tough times when change and disruption dominate and children's emotional health is most at risk. Emotional health, characterised by optimism and confidence based on a strong and positive sense of self, is closely linked to physical health, as we shall see first in the next section on healthy eating.

Encouraging healthy eating habits

Eating involves a great deal more than simply taking in nutrients and calories that we need for living and, in the case of children, growing. In most societies, eating is a complex, family-based social activity and is frequently influenced by strong cultural and religious traditions. It is also closely tied, for young children especially, to the intimate (even occasionally tense) relationship between child and food provider. Over the years, each of us establishes an individual relationship with food that embodies a wide range of childhood experiences, relationships and family patterns.

Humans don't graze constantly like cows or sheep; instead, most adults eat roughly every six hours. Most children need to eat at about four-hourly intervals. They are certainly desperate for food when they return from school. Something that we need to do as frequently as eating quickly sets to a pattern and becomes a routine, part of our daily rhythm. It is important to develop healthy attitudes and habits as early as possible.

HEALTHY HABITS, HEALTHY ATTITUDES

Healthy habits, healthy preferences and healthy attitudes all contribute to healthy eating. The familiar becomes comfortable, so early patterns of eating, good or bad, often stick. It is not just that our taste buds get used to certain foods, flavours and textures (salt, sugar, particular sauces, white or brown bread and so on), we also get used to familiar practices about when, how often and how much we eat, routines that generate expect-ations. Children who like large helpings often live in families in which everyone eats heartily, and children who eat more modestly will often be following the family norm. Eight- to twelve-year-olds are at a critical point: they take more decisions for themselves about what and when they eat and drink – because they are able to reach the cupboards or fridge, may be on their own for short periods, have their own money so can buy what they really like, unrestricted by the limits of the family fridge – and in any case use choices about food to establish their indi-vidual and group identity. Although this might lead to a time of less healthy eating, it is important that our tweenie learns to experiment with and manage the freedom implicit in eating else-where – in the school canteen, the local high street and at friends' houses. This is part of growing autonomy. Trying to maintain control through insisting on calorie- and nutrient-controlled packed lunch boxes, for example, is no longer appropriate. Let them explore, while continuing to model balanced eating at home.

If things go too far, it can be hard to change the way a whole family eats for the benefit of one or two children who are becom-ing heavier than is healthy, but a healthier diet will benefit every-one. It is a good idea to cut down on the fat and sugar intake and increase the amount of fruit, vegetables and fresh food consumed, though not obsessively, and to present these changes as pleasures rather than as a tolerated, unpleasant necessity like medicine. It may be time-consuming and frustrating at the start;

though with persistence, imaginative serving options, our tween-ie's direct assistance in the kitchen and with the certain know-ledge that this is undeniably best for our tweenie, habits and preferences can be shifted. This is neither a nutrition nor a recipe book, so ideas for specific meal plans will have to be found else-where. But, as the taster tips suggest, it is always better to offer the most-desired-but-less-desirable food once or twice a week rather than cut it out completely, because total bans generally lead to secretive guzzling. Fizzy drinks can be a weekend special, with water, milk or fruit juices drunk at other times. Alternatively, the regime could be one sugary drink a day – but not at breakfast! Fries, nuggets or other fried food high in cal-ories can be similarly limited. Growing children need a balanced diet to receive the necessary nutrition, and many tweenies are about to experience a growth spurt in body and brain. A full and varied diet will not only achieve a desirable balance but also foster an adventurous, open and confident attitude to sampling new foods and flavours that may even lead to a more general open-mindedness.

Healthy habits are founded on healthy attitudes – to food and eating and towards the self. These can be undermined if we are not careful. For example, if a child is allowed to go hungry, she may feel neglected, or if forced to eat everything she may feel misunderstood and not respected. Different families in different cultures have widely varied eating customs and attitudes to food. The important thing is to assess whether these contribute to a child's sense of security, significance and connection. Our tween-ie will feel significant and have a positive sense of self that feels worthy of being fed when we:

- Offer her some access to food she especially enjoys.
- Remember her likes and dislikes.
- Treat her the same as all other family members.
- Allow her to decide when she has had enough.

- Do not force her to eat everything.
- Ensure regular mealtimes – including breakfast – so she does not go hungry.

Cooking for the family can be seen as making a direct contribution to everyone's well-being; and if we avoid all talk of dieting while eating a child will realise that eating is not complicated by, or associated with, guilt or self-denial. When eating is seen as a collective, enjoyable and social activity, rather than as merely functional or even a social trial, it helps to foster positive attitudes towards food and a sense of belonging. To reinforce this further, we can invite her to cook with us, limit the food eaten between meals, cook meals that are 'family favourites', have some familiar rituals around eating (such as a candle on the table once a week), share the occasional meal with others and strive to keep mealtimes conflict-free and conversation full. When our tweenie has to eat on her own, we should always try to sit with her to keep her company and use the moment to talk and discuss: to find out about her day, her experiences and her views.

Taster tips for healthy family eating habits

✓ Aim for regular mealtimes and minimise eating between meals.

✓ Try to eat together as a family as much as possible, even if this is only two or three times a week, and assume that everyone will eat the same food.

✓ These family meals could provide the chance to include healthier foods, such as fresh vegetables, that are sometimes hard to include in children's daily diets.

✓ The taste for sugar is habit-forming. Try to keep fizzy drinks for the weekend, and encourage them to drink water, milk or fruit juices as weekday alternatives.

✓ Five daily portions of fruit or vegetables are officially recommended.

✓ Try to find out what is being eaten at school at lunch and in breaks, to offer something different and balance out the diet at home.

✓ Don't put a child on any form of calorie-controlled or fat-free diet without prior professional advice. Worry about moderate obesity, not a little pre-pubertal chubbiness, provided your child is otherwise active.

AVOIDING BATTLES OVER FOOD

We should always try to avoid battles over food, over what, when and how much is eaten. Total bans on any particular food, such as sweets, biscuits or crisps, can be counter-productive, triggering compulsive and secretive bingeing. Battles over what various children will and won't eat can turn mealtimes into nightmares. If feeding our fussy tweenie has become a logistical nightmare, we can try the 'five no-no's' tactic. Let her choose up to five things she is never required to eat. The compromise deal becomes: you don't have to eat any of these, as long as you eat everything else – and stick to it! My step-children were so worried they'd find something else to add in the weeks ahead they never got beyond three or four. It worked like magic.

Enforced diets can lead to battles as well as other problems. Childhood diets are dangerous. No child should be put on a diet without first taking professional advice, even though more children are becoming overweight. Several studies show that children made to diet when young are more likely to develop an eating disorder later. They also show that it is far more effective long-term simply to target *weight stability*, not weight reduction. A clear eating and exercise programme can bring this about. If weight can be stabilised for about two and a half years, natural growth will ensure a return to normal size. Diets don't work usually because children find ways to subvert them and any weight lost is so often regained, plus some.

OBESITY: MANAGING DIET AND EXERCISE

Obesity among the young is the result of eating too much of the wrong food and taking insufficient exercise, and it is growing. The two are interrelated: the heavier you get, the harder it becomes to run about; and the less active you are, the less food you need to maintain any given weight. And then, of course, the less exercise you take, the more time you have . . . to eat! Between the ages of ten and twelve, a child should gain about five kilos each year, but no more. In the UK, one in five of all nine-year-olds are estimated to be overweight and one in ten obese – a rate that has doubled in the last twenty years. Obese teenagers are now developing Type 2 diabetes, previously seen only in extremely overweight adults. Even young children who carry excessive weight are more prone to high blood pressure, blood clots, heart and circulatory problems and serious liver and kidney disease that we associate with adults, and these problems can then plague them for the rest of their life.

It has been estimated that, given current activity levels, children need 25 per cent fewer calories than they did sixty years ago, yet today they consume more calories than then, not fewer. Couch potatoes often munch as they watch TV. Whether at the cinema or at home, sitting in front of a screen is increasingly, even compulsively, linked with eating. Children flop in front of the TV or their computer with snacks after school. Many families eat their meals while watching. On top of this, video rental stores now promote sodas, ice cream, corn chips and popcorn to make home viewing akin to a night out. And when they watch more television, they see more food commercials. American and British children are exposed to something like ten food commercials for every hour that they watch. Most of these promote fast food and snacks high in sugar and fat to establish lifelong habits.

Those who succumb are exposed to an excess of behaviour-changing food additives as well as possible weight problems.

This toxic, snack culture could be undermining children's sense of belonging as well as their health and behaviour. Children who have munched and slurped happily on snacks and pop will have little or no appetite at family mealtimes so may stay away. And as a mum who has spent many hours preparing meals, when these are sniffed at you wish you hadn't bothered and you may give up. A snacking child may feel more bonded to her peers, at least temporarily, but if family eating goes out of the window longer term her family bond could weaken. Of course, the peer bonding may be short-lived and ultimately poisonous if the weight gained attracts the attention of bullies. Serious psychological problems can follow bullying or peer rejection due to being overweight. Eating may then take on a love-hate quality: a source of comfort yet also self-hate as it produces the detestable body and involves a humiliating loss of self-control. Attitudes towards food are primarily taught and learned, but once food becomes entangled with notions of good and evil, or desert and denial, potentially harmful associations become very hard to change.

Taster tips on avoiding over-eating with tweenies

✓ Little and often may be good for babies but it's not good for older children. Regular meals help to establish regular eating habits and regular biorhythms in which the body expects food at set times only.

✓ Snacking should be kept to a minimum. It's now thought that food eaten on the run is not recognised by the brain as proper food, so does not end hunger.

✓ During term time, the mid-morning snack should be food that contains slow-release energy – a sandwich, chunk of bread, a piece of cheese or a cereal bar, not sugar or chocolate. Sugar satisfies hunger only temporarily; then it returns more urgently – the effect of insulin. Sugar also creates an energy burst followed by a lethargic dip, the bane of those who teach between morning break and lunchtime.

✓ Sweet things can be eaten as part of a meal, rather than between meals.

✓ Consider introducing a 'sixty-minute rule': snacks may not be consumed within, say, sixty minutes of a meal, either before or after.

✓ Offer each child the choice of one favoured potato-style snack and buy a restricted number of these each week so the scope for bingeing is removed.

✓ Discuss a range of possible snack alternatives to sweet biscuits, potato or wheat snacks or other snacks cooked instantly in toasters or the microwave. Options might include: a tuna and mayo sandwich, cheese on toast, an apple, cereal bars. A bag of cut-up carrots, cucumber, apple or banana slices can be kept in the fridge so healthy snack alternatives can be consumed without any preparation that may put the kids off. Suggest at least a trial period with these healthier alternatives.

✓ Eating is often a diversion from boredom. Aim to keep children mostly active and busy. Idle hands and thoughts too often wander to kitchen cupboards!

✓ Children who are very hungry before a meal can join in preparing the food to help pass the time.

✓ Encourage moderate portions initially. Second helpings can fill still empty spaces, and if seconds are wanted just because the food was great, the total amount eaten won't be gargantuan.

EATING DISORDERS AMONG EIGHT- TO TWELVE-YEAR-OLDS

Eating disorders among eight- to twelve-year-olds are on the increase. We don't know by exactly how much because the statistics collected relate to different age bands. The director of a specialist children's eating clinic in Birmingham has said: 'They may be twelve when they are referred for treatment, but the seeds are being sown when they are much younger than that. Even in primary school, a lot of children are aware of fat-free products. Dieting is a natural progression for them.' For children of this age, anorexia nervosa, in which people eat so little they lose a considerable and dangerous amount of weight, and compulsive over-eating are the most common disorders. Bulimia nervosa, in which sufferers binge and then purge through vomiting, is found more typically among older teenagers and young adults. Compulsive over-eating is equally common in boys and girls, affects, probably, 5 per cent of the population and tends to run in families. The desire to eat can intensify when children are unhappy, but over-eating can simply have become a habit.

Pre-teens can also be picky and faddy – very selective about what they eat. If they are growing normally, seem active and otherwise healthy, it is best not to get too concerned, but don't encourage it by sending them to friends with a personal 'doggy bag'. However, it just could be the start of something more worrying. If this is our instinct, get help. Forcing her to eat is not usually the answer. If she then becomes angry and feels manipulated, she's more likely to turn it into a serious food fight, which will end with her victorious and in hospital. Make mealtimes as enjoyable as possible: serve things that she likes but don't make an individual meal just for her.

Simon's story

Simon was a bright, sensitive nine-year-old – so bright that his school had considered entering him for a GCSE – when he started to be bullied in school. At home, he began to refuse sweets and chocolates. Although surprised, his mother wasn't unduly worried. But when the self-denial spread to other foods and Simon began to lose weight, the alarm bells rang and she sought medical help. 'He was picked on relentlessly for two years. He lost every shred of self-esteem and wouldn't make eye contact with anyone,' she said. 'He didn't think he was worthy of food yet he became obsessed with it. It was his way of coping, like adults who reach for the bottle.' Simon became so ill he ended up in hospital. After treatment, he changed schools twice and settled happily at secondary school. His mother said, 'It's miserable living with someone with an eating disorder. They become depressed, and extremely angry when you make them eat. We must talk about it and take the shame out of it.'

MANAGING AN EATING DISORDER

Eating disorders are a coping strategy for something experienced as difficult. They are not created to get at us. Although a child may choose to adopt a pattern of disordered eating, she will not have intended to, and has no choice about the consequential eating disorder that can follow. Children cannot be forced to eat so working at it together is the only option. And both parents must also co-operate, as must other children in the family. Rows about the issue will only make it worse. Consistency of approach is important. Brothers and sisters can say, 'We love you to bits but we do not like what you are doing to yourself', thus separating their sibling from her behaviour. Poor self-esteem is very common in children with eating disorders, so one approach is to work hard to make her feel competent, approved of and loved unconditionally for who and as she is, not conditional on how she looks, how well she behaves or how well she does in school. Again, work to increase her sense of security, significance and connection.

Certain personalities seem to be more prone to anorexia – particularly those with perfectionist tendencies. If our child is very keen to do well at school or in sport, has very neat handwriting, wants to be fit and takes lots of exercise, our antennae should be out. It is, of course, fine to be fit, as we discuss next, but it is not fine to burn off so many calories that children effectively self-obliterate.

Taster tips on keeping eating problem-free

✓ Avoid exercising a tight control over food, as well as being directive in other ways (over, for example, music practice, homework, hairstyles and clothes bought and worn). Eating disorders often develop as a way to take control when people feel they have little autonomy elsewhere.

✓ Try not to use sweets or fast foods as a reward: they are more likely to be considered special and become linked to success and approval, being rejected when self-worth is low.

✓ Avoid using sweets as consolation for any emotional upset or injury: eating sugar-based food may become a way children learn to pick themselves up when they feel down.

✓ Don't obsess about healthy eating, dieting, keeping fit, celebrity bodies or ban particular foods from the house. If you feel the need to diet, keep it quiet.

✓ Have fun at mealtimes and enjoy as wide a range of foodstuffs as your budget and inclination allow.

Fit for Use? Action stations!

The other side of the weight coin is activity. Tweenies are becoming increasingly sluggish and inactive. Up to their eyes in electronic media, fearful of playing outdoors and increasingly being driven to school, today's eight- to twelve-year-olds are far more sedentary than they were twenty years ago. Joel, an eleven-year-old, reckons that he spends at least a day a week on his computer and the equivalent of another day watching television. Even when they are at school, British children do little sport – forty-five minutes a week on average according to one study. In one international comparison of time allocated to PE in the curriculum, Britain came last out of twenty-one countries. In another study of young people's general activity rates in a town in eastern England, it was found that only one in twenty took as much exercise as that recommended for a middle-aged man – twenty minutes of strenuous activity three times a week. Fifteen minutes running around at break time is not nearly enough. The result is that children as young as eight are showing the early signs of heart disease, and only 4 per cent of boys and 1 per cent of girls aged eleven to sixteen are reaching levels of physical activity necessary to maintain cardiac health.

The In-between times are also important physically because this is when children begin to develop their strength and skills. They are growing taller and therefore potentially stronger because of puberty, and their capacity to think more abstractly helps them to develop their sporting techniques. They can improve significantly and become deeply proud of their bodies and achievements in the process. It should contribute to their growing confidence. But if their weight prevents them from keeping up with their peers' improvements, instead of feeling successful and pleased, they may feel frustration and shame. If the tweenie years are not only important for establishing healthy habits and routines but also to develop a positive body image and physical competence, now is the time to gird them into action. How?

WALKING TO SCHOOL

It can be hard to organise the mornings to leave enough time to walk to school. Mornings are often mayhem: different children go off in different directions and at different times, all needing our watchful eye; we might have babies who need to be dressed and fed or we might need to leave the house before our tweenie in order to get to work. Driving there might be the only option, so it becomes easier to drop a child off at school on the way, especially if she attends a breakfast club, than walk there and back before setting off. Time is very precious in our pressured existence and the quickest option often wins the day.

However, if it can possibly be organised, it should be, especially if our tweenie takes little exercise at other times in the week. The benefits go beyond keeping weight down and fitness up. Children benefit from the conversations they have with any adult or other child on the way, they can feel more secure because they have a sense of the route between home and school, they can notice a great deal about the changing seasons, nature or local life and residents, and when they have acquired enough road sense and maturity to enable them to walk on their own, the freedom and responsibility they gain contributes significantly to their emotional development. As more people work from home or work flexible hours, there may be other parents with children at the same school living close by who can take our child under their wing. Some schools organise 'walking snakes', an adult-led group of children that collects others on the way. Sometimes, of course, the school is too distant to make walking practical, but even that depends on changing views of what is reasonable. The more we drive our youngster, the more she will consider walking a tiresome, exhausting drag, try to cadge lifts and avoid outings that involve this 'effort'. This is akin to a baby pestering to be carried. They hate to be put down. But we know they must walk and manage otherwise their physical and social development is set back.

EXTRA SPORT AND ACTIVITIES

If it is unavoidable that our pre-teen is driven to and from school and needs to stay in when she gets home as we cannot be there or there's too much homework to be done, it may be time to draw her into extra sport or other physical activities at the weekends. This is definitely preferable to consigning a tweenie to spend more sedentary hours in extra maths or language classes. It is best if these sporting activities are kept low-key. Possibilities are scratch football games in the park or on the common on a Saturday or Sunday morning run by local lads, dads and mums, regular family trips to a swimming pool or swimming classes, athletics at a local sports centre, or occasional visits to an ice rink if there is one close to home. Even tenpin bowling or shopping involves more activity than watching TV. Smaller towns and villages are less likely to have the same range of facilities, but they have the advantage of countryside on the doorstep. If a car ride is necessary to get to the nearest attraction, so be it. If we opt to pay for classes, karate, judo or dance – jazz, Indian, tap, street, ballet – are popular with boys and girls of this age. Less costly are children's groups such as Scouts, Guides and Woodcraft Folk. All these encourage a good measure of running about to let off steam as much as to get healthy.

In many ways, though, it would be more satisfactory if we could allow our children to lead a more free-range, active and vigorous life such as children led fifty or sixty years ago – more playing out, more tree climbing, more cycling, more mucking about, so that we did not need to put them under 'special measures'.

GOING OUT AND ABOUT

One result of children living increasingly behind closed doors – car doors and front doors – is they do not go out and about enough on their own. This affects not only their physical health but their mental health too, the subject of the next section. Growing children need an outdoor environment and a sense of adventure to discover more about what they can do. They need to test the boundaries and get up to mischief, and suffer the consequences if they get it wrong. They can only do that on their own. All children need some private space. When they are driven or bussed to school, they are under adult scrutiny. At school they are watched and monitored. In the safe confines of the home, they are supervised. Even if they are out on their own with friends, the mobile phone encourages adult intrusion, though used by agreement at set times it is able to increase the sense of safety. (See chapter eleven for a full discussion of a range of issues relating to personal safety and sensible risk management.) Both freedom and moderate risk are essential to healthy development. Staying in cars or indoors is no way to develop life skills that help children to feel capable. Avoiding fear makes it grow and fuels the sense of powerlessness. If we confront our fears and cope, it makes them manageable and increases our self-belief and competence. These are what underlie emotional health, our next concern.

Taster tips to get tweenies out and about

✓ Use public transport and walk more when we go out and about at weekends and during the holidays.
✓ Play catch with a ball or frisbie; kick a football, climb trees together.
✓ Encourage bike riding.
✓ Ten- to twelve-year-olds could be sent, in a group with their friends, on adventures to try out local

---

public transport – meeting a challenge to see how many miles they can cover on a one-day bus ticket, or to come home from the swimming baths a different way from their journey there.

✓ Take each member of the family on dog walks, if you own one.

✓ Walk wherever possible, for example to pick up the odd item of shopping, and ask our tweenie to come with us.

✓ Suggest hobbies that require time outdoors: watching out for birds, catching insects in a bug box for identification or drawing; spotting different makes of car.

✓ Encourage walking to school, as discussed above.

Nurturing mental and emotional health

Mental health concerns our state of mind – our beliefs, attitudes and feelings about ourselves and other people. In combination, they influence how we see, relate and respond to the immediate world in which we live. Mentally healthy young people have been described as being able to develop psychologically, emotionally, intellectually and spiritually; to initiate and sustain satisfactory friendships, become aware of others and empathise with them; distinguish right from wrong; and use distress to get help but not to get side-tracked or knocked over by it. Another way to understand mental and emotional health is to see it as an attitude rather than what it helps children to do. From this view, mental health has been described as 'the emotional and spiritual resilience that enables us to enjoy life and to survive pain, suffering and disappointment. It is a positive sense of well-being and an underlying belief in our own worth and the worth of others.' Clearly, then, mental and emotional well-being rests upon a strong sense of self – a clear identity and positive self-esteem, and a sense of basic trust and security.

Information points on possible causes of mental stress and unease in tweenies

- Bullying and friendship problems.
- Family changes, arguments or serious illness in the family.
- Changes of carer: new foster parent, new au pair or minder.
- When a parent is away for a while – for work, caring for an aged relative or in hospital.
- The death of a close family member, especially if it makes you very upset.
- Moving house, especially if it is to a new area.
- Changing school, or changes of teacher.
- School exams or tests.
- Losing a favourite, comfort toy.
- When the atmosphere or routines change at home for whatever reason.
- When the previously familiar becomes unpredictable.

Chapter ten looks at family-related issues that can upset tweenies in more detail. A list of typical symptoms of anxiety, stress and unease is provided in chapter five, page 138.

Sound self-esteem cannot exist without self-knowledge, and the ability to acknowledge and manage one's own emotional responses is part of that. Sometimes called 'emotional literacy', it contributes to mental health as it enables children to be open about their feelings and vulnerabilities and remain safe, instead of engaging in pretence: offering defences or evasions. Emotional literacy improves not only self-awareness, but also awareness of and sensitivity to others. By being able to add another layer of understanding to issues and situations, it also improves our thinking skills.

HOW IS MENTAL HEALTH FOSTERED?

Children need to make sense of what happens to them in their world. If they are helped to understand and feel safe even during difficult times, they are far less likely to end up confused, unsure and distressed. The important thing is to explain as much as possible – what is happening, why it happened, and what might happen next, to be a secure and reliable presence, and to offer as much reassurance as is realistic in the circumstances. We have a clear supportive role to play but individual children also respond differently. Some personalities seem to cope with problems better and bounce back. Some even seem to benefit from adversity because they discover new strengths: a challenge successfully met helps to fortify them for any future ones. Adversity can, then, deepen a child's sense of self if it is managed well. What seems to make a difference to a child's ability to retain her self-belief, adapt and progress despite difficulties is described as resilience. It is certainly an extremely useful quality for a tweenie to possess given the number of changes she must face and it is a helpful way to reflect upon family life because it focuses on the positive: on what goes right for children not on what goes wrong.

RESILIENCE: ENCOURAGING STAYING POWER

Although we say that resilience is the ability to 'bounce back', this phrase actually misrepresents what happens. Resilient individuals who have staying power when the going gets tough do not react mechanistically like a stretched coiled spring returning to the rest position. Staying power involves action, not reaction. This is important. Children with staying power think, feel, perceive and understand themselves and their situation in a way that enables them to stay positive and active, not passive. This is the nub. They believe that they can decide things that will make a difference and help, or they are content to wait but remain optimistic. Essentially, they are able to think in a reflective way, to weigh things up and solve problems, and to put in effort in the hope *and expectation* of a positive outcome. They retain some sense of being in charge. In summary, they have an adequate sense of autonomy so they do not feel dependent on others to make things improve. Tweenies who have most things decided for them, or who are criticised and put down frequently, are more likely to feel helpless and hopeless when faced with a problem, and feel at the mercy of events and other people. Children who display a measure of emotional resilience are, then, able to re-stabilise using a variety of skills, personal attributes and strategies, often helped by a reliable parent or other adult who is able to reinforce self-belief and a realistic optimism.

Information points on resilience

Pioneer researchers in the 1950s studied the life patterns of a group of children as they grew up. They became interested in why more than half the children living in disadvantaged conditions are able to beat the odds and avoid repeating that pattern in their adult lives. In the study, one-third of the children were designated as high risk because they were born into poverty and lived in troubled families, yet one-third of these grew up as competent, caring adults. It was found that, as babies, the resilient children in this high-risk group:

- Were active and affectionate.

- In school, they had a number of interests other than school work.
- Had a positive self-concept.
- Felt they had more personal control over their lives.
- Were more caring, responsible, achievement-oriented.
- Were more autonomous.
- Were mostly growing up in smaller families.
- Had 'the opportunity to establish a close bond with at least one care-giver from whom they received abundant positive attention'.

More recently, the list of helpful experiences has been extended and grouped according to whether they relate to the *child*, the *family* or the local *community*. Our tweenie will cope better with stress if she can communicate well, plan ahead, solve problems as they arise and can see the funny side of things. She will benefit from feeling close to a reliable adult, preferably a parent, who shows care and concern. Having a religious faith seems to help, though we don't know whether the key factor is the sense of belonging that a faith group engenders, clear values, a more fatalistic attitude to adversity or the belief that a deity is looking out for you. Parents of resilient children show affection, supervise effectively, support education, maintain authoritative discipline, keep rows to a minimum and have a good relationship with their partner.

Taster tips on raising a tweenie who has the capacity to be resilient

✓ Give her as much time, attention and affection as you can, so she is sure about your love and feels emotionally safe being close to you, experiences a clear, common bond and feels understood.

✓ Accept and love her on her terms, for who she is.

✓ Encourage friendships inside and outside school, so if things get tough in school she will have other buddies to help her feel okay.

✓ Beware letting electronic games dominate. Children who play these excessively can become hooked on constant stimulation and instant feedback. They also fail to discover other activities they might enjoy and master.

✓ Put some waiting back into wanting. Children should experience that effort is worth it because it produces rewards. The link between effort and outcome that is central to resilience can be blurred when needs and wants are instantly met.

✓ Don't solve all her problems: instead, show her how to go about it, step by step.

✓ Help a child through difficulty and disappointment; don't necessarily act to prevent it from happening.

✓ Don't put her down or let her down: your commitment to and belief in her helps to strengthen her resolve and self-belief.

✓ Help her to be successful in school, but not to the point where she becomes anxious about failing.

DO MANY TWEENIES EXPERIENCE EMOTIONAL PROBLEMS?

More and more children are finding it a struggle to stay optimistic and confident. Overall, it is estimated that, at any one time, at least one in five children and adolescents experience some degree of psychological problem (Health Advisory Service, 1995). At least half as many children aged between five and fifteen, one in ten, experience clinically defined, mental health problems that might last for a year or more that would stop them doing the normal things, such as be able to make friends, go to school and function productively (Office of National Statistics, 2000). This level of distress handicaps a child's ability to be happy. Whether we are getting better at spotting and recording problems or whether life is getting harder for children is an issue to debate. What is clear, though, is that we need to watch out for signs that our tweenie might be troubled or unhappy and be aware of what we can do if she seems either withdrawn or stressed out.

DRAWING THIS TOGETHER

It is part of our duty as a parent to keep our tweenie mentally and physically active and healthy in the short and the long term. Given that children are so much more sedentary now than they were fifty or sixty years ago, it falls to us to ensure they eat a healthy diet and achieve a sensible balance between how much they eat and the amount of exercise they take; children no longer run off surplus calories in the course of a normal day. But we must try not to let food become a problem for us or our child. We have seen that children experience enough pressure, without adding an obsession with food and fitness to the pile, generated by us or by them. Even a confident child can be tipped into not coping by an apparently trivial event, let alone a significant one. If disordered eating – eating too much or not enough – becomes a way of coping, this may permanently damage their physical health. Every aspect of our tweenie's health should be our business – including her sexual health and development, which is the subject of the next chapter.

Ten top take-out tips

- Eat together as a family as much as is practical, preferably around a table – but togetherness is more important than location.
- Sit with your tweenie if she has to eat before or after the main family meal, to provide company and attention.

- Provide a varied and healthy diet but don't focus so much on 'healthy' food that a child feels guilty when eating anything sweet or fatty.
- Always take advice before putting a tweenie on a diet: early dieting can lead to later eating disorders and often don't work even short-term.
- Try not to use sweets or fast foods as a reward or as consolation for any emotional upset or injury: they may become associated with love and success and be rejected when self-worth is low.
- A varied diet of activities – not just homework and computers – will ensure our tweenie gets out and about more to maintain physical health.
- Consider practical ways to make walking to and from school safely a feasible reality to increase the amount of exercise taken, and encourage not only action-based leisure but also family holidays that include action and fun.
- Always protect young skins from any exposure to strong sun with high-factor creams, hats and loose clothing – damage is cumulative over years.
- Remember that behaviour talks. Be watchful for signs of anxiety and stress that include withdrawn or aggressive behaviour, as well as strange pains and changes in eating or sleeping patterns.
- Emotional health rests on a secure sense of self and a reliable, close relationship with at least one parent or other adult. Try to be trustworthy: keep promises, listen attentively to troubles and cut back on criticism during difficult times.

> ### *And Remember!*
>
> Avoid turning food battles into power battles.
>
> Computer play demands little from parents, but it can demand little from tweenies too.
>
> Healthy brains and bodies need physical activity, especially during this key phase of development.

9

ALL CHANGE:

Growing up Confident about Sex and Puberty

IT IS INTERESTING TO NOTE that society's alarm and apparent panic over sex relates almost exclusively to the tweenie age group. It is the eight-to-twelves whom we fear will be catapulted into precocious sexuality by wearing little G-string panties and skimpy tops bearing provocative wording. It is the eight- or ten-year-old, not the four- or fourteen-year-old, whom we worry will be confused and disturbed by more explicit sexual references and relationships in television programmes during and after 'family viewing' time. It is our tweenie, much more than our teenager, whose innocence we feel should not be stained with the detail offered in magazines about the range of human sexual behaviour or advice on particular practice. And we imagine that paedophiles are more inclined to prey on pre-pubescent children than on fully fledged adolescents because tweenies are more unsuspecting and easier to con. It is also, generally, parents of children of this age group who question the content of schools' sex education lessons. It feels like a critical time. Our tweenies are on a cusp and parents are understandably anxious.

These In-between years are significant as the time children increase their sexual awareness: they add to their previously hazy knowledge base but are predominantly inactive. In fact, sex is typically seen as disgusting. Tweenies should move forward inch by inch, from confusion towards comprehension via apprehension: the danger is they are being confronted with a glut of images and information before they are ready to absorb and comprehend it. While they seem to know a great deal more about sex than we ever did at their age, it is debatable whether they understand anything better as a consequence. In fact, what they know could be making them feel more anxious about sex and growing up, not less; in which case we should be more troubled by their worries than by ours, for their worries are often based on misconceptions and can do far more damage. Instead of bemoaning what they are being 'forced' to know, we should be concerned about the sense they make of what they know. If we accept that our most important role as a parent or carer of a tweenie is to help them to understand their world and be confident about growing up, we should check regularly whether they feel comfortable with what they hear and see in relation to sex. If they are not, we should find ways to put them at ease. Playground talk can be wide of the mark; knowing too much before they are ready can confuse, terrify or imply that 'everybody's doing it' and add to pressure. It is extremely important to talk within the family about sex to 'normalise' it, even with tweenies.

Tweenies may also become anxious or confused if we panic about their natural inclination to explore their gender identity in play because we see it as sexual. It is normal for any eight-to twelve-year-old girl to want to paint her nails, try on our high-heeled shoes and muck about with make-up and hairstyles (and don't be troubled if any boy shares this fascination). It is normal for any tweenie-aged boy to 'try on' his masculinity by investigating his and his friends' bodies, talk a bit 'dirty' about male and female bodies (and some girls choose to do this too). They are not being sexually precocious, just boys and girls role-playing and role-swapping to help themselves feel more prepared as they approach adulthood. It is the commercial exploitation of this natural tendency – tweenie make-up sets, mock or real body piercing, high fashion clothing and the slant of some advertising, for example – that feels so inappropriately sexual and wrong. And it is also potentially harmful to tweenies' development because, by offering these products, companies are directing tweenies as to how and when to be, instead of allowing our children to discover these possibilities in their own time and way – exploring at their own pace.

This chapter looks in more detail at whether and how we should protect our tweenie in a sexualised society and at how we can contribute to sex education and talk about sexual health issues at home, and offers detailed advice. It begins with a review of puberty and suggests how to help our tweenie enter this significant stage of life with confidence.

Puberty: changing inside and out

Puberty is, of course, inevitable. Though we might want our 'babies' to stay young and adorable for ever, we cannot hold it back. It is also progressive. It starts when no one is expecting it, and this can be the hardest thing for parents to accept – puberty begins when children are so unsuspecting, so innocent. The changes seem to be stuck on, or the work of some inner, alien being that is taking over, something we need to protect them from; certainly nothing to do with them, which is almost true: it is happening to them but it is not something they have willed. The early indications – the occasional underarm hair, breast buds, hair on the upper lip or voice changes – seem out of character. They are clearly still young boys and girls; yet, as in a chrysalis, the adult is growing within. One in six girls now show some sign of puberty at the age of eight. Girls' periods can start as early as nine and as late as sixteen, but the average age is eleven to twelve. Boys are later starters and the signs are not only less obvious, but also more likely to be hidden behind towels and doors.

Most boys enter puberty between thirteen and fourteen, but it can also be either sixteen or twelve. Male puberty is marked by the appearance of pubic hair, the voice breaking, hair on the upper lip, genital enlargement and the emission of semen, sometimes at night as a 'wet dream'. Some boys shoot up in height quickly at this time; others grow more slowly over longer. Feet may grow first, causing the clumsiness so typical of young and pre-adolescents. Girls become noticeably taller from about eleven or twelve. Around the same time, their pubic and underarm hair will start to thicken and a moistening vaginal discharge will appear. A girl may be full-breasted at twelve, or not until fifteen. The range in pattern of development among both girls and boys is enormous; so the best guidance is to welcome the process and accept it as normal as, when and how it occurs.

WHY DOES PUBERTY START WHEN IT DOES AND IS IT STARTING EARLIER?

The age of onset of puberty is linked most strongly to genetics and family history but it also seems to be influenced by nutrition and weight. Scientists remain unsure about what precisely triggers puberty, but they believe that when children attain a certain body-mass index (weight related to height), the brain triggers the pituitary gland to release more of the hormones that usher in the central phase. Although we understand puberty to be the time during which the reproductive organs mature, other significant physical changes take place at the same time. During the six or so years, our hearts and lungs double in size, the blood's composition changes completely, muscles thicken, brains undergo a kind of refit and we grow, and grow. It is hardly surprising that it creates a major disturbance.

Despite the wide assumption that puberty now starts earlier, it has not been clearly proven. Potentially useful studies have been either too small to tell a convincing story, or too different to enable the results to be compared. It is possible that the first indications of puberty are appearing earlier but the age at which girls start their periods, known as menarche, is remaining unchanged. However, in Japan the average age of menarche has been falling steadily, by five months in total since a particular study began forty years ago. This trend is explained by improved nutrition and health. In the UK, children's height and weight is certainly still increasing, for boys as well as girls, so we might assume the same trend will be found here. We certainly know that underweight adolescent girls with eating disorders lose their periods. We also know there has been an increase in obesity in children. We might, therefore, conclude that the age of puberty is falling here and will continue to do so.

WORRIES AROUND PUBERTY, ESPECIALLY EARLY PUBERTY

Our female tweenie may feel deeply uncomfortable about growing up too soon, having her body change before those of her friends, and certainly before she is physically or emotionally prepared for it. We may say it's great that she's 'growing up' and becoming a woman, but a nine- or ten-year-old is unlikely to be impressed. If family history indicates an early menarche, it would be helpful to be straightforward about times and practicalities when other females in the family menstruate. Late-developers can feel different, too; but in relation to the eight- to- twelves, the more common challenge is how to help them cope with the practicalities of periods when full puberty arrives early and, for other children, address their worries about when it is likely to happen and what it will be like when it does.

Sexual orientation is another worry that often emerges towards the end of the In-between years. Same sex 'crushes', sometimes focused on someone older, are very common at this age for both boys and girls as they experiment with different types of social attachment outside the family. They may need assurance from parents if they get teased about their interest or are troubled by their feelings. It doesn't mean they will feel this way for all time. And one delightful feature of today's teenage girls compared with my youth is their openness about displaying friendship and affection with enveloping hugs. As tweenies approach adolescence, they may also want to mark their growing independence by becoming less intimate with parents. They will still feel closely attached but may not feel the same need to express it. Happily, girls are able to meet their continuing need for hugs and cuddles from friends, or even teddies, instead, but boys usually have to wait a few years before they can rediscover physical comfort, this time with girl friends. While they wait, they may question whether they are lovable and may use sexual experimentation with peers to satisfy both their curiosity and their wish for physical closeness. Pets such as cats and dogs can be useful at this time as they can provide uninhibited and uncomplicated surrogate warmth and softness.

HELPING GIRLS AS THEY ENTER PUBERTY

Mothers are usually intimately involved in their daughter's puberty. Through their greater physical closeness, they notice the arrival of underarm hair, pubic hair, and the breast buds, which then fill out. Mothers anticipate and get involved when periods start because there are plenty of signs and young girls especially need support, demonstrations and reassurance. Menstruation is likely to begin after a growth spurt and weight gain and when a girl's hips fill out, but there are no absolute rules. If you are a father with full caring duties, you will be aware of at least early breast development and your daughter's growth. You will be able to prepare her or you might ask a close female to raise the issue if it is one you want to avoid. Occasionally, a girl will not let either parent know when her period has started. This is not uncommon and may reflect either

her confidence or her wish for some privacy about this aspect of her life.

What we can do to help our daughter

Even if we believe our daughter has learned about periods and how to manage them at school, it is important we should also discuss this. We can explain the sanitary supplies we will have bought and put aside for her use in preparation.

If our daughter starts her period while at primary school, we should inform her teacher and check if there are designated disposal bins or emergency supplies available. At least one girl in ten start their periods in primary school. If our daughter is one of these, she is likely to feel very alone. She won't know that one or two others will have joined the club too. We should keep a record of the flow so we can help her be prepared each month, though it may take a while for a clear pattern to become established. Pads or towels, not tampons, are the appropriate form of sanitary protection for young girls, and spare towels and disposal bags can be placed discreetly in her school bag. Discuss with her a practical routine for towel changes given the pattern and commitments of her school day and check whether her underwear accommodates the pads comfortably. It is possible that she will find these times of the month stressful because she will be on constant watch for teasing and accidents. Realise that she may feel very alone and not at all grown-up and womanly about what has happened to her. Tolerate childish outbursts on her return home that may release any tension. Tell her that her teachers know and can help if she needs it.

HELPING BOYS AS THEY ENTER PUBERTY

Boys' puberty usually takes place behind locked doors and very well-wrapped, cover-all towels. In fact, one might almost say that in the process of separating from 'mummy' they become one, of the Egyptian variety! Men are so often hopeless at discussing sexual matters in an intimate and biological way with their sons. They feel far more comfortable with the 'Masonic', nods and winks, method of communication, sending secret signs and uttering strange knowing grunts that are supposed to indicate initiation to the brotherhood. It can be left to the mum to try to explain the upcoming bodily changes, if she is brave enough. It might be thought unnecessary, given that schools are now required by law to offer sex education, but there are dangers if we opt out, as we discuss in a later section. If we say nothing, we appear to ignore something earth-shattering and intensely personal that's happening to him, which will not score very high on his 'significance' scale.

Rather than staying silent, we can direct our son to a suitable website, if he hasn't got there already, or, even better, buy a book written specifically for pubescent boys. Some are listed in the resources section at the end of this book. By taking either or both of these steps, we have shown we have noticed; we have shown we care. Either action lets him choose the right moment to click and repeat click, or read and reread, as often as he wants. The earlier we make it available, the sooner he will be able to rest easy about the unfamiliar things he hears or notices in himself. Choose the moment in response to possible changes: if we buy too soon we may foreshorten that valuable period of childhood innocence.

What we can do to help our son

Respect his physical privacy and lay off the teasing. If we can't resist, we should at least be respectful and loving. Be sensitive about when to cover up; if our home has been a happy nudist colony, gauge the time to embrace modesty – probably by the time he reaches the age of twelve. Beware putting a box of tissues in his bedroom. Though it is normal to masturbate he'll find his own, less obvious ways to deal with it. Let him know we are available to answer any questions he may have, about sex, relationships, girls' development, contraception, sexually transmitted diseases, anything. Young boys are increasingly reporting that they learn about sex from girls', as opposed to 'girlie', magazines. If we find one of these around, or see him reading his sister's, it could be the right time to talk. Be understanding if we do find a 'girlie' magazine or video that many boys seek out around the age of eleven or twelve. Their motivation will be a natural curiosity as much as physical pleasure. However we should not tolerate the possession of hardcore pornographic magazines or films or any inappropriate sexual behaviour or macho, sexually abusive language. Any parental material should be kept well away; although some may think this could 'normalise' his exploration, his sex, and ours, should be left private.

HEADY STUFF: BRAINS CHANGE TOO

It's not only tweenies' bodies that are on the move; their brains undergo a refit as well. Several studies show that, as children enter puberty, there is a sudden increase in neural activity in the prefrontal cortex of the brain as millions of new connections are made. We now know that this heightened activity starts at around ten, peaks at eleven or twelve, stabilises at fifteen but does not fully return to a normal pre-pubertal or adult rate of activity until the age of eighteen. This activity is particularly significant because the prefrontal cortex plays an important role in the assessment of social relationships, as well as planning and control of our social behaviour. While this rewiring is taking place, young people have a significantly reduced ability to understand emotions and read social situations. The eleven-year-olds were already 20 per cent slower at identifying emotions such as anger, happiness or sadness. In other words, social and emotional situations are likely to become confusing, children may find other points of view puzzling, and they will become more frustrated and exasperated and more prone to 'losing it'.

This heightened neural activity happens as the brain completes its most significant developmental phase following birth, which takes ten years. By then, the brain is adult size. Having reached full size, 'disconnected' rarely used synaptic connections and retained only those regularly active, it seems the brain has a final 'shake-up' to find a comfortable and efficient arrangement for longer-term, adult working. The process can be likened to the large electronic indicator boards in train stations that clatter en masse as the computer searches relevant information about the next cohort of train departures. While it is whirring, you have no idea how you are going to get to where you want to be – or even which platform you are to start from. Imagine that going on not for mere seconds but years. Added to this, our tweenies are, in effect, being told over the public address system about far more trains and journeys than they thought existed. These are the messages sent about their future sexual journey by magazines, clothing manufacturers and the public media.

Shielding our child in a sexualised society

Commercial companies are increasingly using sex to market their goods to tweenies. This is worrying many parents and commentators. It seems to violate the long-accepted boundary between childhood and adulthood. Underwear and skimpy tops are being sold for eight-year-olds and younger printed with provocative phrases and sexual innuendos. The thong-style pants ape a design that, until recently when they became fashionable, was distinctly 'adult', and only sold via specialised, usually mail-order, pornography-related outlets. Tweenie magazines contain articles on how to kiss; jewellery shops that market piercing and trinkets to young girls have mushroomed; and cosmetics and body fresheners are being packaged and pitched at tweenies. Instead of dabbing and daubing with Mum's cast-offs, one stage up from face paints, tweenies now have their own 'make-up' sets. Some nine-year-olds wear make-up to school, and one mother on a television programme had given her ten-year-old a professional 'make-over' as a birthday present 'so she knows how to do it properly', as well as a trip to the hairdresser for highlights. If all this is wrong, what has gone wrong and what can we as parents or carers do to shield our child from the worst excesses?

FORGING A SENSIBLE APPROACH

These developments cannot be good for our young children and should be resisted. The greatest potential danger is not that an inappropriate heightening of sexual awareness will encourage pre-teen sex and teenage parenthood, or that 'tarty tweenies' will act as beacons to predatory paedophiles, though this is a possibility, but that this subtle pressure to be more grown up, more 'female', more self- and beauty-aware encourages young, vulnerable and impressionable girls and boys to believe that they are not okay as they are. It adds a further destructive layer to today's tweenies' growing awareness of body image and their desire to be attractive and slim. In other words, it plants and feeds self-doubt. It is quite safe for young girls to try on their older sister's or mother's brassiere for fun, streak their hair with easy-to-wash-out coloured powder, teeter in their high heels or wriggle into their disco-style clothes. In this case, tweenies are merely playing: paddling in the shallows of the great sea that is their future. It is far more insidious for tweenies to be persuaded to jump in: to want a padded bra to appear bigger-breasted before a girl has any real need for support; to want their own quality, as opposed to play, cosmetics in order to look acceptable; or to have real manicures in nail bars or their hair professionally coloured and spiked to impress friends. The play version of growing up they happily grow out of. The more realistic version accords value and status to the altered state, keeps it desirable and imprints a profound sense of inadequacy for those who feel they cannot be beautiful or attractive, who cannot be thin, whose breast development is a long way off and who chew their nails or have untamable hair on their head or arms and legs.

Of course, some girls like to be mini versions of their mother or their big sister, and some mothers get a kick from kitting out their daughter as a carbon copy of them, as do some football-crazy fathers who dress sons in matching strip – or some celebrities who order matching 'designer' mini-outfits aka David Beckham. We all like our children to be like us, even though it's actually healthier and easier for children if we applaud and respect their difference, not their similarity. It may be fun, but it is simply not necessary.

SEX IN MAGAZINES AND ON TV

The front covers of girls' tweenie magazines at first glance look very like those aimed at teenagers, both young and old. It is therefore very easy to take the view that they contain similar material and want to keep them well away. However, most of those pitched at our In-between children do not peddle sex or encourage inappropriate behaviour. From a selective survey (*Bubble, Star Girl, Go Girl* and *Girl Talk*), those pitched at the age group we are interested in offer lots of celebrity gossip about pop idols, free posters of these – and of cute animals; information about dance moves so tweenies can learn to wriggle like their idols; a guide to available funky pens and pencils and mobile phone extras; articles on sleepovers, getting upset when a pet dies and about how to make things; puzzles, cartoon strips based on TV soaps and pop bands and simple horoscopes. Any emerging interest in boys is focused on pop idols, not personal boy-girl relationships. Front cover freebies included jewellery, stationery and a sample of solid perfume. These magazines mirror tweenie interests; they do not fan a precocious sexual concern.

Magazines such as *Mizz* aimed at the next age group, the young teens, have older, more obviously and heavily made-up girls on the front who look about fourteen. These differ in that they start to have problem pages and make-up tips, and articles on how to impress a boy a reader likes. There can be features on magic and mysticism, on health (why sleep is important, for example), and friendship problems. *Sneak* and *It's Hot* both focus on pop celebrities, for lads and girls.

For a quick guide to which magazine is right for our tweenie, check the contents, look for a problem page, at the issues raised there and the age given of those writing in. If we are more worried about an emerging obsession with celebrities than our tweenie's wish to try sparkly make-up, that might be a reason to make them pay for a magazine from their pocket money; they then forgo something else and are forced to assess their priorities.

Sex on television is hard to escape. No one would want to return to the time when children were sent from the room the minute sexual talk or action became too 'fruity', for that creates the fear and ignorance that bedevilled so many in the past. Younger children don't always take in what they see, especially if they don't spot its significance. If issues such as under-age or premarital sex, infidelity or oral sex emerge during family viewing unanticipated, we could ask an open question at the end of the programme if there was anything our child wishes to talk about or have explained. If it passed him by, there's probably no damage done. If it created confusion or alarm, it can be talked about and explained. However, if we expect a programme to contain 'adult' material it is probably better for nobody to watch or to engage our tweenie in an alternative activity.

Taster tips: guidelines on keeping sex at bay

✓ If a sexy-styled item is not an essential 'must have', don't buy it. Always opt instead for the regular version saying, 'You are lovely as you are. You'll be more ready for this in a few years' time.' Any sulk will not last, it will reinforce your authority and it may, even, persuade the marketers that this pitch was a mistake.

✓ Keep play at 'being a grown-up' how and where it should be – playful, and in the home and off the streets. Collect discarded clothing, cosmetics and shoes, hats and so on in a 'dressing-up' bag, so being a man or woman can be tried on for size while child-hood and a child's self are respected and preserved. Growing up is about far, far more than becoming sexually alluring or active.

✓ Realise that it is far more important and healthy for a tweenie to work on who he is inside than on his exter-nal appearance.

✓ If we show appropriate physical affection to our part-ner through hugs, kisses and handholding, it helps to place intimacy in a domestic and loving context, not left to wild imaginings.

✓ Ask older siblings to be careful about what they say or do in the presence or hearing of our tweenie.

✓ Avoid equating looking good or attractive with look-ing sexy. Elegance, style, confidence, originality, artistry and creativity are all qualities to commend in appearance that don't depend on flaunting flesh.

Sexual health and education: talking about sex at home and at school

Evidence from Europe suggests that when parents talk openly and fully to their children about sex, the first sexual experience is delayed, sex is more likely to be viewed as part of a relationship and the emerging adult is more likely to take appropriate responsibility. This difficult subject should not be left to schools. We cannot know what individual teachers will cover or miss out, or how well they will cover it. I remember sitting on my son's bed one evening during his junior school years and beginning to talk to him about sex and relationships. 'Don't worry, Mum,' he said. 'We've done this at school so I know all about it.' 'So you know that men and women have sex as a loving act because it feels nice even when they don't want to have a baby?' I replied. His eyes popped out of his head. 'Do they?' he exclaimed, in amazement. Another issue is that children develop at different times. The moment selected by the school to run a sex education lesson for our tweenie's class may be the wrong moment for our child. He may simply not be ready to hear it so the information will be giggled over, not absorbed, and the learning opportunity wasted. Even we can't guarantee to pick the best time, but being around to field any questions and watch out for suitable triggers means we are better placed than the school, and we have more chances to try.

Of course, even when sex education is not being formally taught as part of the personal, social and health education curriculum in school, children will try to teach each other. They pick up part-truths, put their own gloss on things they only half understand, and try to gain status from being all-knowing, and sometimes all-doing, so make things up along the way. For tweenies, in relation to sex and the playground, a little knowledge usually goes a surprisingly long way! And in relation to our own child, this is the dangerous bit. He can find what he hears disturbing. A friend told me when I was eleven or twelve that her uncle 'who's a doctor so he should know', had explained that before a man and woman make love, the man 'runs his hands all over her body'. I was revolted by this thought, and desperately hoped I might be able to avoid sex altogether. It is not enough to tell our child not to believe everything they hear at school, because they won't know which bits to believe and which bits not.

The best reassurance to offer is that physical intimacy is something that older people do, that it's very hard to understand and may seem peculiar and yucky, but they will feel okay about it with the right person and when *they* are ready for it – or when it is allowed depending on cultural expectations. We put the ball in their court so they feel in control. It is also imperative to impress that no adult has any right to see or do anything to our child's body that seems strange or feels uncomfortable, and he should speak up if someone tries. And it is never too early to state that they are lovely as they are and should be loved by others for who they are, not for what they enable someone to do to them or because they look a certain way that people call sexy.

Time to Talk is an initiative developed by Parentline Plus to encourage parents to talk about sex and relationships with their children. Their leaflet offers suggestions on ways to introduce the subject. It recommends that talking about sex start early and that it be an ongoing process rather than separate unrelated conversations. There is also a quiz on the Parentline Plus website that helps parents think about new ways to go about raising the subject with their children. The Family Planning Association offers a video to guide parents on the same subject that many regard highly. Messages about sex and relationships are everywhere – so not talking about these subjects at home suggests to children that sex is still a taboo subject and something that is difficult for everyone to talk about, even with their own future partners. Children want and need to know about their parents' values and beliefs, and boys certainly need to be shown a neutral and respectful language to use in relation to sex and girls that is different from the cruder versions they may hear spoken by their peers.

It is particularly important to talk about sex in an open manner because children today see many patterns and styles of relationships within their immediate and wider families. Parents who remain married to each other tend to keep their physical relationship private, which makes it easy for any tweenie or teenager in the family to pretend that nothing 'like that' happens any longer. That is what they want and need to believe, for sex itself, let alone parental sex, is difficult to comprehend at aged ten or even twelve. If it can be put in a general box called 'love', it can be more easily understood. However, now that divorce, serial monogamy and teenage sex are more common and openly accepted, more children are likely to be more aware of sexual activity, usually an important part of any emergent relationship even among older couples. If older siblings are allowed to have their boy- and girl-friends stay overnight, an explanation should be provided so the growing child can appreciate when it might be acceptable or advisable to start a sexual relationship and when not.

Taster tips on talking about sex

✓ Use everyday triggers, such as TV soaps and other programmes, their own magazines, family events such as weddings, births or break-ups, the behaviour of animals and family pets or even the quite rude jokes they begin to tell.

✓ Talk about sex as an important way to express love, closeness and sharing as part of a deep relationship as well as the mechanics of periods, contraception, puberty and the facts of life. Sex should be the ultimate expression of a relationship that has grown slowly – not a quick way to impress your mates.

> ✓ Always challenge any seriously crude or sexually
> degrading comments from anyone in the family, but
> don't get upset if your son or daughter draws explicit
> pictures of genitalia with friends, uses bald language
> or experiments with masturbation.
>
> ✓ Make it clear that a child's body is his or her own and
> is private. No adult or older child is to touch it or do
> anything that seems strange or unusual. No one
> should ask for secrets to be kept from you that involve
> any physical contact or any request to do something
> to someone else.

When a group of twelve-year-old boys were invited to suggest
reasons for not having early sex, rather than refer to such matters
as sexually transmitted diseases they mentioned that they might
not be able to do it, they might not be good at it, they might
get laughed at after by the girl, they feared their penis would be
considered small. These responses show boys harbour a great
deal of anxiety. No doubt girls do too. Peer pressure and ex-
aggerated expectations can therefore work both ways and deter
sexual activity as well as encourage it. Perhaps the most sound
advice parents can offer is to acknowledge that having intercourse is a very big step, that being worried about it is only
natural and the best thing is not to hurry it or be pressed into
it. When the time is right and when the person is right, it will
feel right.

SEX EDUCATION LESSONS AT SCHOOL

Secondary schools are required by law to deliver lessons on sex
and relationships but primary schools are not so obliged.
However, primary schools have to cover personal development,
health and safety, relationships and active citizenship as part of
the personal, social and health education curriculum, so it is

highly likely some of the essential facts about reproduction will be explained. It is normal to be worried about what our child might be told in these lessons. We would prefer it not to cover information that might confuse our child and for it to be consistent with our approach. Many schools offer parents the chance to hear about the lesson content in advance. Anyone who is concerned should contact the school to discuss the subject. We should remember, though, that many teachers have a great deal of experience and know what children tend to know, what level of understanding they can cope with and how best to present information to them. Having said this, it took many years for one teacher who delivers sex education lessons to realise that up to the age of about nine, children watch videos of pregnancy and birth and identify with the baby – reflecting egocentrically on their own origins. Only from nine or ten onwards will they see themselves as the person potentially having the sex and the baby and realise the value of contraception or delay.

SEXUAL HEALTH AND PREGNANCY

It would seem impossible to most parents of tweenies that their eleven- or twelve-year-old could be either currently or imminently sexually active. Pre-teen sex is still not the norm but evidence suggests it is becoming more common, so we should be vigilant and show that we consider embarking on a sexual relationship to be a serious step. In a report published by ChildLine in 1999 detailing the calls about teenage pregnancy and young parenthood, it stated that of the 7,317 girls calling about pregnancy in 1997–8, almost 80 per cent were under sixteen and some were as young as twelve. 'Most of our callers are between ten and fifteen . . . Children as young as twelve are having sexual relationships, often unplanned or secretly, sometimes as part of a longer term relationship . . . in the main, young people's early sexual experiences do not seem to be planned or even explicitly chosen. Peer pressure, pressure from boyfriends, too much alcohol and sheer opportunity all played a part. Young people generally knew about the facts of life and contraception, but they did not seem to have put their knowledge into practice.'

One secondary school in London is aware that it has a handful of twelve-year-old pupils who attend registration but then leave the premises to earn money from soliciting. Some of their clients are fellow classmates who similarly signed in then bunked. This account should not cause all parents of tweenies to panic, because it is far from the norm, but it is proof that some boys and girls are sexually active at twelve and we should appreciate that our eleven- and twelve-year-old could be aware of their peers being sexually active, though they may not necessarily be tempted to follow suit. In one area of the UK that has the sixth highest teenage conception rates, a group of teenage girls agreed that losing one's virginity had carried great status. They explained that they separate their 'recreational sex' (one-night stands with multiple partners, for which they use contraception) from sex with a regular partner (for which contraception was only sometimes used). The girls estimated that two-thirds of their sex was unprotected. These girls were young teenagers, not tweenies, but it demonstrates that attitudes to sex are changing and sexual experimentation is something older tweenies are beginning to explore. We should not be complacent, believing that our eleven- or twelve-year-old could 'never do that'.

Against this background, our tweenies need our continued warmth, attention, approval and conversation in order to feel secure and cared for – so they have less need to look for misplaced and misconstrued intimacy in alternative, often temporary and inappropriate, sexual relationships forged either locally or on the net.

There are no obvious signs to look out for that might suggest a tweenie could be engaging in inappropriate sexual behaviour. They would clearly need to have the opportunity, so if they seem keen to be out a lot, are significantly more interested in how they look, seem more assertive or truculent, that might suggest some sexual involvement. But this is quite typical behaviour for pre-teens; so before we panic, consider if any event might explain a developing interest. If the family has been through a hard time, or if we have recently found a new partner who might be spending more time with us at home, our tweenie might feel pushed aside or upset, so might feel valued by and vulnerable to sexual attention. Friends can have a big influence, too. Ultimately, the best protection is openness, so we should talk as freely as we feel able.

Information points on pre-teen and teenage sexual behaviour and pregnancy

National statistics on teenage pregnancy rates show that after a worrying and prolonged rise, they have now begun to fall slightly. Now, fewer pregnancies come to term.

- In 2001, two twelve-year-old girls gave birth to live babies.
- Falling educational achievement seems to be a more significant factor in teenage pregnancy than absolute levels of achievement. Teenage mothers were likely to have experienced three consecutive years of falling test and exam results, a pattern that can begin in the tweenie years.
- The higher the educational aspirations of girls, the more girls regret their first sexual intercourse.
- Educational achievement does not, however, seem to raise the age at which girls lose their virginity.

DRAWING THIS TOGETHER

The years between eight and twelve mark the dawning and development of other-directed, interpersonal, sexual awareness. During this time, our children will experience the first physical and hormonal changes associated with puberty; they begin to explore what it means to be female or male and sexual, both in terms of who they are and how they behave; and they confront and absorb a great deal of information about the sexual side of adult relationships. There is a huge and confusing amount to take in on a mental journey that will involve fear, disgust, humour, curiosity, nerves and very mixed messages about whether looking sexy or sex itself is okay or not okay. We cannot hide or shelter them from it, nor should we. The tweenie years are valuable as an opportunity for them to acquire, with our help, the attitudinal armoury with which to shield and protect themselves so they may parry or play as they later feel is appropriate.

Children tend to be more impressionable and vulnerable to sexual exploitation and gratification when they feel uncertain and under stress. Family problems that seem to threaten accepted securities are one source, and it is how to support tweenies as they face a range of difficulties that we turn to next.

Ten top take-out tips

- The pre-teen years are crucial for making it feel normal to talk about sex and relationships at home. Use their questions, TV programmes or the birth of a baby to raise the subject regularly. Include both facts and personal views and values.
- Make it absolutely clear that the age of consent for legal penetrative *and oral* sex is sixteen years of age. Any boy or man who has sex with a girl under the age of sixteen is committing statutory rape and can be charged, and this may soon apply to oral sex.
- Reflect on our own sexual behaviour and the lessons it might send. Remain discreet about personal relationships.

- Be tolerant of the mood swings that can sway children in early puberty: when children feel loved and lovable as they are, they're more likely to expect others to do the same.
- Avoid sexual stereotyping and criticism. Allow both sons and daughters to see a future full of hope and possibility and to be proud of something they cannot change: their gender.
- Consider whether the freedom they have could expose them to sexual risk and temptation.
- Foster accepting, respectful, loving and nurturing relationships between everyone at home as the most effective sexual protection, for early sexual intercourse won't then be used to find intimacy, approval or self-respect.
- Children who are given appropriate autonomy and responsibility will be less likely to flaunt lost virginity as a badge of maturity.
- Investigate the cause if schoolwork starts to slip. Confidence tumbles are a risk factor for early sexual experimentation.
- Stress that physical and sexual abuse can take place within personal relationships. Being pressured to engage in any sexual touching that feels wrong or to watch any sexually explicit video is a form of sexual abuse.

And Remember!

Knowledge creates confidence and power: make sure you and they know all the facts.

It's natural to explore gender, but not for this tendency to be exploited commercially.

Don't just deplore what they know, check the sense they make of what they know.

10
FAMILY UPSETS:
Supporting Children When There Are Problems

ONE OF THE DEEP FRUSTRATIONS of being a parent is that it is not in our power to ensure that family life is always calm and nurturing. The simple business of living close to other people, regardless of any particular difficulty, is not always that simple; and we may also have specific financial pressures, be depressed or ill, have a marital problem, a bereavement to come to terms with, elderly parents or an unwell child to care for or new partners and their children to weave into our life. Even apparently rock-solid families have times when inside or outside pressures can strain our most precious relationships.

It is not unusual, either, for one problem to create another, because the associated tensions can make us short-tempered and intolerant, especially with our children who can then decide to test us to our limits just when we have fewer reserves to understand why or respond well. But, separate from this, children also have their own problems. Far from being too young to feel stress, in effect they get a double dose – theirs, and ours handed on. Children can be more troubled by stress than adults, partly because their time horizons are so short but also they are inexperienced. They tend to assume now is for ever, that 'normality' will not resume and that things won't change for the better.

Our role is to help our child maintain faith in herself and be optimistic about the future as she strives to understand and adapt.

This chapter explains what parents, individual children and families as a whole find difficult and explores the dynamics of difficulty – how parents and children tend to react when stressed, suggesting how we can help our tweenie through these times by providing effective and appropriate support. The first section makes us aware of experiences that either adults or children can find problematic, including bereavement, and how these can lead to changed and more difficult behaviour on both sides. The second section focuses on three specific family-based experiences that present difficulties: separation and divorce, establishing stepfamilies, and living with violence. It considers how these may impact on eight- to twelve-year-olds in particular and what support they need. The chapter ends with a more general review of tweenies' needs during stressful times and suggests key responses that will ensure an easier, smoother path through the problem, whatever it might be, enabling our tweenie to emerge more sensitive, insightful, self-aware and with greater confidence as a result.

The Dynamics of Difficulty

Tweenies live with our troubles because most adults find it virtually impossible to keep the really big ones under wraps. We come across as withdrawn, strange and often short-tempered as well. We are so self-absorbed we're simply not as well attuned to them as we were before. We may ignore the bad behaviour that we used to jump on. We may be silent or moody. We can become absent-minded, even about essential tasks such as washing school kit, signing a school form, buying something they need and even, sometimes, noticing and preparing for mealtimes. And we will certainly be less patient. Feeling more insecure and vulnerable, we can respond even to minor challenges in a far more defensive or confrontational manner. We are therefore not only less available, but also more unpredictable and likely to be ratty when we surface.

Children don't like it when life feels different. Even older tweenies can assume they are the cause or that they should have prevented the problem because, as they now feel more competent, they may be inclined to take on more responsibility and guilt. Ironically, their attempts to pull life back to 'normal' often have the opposite effect. They play up to get reassurance from, they hope, loving attention but end up more sad and confused when the result is further harsh words and hostility that increase the insecurity. Rather than add the cloud of mystery to the confusion by keeping everything secret, tweenies are old enough to be told at least something about most problems, even if these are complex. Some typical ones are reviewed below.

SOURCES AND EXPLANATIONS OF STRESS: WHY ARE SOME EVENTS SO UNSETTLING?

Stress tests list a variety of 'life events' relevant to adults and place them in order according to how much, typically, they affect us. Common sources of stress for adults (in no particular order) include money problems; work demands or difficulties or lack of work; arguments with a partner, other family member or children; relationship breakdown and the ensuing separation, new relationships and creating new families; physical or mental health problems; close family bereavements; living with violence or addiction; moving house; car accidents and house break-ins. Many parents now report the six months it takes to choose and receive a secondary school place for their eleven-year-old to be surprisingly stressful. If we inspect the events closely, we can observe certain common features and implications that explain why people become so unsettled by them. Children's experiences can contain the same features, hence something that seems trivial to us can none the less cause our child deep distress.

Incidents that score highest in stress tests for adults are death, relationship breakdown and divorce (a form of bereavement), and having to live apart from someone we care about for extended periods. Each of these events involves a disruption or end to a key relationship through which we experience and understand ourselves. When these relationships end, it feels as though our very being is challenged and undermined. The second group of events with slightly lower scores includes marriage, pregnancy, promotion, retirement and redundancy. What links each event in this group is the acquisition of a new identity or role – a change that could create uncertainty, financial worries or fear of the judgements of others. Even apparently welcomed changes, such as marriage, can thus be stressful. Stress-inducing events that score lowest are those that simply involve a change in routines and habits. Change, of course, is the theme that connects them all. Some of the changes in the list above are predictable and broadly within our control, while some are predictable yet outside it, as in a terminal illness. Other events happen out of the blue, and these tend to be more unsettling because they rock our security and make us feel powerless and inadequate, not to mention angry. Tweenies, of course, find the same kinds of features upsetting. Having looked at why certain difficulties are upsetting, we are in a better position to empathise with our child's troubles.

STRESSES THAT TWEENIES EXPERIENCE AS UPSETTING

Tweenies' troubles can range from the apparently trivial to the obviously difficult. Growing up brings with it normal anxieties and problems but some children face distress unequal to their years. In order to be able to offer support in every case, we need to scale down our definition of a problem to match the narrower scope of our tweenie's life and be sensitive to the features of stressful events discussed above that could be present for her. Looking at the most apparently trivial issues first, most children hate their routines to be disturbed. Experiences such as school changes or a new teacher could raise worries about their new role, how they should behave and whether they will be liked or be successful. Tweenies can become very reliant on close friends for self-affirmation, as we saw in chapter five, so being rejected or losing a best friend through a house move could be akin to a divorce or bereavement. The table below offers a range of examples of apparently unexceptional incidents that our tweenie could find difficult, placed next to those that are more obviously difficult. We should not forget that stress is cumulative. As Tricia's story told below shows, an unfortunate coincidence of major difficulties can lead to a depth of distress that may genuinely threaten long-term emotional health. In fact, a child can be tipped from coping into not coping by an apparently insignificant event.

Examples of incidents that our child could, or is likely to, find difficult

COULD FIND STRESSFUL	IS LIKELY TO FIND STRESSFUL
1 Loss of a key relationship that provides security and care	
• parent away visiting or travelling	• arguments or violence between parents – and feeling marooned in-between them
• end of parent's subsequent relationship	• parent in prison
• parent absent in hospital	• non-resident parent being in irregular contact
• familiar carer leaving	• resident parent criticising / excluding other
• parent starting, or starting full-time, work	• serious parental illness
• death of a pet	• losing touch with a divorced or separated parent
• older sibling leaving home	
• being 'dumped' by a friend	

COULD FIND STRESSFUL	IS LIKELY TO FIND STRESSFUL

2 Change in status, identity or self-image

• arguments with friends	• new step-siblings (could alter birth position)
• start of school year	
• poor result in a school or other test	• starting a new school
	• bullying
• being ill, or the end of a long illness	• new baby
	• parent takes up with a new partner
• puberty	
• change of surname	

3 Change in routines

• parent beginning a different job	• change in childminder
• childminder taking on a new charge	• moving house and new journeys
• start and end of school holidays	
• grandparent requiring more support	
• changes to parent's shift or work rota	
• parent working at home, not office	
• any additional after-school activity	

4 When things happen 'out of the blue', unpredictably

• parent returning late without notice	• any violence, to a child or loved adult
• going out in the evening without notice	• drunken behaviour
	• parent death following an accident
	• parent's moodiness
	• swings in parent's expectations or behaviour

Tricia's story

Tricia was eight and had recently moved to a new school when her father left home to live with another woman. It came as a big shock to everyone, her mother included. Initially, Tricia managed well, as did her siblings, but this upset was followed over the next two years by other difficulties. First, her mother's father died – he had brought up her mum alone so she was devastated. Then her maternal aunt died after a difficult illness. Naturally, her mum became quite distracted and Tricia spent a fair amount of time in her room, leaving her mum alone and avoiding their growing arguments. When she was ten, she discovered a lawyer's letter that confirmed her parents' legal divorce – the finality was a shock and she was upset that she had not been told. Later that year, her father remarried while on holiday without telling his children or inviting them. Things weren't too good for Tricia at school either. That year she had felt picked on by her teacher and was bullied a little, though she had close friends too. She was therefore glad to start afresh at aged eleven in a new school – but things didn't improve. Her new, professed 'best friend' began to bully her seriously. She began to fear school and after a bout of glandular fever, during which she had to miss quite a bit, she became depressed and stayed away more. Visits to her father became less regular, her parents sometimes disputed how to manage her depression, and the 'happy' news that she now had a baby half-sister increased her unhappiness. With a lot of love, time, understanding and unwavering acceptance and support from her mother, Tricia has been able to find herself again and rebuild her confidence.

BEREAVEMENT: LOSING SOMEONE WHO MATTERS

Some events are obviously harder for tweenies to understand and manage and the bereavement of a close family member is one of these. The loss and grief experienced by a young person when someone who matters dies is intense in itself, but it can also raise uncomfortable questions about who else could die, and when. Younger tweenies are still prone to imagine wild things, so they may not be able to distinguish a life-threatening illness from a mild one and may become unnecessarily anxious over a passing problem. One eight-year-old girl believed her father's illness to be catching so thought she might die. Different children respond differently, so our pre-teen may become withdrawn, clingy, aggressive or liable to tantrums as a consequence of her insecurity and confusion, or a mixture of these at different times. She may also find it hard to sleep or be troubled by disturbing dreams, and the resulting exhaustion could intensify her anxiety, producing headaches or tummy aches on top. 'The biggest change in my life,' wrote one contributor to the Children's Express website, 'was when my father died. I was nine and it was a major event. My older brother started telling me what to do, and my mother became quieter. I always think one day I'll come home and there'll be a new man sitting where my dad used to.'

We can help a child to comprehend a death with support both before an anticipated event and after. Beforehand, we can: keep her appropriately informed of developments; provide her with an opportunity to talk about the likely impact – not only how things will or could be different but also what will remain the same; discuss how best to say goodbye and whether it feels right to offer any final token of appreciation. It will be important to reassure any child that she is in no way responsible.

Coming to terms with a death after it has happened can be very difficult even with satisfactory preparation. Even older pre-teens may block the emotion attached to the death and act as though they feel nothing; and while this pretence may offer immediate comfort, exploring reactions generally helps to settle a child and move on. Silence may seem to provide mutual protection (if they are quiet, maybe they're okay so I won't reopen wounds) but can maintain damaging misconceptions. Raising the subject may be easier if the initial focus is on the person's life and personality, moving later to any implications of the finality of the death. Another typical response from a pre-teen child is to ask lots of questions of fact and explanation. Tweenies are capable of showing great interest in the biological aspects of death; for example, what illness caused the death, how did it develop, why couldn't it have been stopped, what happens in the body when someone dies and what happens when the person is buried or cremated? Those able to make sense of the permanence of death can appreciate the notion of someone going away for ever, not moving, eating, laughing or being: for this reason, they may experience deeper loss than a younger child. Their questions may seem callous but are natural and should be answered as straightforwardly as possible. The important thing is that the death can be talked about at any time when our child feels the need, remembering that she will experience the event in her own individual way, which means that children need both individual time and collective, family time to explore what it all means. Not only is it impossible for a child to assemble all thoughts and queries during one convenient moment that we allocate for discussion, but also her feelings are likely to change over time – from denial, to anger, to guilt.

And children do feel considerable guilt; they often sense that something they did may be to blame, especially if the relationship was conflictual. It is essential that they are told, repeatedly, that nothing they could have said or done could have prevented the death from happening. A nine-year-old boy drew a picture of him standing over a broken vase between angry parents. He believed it was his clumsiness that had made his dad get ill.

Mital, aged ten, thought that he had caused his father's death, because he had become angry and had spilled some milk deliberately that same morning. His father had been ill for a while, and Mital thought the illness was his punishment for eating beef hamburgers at school (he was vegetarian and a Hindu). He imagined that the string necklace he wore, a religious symbol of blessing, would tighten like a noose to remind him when he did something wrong. When his mother learned all this, she was able to free him from his burden and his relief was visible.

Of course, children do not always want to talk; some find great consolation and security in normality and value a speedy return to school, for example, as a relief from the company of grief-stricken relatives. It is very normal, too, for a child to jump in and out of grief, wanting to have fun one moment and be sad the next, which should not be taken as disrespectful. Whatever our child's need, we should try to be there and talk, or remain quiet, as required.

Taster tips on responding to actual or anticipated bereavements

✓ Older children make better sense of events if we use straightforward language. They may feel offended or manipulated by phrases such as 'passing away' or 'going to heaven'.

✓ Be as truthful as possible about the likelihood of death, or why it has happened if it was sudden. Provide an opportunity to say goodbye, even if this is uncomfortable: say, at a last hospital visit, 'This could be the last time we see . . .'

✓ Always prepare a child for the death of someone close if it is known, and acknowledge her feelings. 'It is very sad that Daddy is very ill and is going to die soon. Sometimes I feel very angry about it and even

---

scared and I expect you do too. But it's harder for him and we must help him and love him lots and do our best to have good times now.'

✓ If you, as a parent, have an illness that could be terminal, provide plenty of opportunity to talk with all children about the likely impact, especially in terms of their practical care if you are parenting alone.

✓ Make it absolutely clear that a child is in no way responsible for the illness.

✓ Prepare a collection of memory items – letters describing your family and personal history, tapes, videos, favourite music, clothes, jewellery or trinkets, so these can be viewed in the future to maintain a connecting thread and used to answer questions.

✓ Begin any conversation with questions. Ask what they think has been happening, or what they want to know, rather than directly telling. Any misconceptions can then be addressed and the discussion can be individually focused.

✓ Don't hide your grief. Explain that you are feeling very sad today, so they can understand and explore their own feelings safely and freely.

✓ When a death is unexpected, our child should learn about it from us, in a quiet place and as soon as possible after it happened, preferably with relevant family members present.

✓ Involve them in planning the funeral and remembrance service, especially if a brother or sister dies, so they feel closely involved and important, not forgotten. Try to sit together at the ceremony, or ensure someone else whom they know well sits close instead.

✓ Emphasise that it is only the body that is put in the ground or is burned and that the person cannot feel anything.

✔ Create and reinforce memories. Talk about the person, what he or she has left behind in terms of memories and personal or even material gifts. This will affirm that out of sight does not mean out of mind.

✔ Ask them which belongings, if any, of the deceased person they would like to keep as their personal memento.

✔ Acknowledge anniversaries of the death and remember the person at other special family events.

✔ Keep some regular time free for you and your tweenie during which she is the clear focus, not the recently deceased person, unless she raises this.

✔ Maintain normal routines and rules and reassure them that they are still loved and will be cared for by you and that you remain healthy.

When a favourite pet dies

Children can form very close attachments to family pets so the grief on its death can be deeply felt. Stephen, twelve, groomed his pet rabbit before the garden burial, to feel his soft fur for the last time and to honour the animal before the final farewell. To acknowledge this close relationship, we should bury any pet with an appropriate degree of ceremony and respect, having asked first what should happen. A promise to buy a replacement may stem the tears in the short term but we should realise it was this particular animal that was special. It is better to wait a short while before we offer to buy another.

Taster tips on when a pet dies

✔ Prepare them for bad news; sit them down and treat it seriously.

✓ If possible, let the animal be seen before it is buried or otherwise disposed of, delaying this until after school where possible and relevant.

✓ If the pet is to be taken to the vet to be put down, let final farewells be said, with cuddles, little poems or prayers.

✓ Invite views about how to mark the event or the grave and how to conduct any ceremony.

✓ Offer to put a photo of the pet in the living area or child's bedroom.

The impact of family troubles

Having a 'family relationship problem' is one of the top four reasons that young people call ChildLine, the national children's helpline. This category, when combined with sexual and physical abuse (both of which occur most frequently in families), explains 47 per cent of the calls received from ten-year-olds, compared with 40 per cent for all age groups. Physical abuse is the most common complaint of young callers, especially boys, which shows that families can cause children distress as well as be a source of comfort. This section looks at a selected range of family troubles and at how we can mitigate any potentially negative impact on our pre-teen child.

WHEN THE PARENTS' RELATIONSHIP ENDS

Perhaps any family's greatest difficulty is when the parents' relationship ends. With about four in ten marriages ending in divorce or separation, more and more children will experience family change. Over 70 per cent of children whose parents divorce are under ten. If live-in partnerships are included, the percentage of tweenies so affected will be even higher, because we know that cohabiting couples tend to end their relationships sooner.

No two relationships are the same, and no two endings of any relationship are the same. A divorce or separation can be acrimonious or amicable, be anticipated or come as a complete surprise. Few children welcome the experience of family breakdown or divorce, however it comes about. None the less, children have particular needs at different stages of development, and these may determine how well they adapt to living between two different homes or seeing one parent less often. If we review the particular needs and views of tweenies, this will highlight where they may be especially vulnerable and require extra support.

Information points: What research shows is best for children

- The most important thing to children was that both parents remained emotionally and practically committed to them after the divorce.
- Young children coped with their emotional difficulties in a number of ways, including distracting themselves through playing or learning new things, withdrawing by sleeping and displaying anger and distress.
- For children who needed support, the crucial element in their choice of who to turn to was trust, though it often took time for that trust to become established.
- The quality of children's key relationship with an adult or siblings can create more stability than a blood relationship.
- The freedom not to talk to school friends or teachers if they did not trust that school was a safe place.
- 'Doing' may be more important for some children than talking; for example, playing games or learning practical skills in a general way rather than being asked to talk to a strange adult such as a counsellor.

Facing Family Change, Joseph Rowntree Foundation, *findings*

Needs that are particular to tweenies will relate to their stage of development: in other words, to the bedding-in of confidence and personal and gender identity; to puberty; their ability to think in more grown-up ways and handle more direct answers to their questions; and their increasing reliance on friends. For example, parental breakdown and acrimony could delay the flourishing of confidence that would normally occur during the pre-teen years and make friendships more difficult. An eight- or nine-year-old boy may feel particularly let down if his father leaves just when he needs to identify more closely with him. Although girls also need a father's love and admiration, their significant role model at this stage is more likely to be their mother who is also most likely to stay. And if a new male partner joins the family soon after, there is the chance that a resentful or angry son could be less welcoming, become more competitive and be less ready to accept direction from him. Girls may have a hard time managing family changes alongside the arrival of periods. If they feel special to their fathers it can make them more confident about their changing self and future relationships with boys. Should an adored father produce a baby girl with a new partner at this stage, without special attention his pre-teen daughter could feel very hurt and rejected.

Overall, it is generally beneficial for the emotional welfare of both girls and boys that the departing parent – mother or father – remains in regular touch and demonstrates an ongoing commitment to the individual child as well as respect for the family that was – and still is, because the child's birth parents remain just that even when they no longer live together. If it is at all possible (though, sadly, it is often not so), our tweenies will value the occasional get-together of both parents with brothers and sisters and even new partners to mark special events such as birthdays and achievements, provided no sparks fly. This will help to keep important the part of childhood that occurred before the break-up, demonstrate that parents can still co-operate in the children's interests and thereby ensure each child remains intact rather than fractured following the split.

Taster tips if you are living apart from your tweenie

✓ Be assured that whatever the circumstances, you still matter to your child. Children are, in general, hugely forgiving of parents and will value your love and attention.

✓ Be sensitive to a tweenie's need for extra support and attention at times of other changes, such as school transfer, puberty, any illness or house move.

✓ Let them know they matter to you by keeping in touch, if not in person then through, cards, letters, postcards, e-mails, telephone calls or text messages. Correspond with each child separately and try to refer to particular events that have been special to them. Don't give up if you get no response: they could be angry or feel let down.

✓ When they visit, do ordinary things rather than fete them with special treats. Children prefer it this way.

✓ Accept that their developing personal and social life is very important to them. Work around this and let them be open and honest about their preferred visiting arrangements in regular reviews.

✓ Treat them as if they have rights in your new home so they feel they belong there too.

Researchers at the University of Leeds asked a range of children for their views of parents splitting up. The quotes that follow, from children who chose assumed names, are taken from two reports, one published by the Joseph Rowntree Foundation and the other by Young Voice, an organisation that seeks to make young people's views count.

Tuning in to tweenies

'There's nothing a child can do [if parents split up]. It's because it's their parents. There's no point in getting involved because it might make things worse.'

Q: So what's the best thing to do?

'Try and forget what's happened and get on with normal life.' Elise (aged ten)

'It's going to start to go worser than it is now, even though I don't like it and I'm nearly in tears. Because there's a new baby coming and think of it – pram, baby chair, "Why is it crying?". It's going to be much harder now . . . it feels a lot more [sigh] how do I say it? Er, lot more per cent that I won't see him a lot.' JJ (aged ten)

'Every time I go to bed I think this is all a dream . . . One day I'll wake up and say "Hi Mum", and Dad will be there and I'll say "Dad, what are you doing here?" I know it's not true. I think to myself, "What are you talking about" but I wish . . . and just think in my mind, "I hope it's true".' JJ (aged ten)

Where to live, which parent to live with?

Living between two homes, or living without one or other parent, is easy for some children to manage but not for all. The following experiences of a group of young people who agreed to speak show this clearly. Bob, twelve, said, 'About a year ago I would come home from a weekend with Dad, and find it very hard to re-adjust – sometimes it's just too much. Mum was always very understanding, and I used to have a lot of Mondays off school and then by Tuesday I'd be fine.' Caroline, aged seventeen, declared, 'It didn't work for me having two bases because you've got like two bedrooms and two of everything and I was getting mixed up who I was.' On the other hand, Lisa, eight, said, 'It isn't difficult for me. You walk into Dad's house, you think, "Ah, late night tonight, stories, cornetto" and at Mum's you think, "Ah, nice early night tonight, nice little bowl of cereal and some lovely hot chocolate".'

Chelsea, eight, was confused in a more practical way: 'At school, if they ask us to draw a picture of our home, I tell the teacher I've got two homes and they just say you choose which one to draw. So it's hard, so what I have to do is take it in turns to draw each house, but once I drew Mum's house and inside it I drew my Dad's room.' Elizabeth, nine, described something similar: 'Sometimes I get confused on Mondays and after school, if I've just been at my mum's, sometimes I go to my mum's instead of my dad's.' Tom, twelve, felt the transfer difficulty was eased by having school as a buffer. 'It's okay for me because we don't move from one house straight to the other. We normally go from school to the other house, then it's all right because we can say goodbye in the morning and we'll be able to forget about it in school.'

These quotes from *Parent Problems!* show that it is not easy for children to split themselves between two homes, emotionally or practically, even where the arrangement is amicable. Children hate to have to divide their loyalties and take care not to give hurt or show favouritism. Sometimes the solution is negative: 'I only get upset after I have seen my dad, then I get better, then he comes along and then I get upset again and so I said the perfect way is that I just don't see him' (eleven-year-old); but sometimes it is positive: 'I'm happy that both my parents are happier now. It's been worth it for that' (twelve-year-old). So relationships do falter and good can come out of it; and we can move on and try to make the next stage work for everyone too.

Taster tips on managing relationship break-up

✓ Provide opportunities for them to talk and express any angry and upset feelings.

✓ Describe as honestly as you can what is happening or what might happen.

✓ Reassure them that they're not in any way to blame, that they are still loved very much by both parents and that although things may be hard for a while, you'll always be there for them.

✓ Be honest about your regrets and sadness, but offload your distress on your friends, not your children.

✓ Listen when they want to talk, otherwise they may feel unloved and ignored, which can affect their confidence.

✓ Involve them in as many decisions as are appropriate about the family, but don't involve them in the arguments between you and the other parent.

✓ Don't make them take sides or use them as your spy to gather information.

✓ Allow them to carry on loving and respecting the other parent. Being rude about the person you are parting from in a child's hearing can cause immense difficulty.

✓ Allow them to keep and display photos of their non-resident parent in their bedroom, even if you feel that person has let you down. Your child needs to keep that parent 'in mind' to maintain her emotional bond and a photo may convince that the thoughtfulness is being reciprocated.

✓ Assure them that you will keep in contact with the grandparents, cousins and aunts on both sides of the family, for as long as it feels natural and enjoyable.

✓ If your child does not want to see her departing parent, realise she could just be hurt and angry. Don't whoop with joy because she's taken your side and block any meeting; instead give her something to respect about the parent, say contact now is important because she could need and value the relationship in the future; but create a timetable that reflects her preferences.

IN STEP? NEW FAMILIES: A WORLD WITHOUT A BEGINNING

The loss of the family structure can be very upsetting for children. They can become even more confused and resentful when new people enter their lives as partners of parents, step-parents or stepsisters or -brothers and the adults attempt to recreate what has been lost, which is impossible. One in eight children are likely to grow up in a stepfamily and one in three marriages are remarriages. Stepfamilies are becoming far more common. Some stepfamilies work brilliantly; others never gel. But where they do work, they can be a rich source of comfort to parents, step-parents and all the children involved, and the relationships can remain lifelong and valuable.

Stepfamilies, unlike original families, create an entire world for those involved that has no natural beginning or path of becoming. Children are chary of change, especially if they don't know what's in store. Families take time to develop to the point where they assume a connected identity for all those who live in and around them. It is a common error to think that a stepfamily inevitably will become a secure, cosy unit, quickly re-creating what has been lost. Success is rarely instant; it takes time, patience, understanding and compromise, especially on the part of the adults who hold the key. What are the factors that help to make stepfamilies 'work'?

Researchers say that what seems to matter most in terms of children's emotional and academic development is if a child feels safe with and warmly supported by at least one parent; in other words, the quality of the central relationship is more important than the particular structure of any family. 'Warmly supported by' means listened to and understood, cuddled and cared for. The biggest difficulty may be persuading our own child that she is special to us while trying to treat all children in the step-family fairly. If there is an obvious conflict between the two, we should always err on the side of our own children; but it need not be that difficult if we ensure that family rules apply to every-one, birthdays are celebrated similarly and clothes and treats are bought on a similar basis, while reserving some special time for a special relationship with our child on both a regular and spon-taneous basis, especially in the early months and years.

It is hard to characterise common features of stepfamilies, for there is a greater variation between stepfamilies than between original families. Someone who has interviewed a large number of stepfamilies commented that for every apparent pattern, she could identify an equally clear, opposite pattern. The best way to help reformed families to gel is to apply the general prin-ciples of good relationships discussed throughout this book, and the experience of stepchildren as recorded here is particularly valuable.

Taster tips on helping stepfamilies 'gel', supported by stepchildren

✓ Don't try to buy any child's affection with presents.
✓ Earn your partner's children's trust and respect before you try to discipline them.
✓ Don't force the new stepfamily on children: 'Let every-one come to terms with it gradually, in a "drip-fed" way, because you can't create instant happy families.

Make sure everyone feels welcome and not out of
place.' Bill, twelve

✓ Never 'bounce' children. Warn them in advance of any
new relationship or new developments and of any
other children involved.

✓ Accept it will take time: 'I felt as if he was rejecting
us as a family although he didn't mean that. We were
going somewhere one day with her and her children
and he said, "It'll be like a family outing" and I went,
"No, it won't!"'

✓ Accept that not all pieces of the new family jigsaw
will fit: 'I got used to her and she's really nice. But I
don't talk much to her daughters – we're on different
wavelengths.' Mike, fourteen

Parent Problems! Young Voice

Families are necessarily organic; they take time to grow and
shape, and there is certainly no one model, or even one type of
model, that fits all. It is for each child to give and to take what
she feels she can or needs during any period of adjustment and
thereafter, and for each adult to accept that the stepfamily may,
or may not, be a particular child's natural centre of gravity. As
one of the adult players, we must appreciate that any resentment, guilt or jealousy we feel should not dominate or dim our
child's. We have to accept that whilst we naturally try to do our
best, our efforts may not be appreciated or valued immediately
and we're unlikely to do everything right. Nevertheless, with
time, tolerance, trust, tact, talk and tenderness, stepfamilies can
and do become a stable, healing and emotionally sustaining base
for each of the participants.

FAMILY IN-FIGHTING: WHEN IT GETS ROUGH AS WELL AS TOUGH

Verbal and physical violence is part of the human condition. Families are not immune though this does not make either violence, or any other form of abuse, acceptable. Living close together as most families do, the experience is often intense and can become rough, with children sometimes either receiving harsh treatment or witnessing parents or siblings coming to verbal and physical blows.

Children can be deeply upset by heated and abusive verbal arguments as well as by physical violence, especially when one sometimes leads to the other. Simon, eleven, and Julie, eight, said they would sit on the top stair hugging each other and crying when the words were flying between their parents below them after their bedtime. Every time they heard a raised voice, they would crane to hear whether it was a laugh or a cry and then stay awake in case it got nasty. Alex, twelve, would put friends off from coming to his house, arranging instead to go over to them in case his parents embarrassed him with one of their regular and deeply upsetting verbal set-tos. He hated to hear his mum belittle his dad. Simon said he would jump about shouting 'Stop it!' in a desperate but ineffectual way, trying to get his parents' attention if there were big arguments but mostly he'd just go and hide away in his bedroom.

About 3 million children actually witness incidents of domestic violence every year and many more are aware of it. It is estimated that in nine out of ten incidents, a child will be in the next room and therefore know of and be frightened by what they hear. We are becoming increasingly aware that simply witnessing or hearing over-heated rows between parents or parent and partner can seriously disturb children. Peta, nine, said, 'I've only really heard it, but I've never really seen it . . . I was thinking that my dad was hurting my mum. I could hear the conversations they were having and Mum was saying, "Stop it!", but, every time, I was crying and I didn't really want to listen. It was quite hard going back to sleep because, mostly, I've been in my bed most of the times . . . It's usually woken me up.' The distress can affect their performance in school in the short term and their attitudes, behaviour and relationships in the longer term. Susanna, twelve: 'I'm not learning very much . . . Sometimes 'cause I daydream, and just thinking when my dad hit me, and I want to really cry but I don't want to tell anybody. So I try not to cry and then I just don't do my work.'

When children are emotionally attached to either or both parties involved in the crossfire, they can become very confused and uncertain about whom to love or trust. Children may also feel both incompetent and guilty, being unable to prevent any particular incident, and deeply insecure and anxious in anticipation of the next episode, because they are rarely one-offs. Errol, eight, explained, 'You know how it made me feel? It affected me a lot. It gets me all muddled and weird. I feel like it's all pressing outwards inside my head. I think it has frozen me up a bit inside . . . I tried to help. I tried to guard my mum so he couldn't hurt her. I didn't talk to anyone about it – anyone. I used to run downstairs to see Mum was okay.' It is quite common for a child to prefer to stay at home to police and protect, rather than go to school; but others may welcome school as a safe haven where they can leave their troubles behind and relax. Some even admit to being naughty to get a detention to put off going home.

Children's views of rough behaviour in families have been recorded in a booklet published by *Young Voice*. The contributions above have been selected from that. Some of these children's experiences are also recorded below.

Tuning in to tweenies: what children in rough homes say they need

'They need their mums to help them and talk to them. The children need their aunties. They need their friends when there are problems in the house.' Aziza, twelve 'A counsellor, or someone like that. Someone that would just take them out, and that, and that would make it easier for them. Make them feel good about themselves and make them feel it wasn't their fault.' Melanie, twelve

'Children need to take clothes with them if they have to leave home. They need to have friends and relatives to give them a good home, a nice clean home. The children need blankets, coats, and everything else you would have in a home.' Mona, eight

'Somewhere they can go, like when their parents are arguing, that they can get out of the house.' Tasha, twelve

'I don't think children like it when they have to talk about their problems. You should be able to just play, or do pictures, or even write a little book, saying everything, and give it in every single day, showing how you feel and they could put it somewhere safe so no one else can read it. That would be good. I just don't like saying it straight away.' Susanna, twelve

Stop Hitting Mum! Young Voice

So any parent being treated roughly has a double difficulty – to ensure their own safety and that of their children. But there are things we can do to help any child cope, in addition to the suggestions offered by the children above.

Taster tips on supporting children when family life gets rough

✓ Reassure them that they have not caused the problems and have absolutely no reason to feel guilty. If a child is treated badly, she must be told emphatically that it does not mean there is anything wrong or bad about her.

✓ Reassure them that they are still loved and wanted, by everyone hopefully, and offer physical consolation and cuddles so they don't learn to fear or mistrust all forms of physical contact.

✓ Maintain routines as far as possible to bolster a sense of security. When they are away from you, find ways to stay in touch, perhaps with a text message, so they know you are still safe.

✓ Try to find reasons that a child might understand to explain the current problem, if it is new development, or why it has re-emerged.

✓ If a child is in physical danger, it is imperative that help is sought or a safer place to live is found. A child's safety is any parent's first and foremost responsibility.

✓ Be tolerant of tears, which may flow very readily when raised voices stir memories, or of irritability that stems from poor sleep patterns.

✓ Seek help to find strategies for yourself and others that might reduce the amount of violence in the home, for the adults' benefit and the children's.

Supporting sensitively: a five-point guide to giving emotional first aid

The taster tips above offer specific practical advice for particular situations. This section suggests general guidelines that will be helpful whatever the difficulty facing us, or our child.

Children who experience insecurity and unhappiness may reject school, fall out with their friends, concentrate less at school, become less willing to play out or socialise and more dependent. Just when a tweenie needs to be out exploring and tasting more freedom, she may have neither the energy nor the inclination to do so. To help them cope at these times, children need:

• Structure and security.
• Their feelings acknowledged and validated.
• Regular updates on developments.
• Plenty of love and commitment.
• A parent who is emotionally available to talk and console, having looked after his or her own needs.

MAINTAINING STRUCTURE AND SECURITY

Changes often upset family patterns that children rely on for comfort, so during difficult times it is very important to keep as many of the usual routines going. Routines can help to support a child even if she feels very wobbly inside. If you normally take a child to school, try not to miss too many trips; or if that is the big change because, for example, you are in hospital, the alternative carer should maintain the familiar evening routines.

• Try to keep school attendance regular. The odd day off school may help, but certainly not too many, and never so many so that re-entering school becomes an issue.
• After-school activities should be kept going – up to a point.

Where a child has had a heavy commitment – absolutely manageable when things were calm – it might be sensible to drop one or two things to avoid getting over-tired. Ask her what she thinks she can realistically keep going. Distress can be exhausting, and none of us can manage nearly as much as when we feel strong.

- If weekend arrangements have to change, keep at least some of the time free for doing very familiar things.
- Try to make it possible for friendships to continue, even if you have moved away from an area and a journey is involved. The distance may feel smaller if photos of friends, taken before any move, are pinned up somewhere. This will help a child who is temporarily isolated to feel in touch and attached, reinforced with regular telephone calls if that's feasible.

ENCOURAGE THEM TO TALK ABOUT HOW THEY FEEL

Assume she knows what's been taking place and let her know that you know. As we have seen, many children feign ignorance and innocence. She could be feeling angry, anxious, frightened, jealous, guilty, insulted or unloved – or none of these, depending on the circumstances. But it is wise to encourage her to talk about her thoughts and reactions if that's possible, provided you are in a quiet place and have plenty of time.

If the issue is one that could distress you, all the more reason to bring it into the open, as her wish to protect you could explain any pretence of not knowing or not feeling sad. Yet it's our job to support and protect our child, not the other way round. Once she opens up, she should not be rushed or interrupted. It is important to demonstrate total respect for what she has to say and how she needs to say it, even if she expresses anger against you or someone else that you care for. It is also important to validate her perceptions so she feels she can rely on her view of things. If we want to put forward a different interpretation of events, add this as an alternative possibility, or present it as your view to be placed alongside hers. Don't declare that she is wrong or insensitive to speak out. Honesty should be encouraged.

Having said this, some children just don't want to talk. They prefer to work things through on their own – in their heads, as it were, while being active or doing normal things. As one report concluded, 'doing' may be more important for some children than talking; for example, playing games or learning practical skills in a general way rather than 'forced' disclosure to an unfamiliar adult such as a counsellor. Children will open up when they can trust the listener to hear them accurately and to treat the information as confidential. Many children do not want to talk to friends for fear their troubles may be passed on as gossip.

- Don't force any discussion. Always give them permission to refuse, using a phrase such as 'I wondered if you might be ready to talk about . . . is this a good time?' and let them say no, so when it takes place it is always on their terms.
- Try opening the discussion indirectly, by raising someone else's experiences, or your own, but not so that they have to mop up your tears!
- Make sure there's plenty of time and the place is private. Remember that people often hold back the really important stuff until the listener is on the point of leaving – so try to appear to bring it to an end at least fifteen minutes before you have to, so there is always time to talk through that slipped-in worry.
- Boys sometimes find it easier to talk if they are doing something else at the same time so don't have to speak face to face.
- Make it clear at the end that you're happy to chat again whenever it helps. Thoughts and feelings are layered; the ones that are easiest to talk about tend to get raised first, leaving deeper, often more important ones unaired until a further opportunity.

LET THEM KNOW WHAT'S HAPPENING

What both children and adults find difficult is uncertainty, so children need regular updates on developments. When children are consulted and kept informed of key changes, they feel more involved, more secure and less at the mercy of events and other people. This will also help them to realise we care enough to think about them and their interests, even when we are absorbed and distracted, and that we trust them with the information and respect their ability to comprehend and understand.

- Give notice beforehand of what is likely to happen, confirm that it is happening, and after explain why something happened, if it happened unexpectedly.
- Explain any unexpected absences, variations in routines and important changes in your life, especially about partners. ('He's becoming more important to me and it's likely he'll be spending more time here. How might you feel about that?')
- Try to offer some choices about the direction of any changes, especially if the decisions will have a practical impact on her life, so she doesn't feel excluded.

OFFER EXTRA LOVE AND COMMITMENT

The bottom line is that children can be amazingly resilient and overcome enormous difficulties if they have a good relationship with the main caring parent: when they feel parents are there for them and are warm, reliable and caring. Talking, playing together, showing understanding and being around more will help any child to trust your love and feel wanted and safe, which will help her to cope with just about anything.

- Answer her questions honestly and take her worries seriously.
- Tell her you love her and she can come to you any time she feels upset.
- Try to spend more time with her so she feels rooted and secure

and safe in one part of her life. She may need to spend more time with friends, but this should not crowd out time that she would otherwise have spent with you.

- Suggest a trip to the cinema together, a simple pizza or meal out or just a walk, to have some 'togetherness time' and to show you enjoy her company.
- Be gentle and understanding if she becomes rude or naughty. It's usually a sign that she needs your attention and is feeling rotten. However, she shouldn't be over-indulged if this totally overturns the normal rules and routines.

LOOK AFTER YOURSELF

It is important to meet our own needs when the family or our child is having a difficult time. We can only give our time and attention to others if we feel strong enough and have sufficient emotional energy to give. Caring for ourselves means making sure we get enough rest, having quiet time to reflect on the situation and taking some moderate exercise. It helps if we can find the time to do simple things that we generally enjoy, such as meeting a friend for coffee, and talking things through with brothers, sisters or parents who are close can be very beneficial. If we can't cope, neither can our children.

- Reduce the overall pressure. Drop unnecessary jobs when you can. Commitments often seem more manageable once we have listed them in order of urgency, and focus on the important one first.
- Make it clear to the family what you need. For example, you are entitled to have some time alone and some social life.
- Feel better about yourself by listing your good points and your successes. Do this with a friend if it will help.
- Think about what helps you to calm down, relax and recharge. Try to build it in to your day or week.
- Listen and talk more within the family. Everyone benefits if

they are honest with each other about feeling hard done by, angry, sad or lonely, instead of allowing resentment to grow. Talking to friends can also help.

DRAWING THIS TOGETHER

Although we cannot usually prevent unsettling events from affecting our children, we can help them to cope. Children can come through difficulties when they feel understood and reliably supported, are given space to reflect and talk and when a degree of comfortable familiarity is maintained. Above all, they need someone to listen calmly to their sometimes hostile or distorted view of the situation. We are the grown-ups, and any antagonism or exaggeration should not be viewed as a personal attack but be understood as a product of natural confusion, disappointment, loneliness, fear or self-interest. Pre-teens, like all of us, are very capable of distortion, fantasy, deep feeling and guilt. Offering a genuine account of the truth that is kind yet not brutal will help them to make sense of their world, anticipate the future, maintain their trust and faith in you and themselves and absolve them of guilt. If we also consult on key decisions, our tweenie can emerge more resourceful and sensitive and with greater self-respect. A good relationship with a parent or other key adult is known to act as a restraint or protection as a child confronts challenge and temptation outside the home, the subject of the next chapter. As our tweenie begins to explore risks and daring, we should keep these guidelines in mind.

Ten top take-out tips

- Make it absolutely clear that your tweenie is not responsible or to blame in any way for what has happened. Nothing she might have said or done could have changed anything.
- If someone close to them had has to leave, permanently or temporarily, ensure that out of sight does not mean out of mind.

- During any disruptive changes, keep other aspects of life as normal and regular as possible.
- Talk whenever there's an opportunity but always check first if there's anything they want to know about.
- New partners should be clear that your children come first.
- Children should know if you get a new partner that you are still there for them 100 per cent.
- Appreciate that any friendship problem can be enormously destabilising for a tweenie.
- Allow your child to love, respect, revere and hold in mind an absent parent.
- Look out for the features of small-scale difficulties that could have a full-sized emotional impact.
- Remember the dynamics of difficulty: if they play up they could need reassurance not reprimands.

And Remember!

Don't let our problems overshadow theirs. Always listen, and believe what you hear.

Children respond differently; let each one identify what help she wants, and be there.

If you could be the cause of their distress, consider what you might change.

11

SAFE AND SECURE?

Courting Danger and Flirting with Risk

CHILDREN HAVE AN UNRELENTING FASCINATION with the forbidden. It is always there but it becomes more evident at key stages in their development when children get fresh yearnings to be more independent. Their interest in probing the prohibited relates in large part to self-respect. It is more a statement of their autonomy than a wish to outrage or confront. Children assert, in effect, 'I am my own person. I am not a goody-goody, just doing what I'm told. This is what I shall do to prove it.' Courting a measure of danger is also a constituent of play and having fun, as we saw in chapter seven, part of exploring their new freedom and acquiring greater competence: they want to use their growing strength and confidence to master things that used to frighten them. Children also need to explore the boundaries and get up to mischief, which is not the same thing as openly defying the law and intentionally threatening their own or other people's safety. Kept safe and in proportion, taking risks is a healthy part of growing up and will happen as children gain more freedom. But our eight- to twelve-year-olds do need to stay, as it were, in the shallow end of risk; stray out of their depth and they could face real danger.

While most pre-teens enjoy the innocent thrill of things like scary funfair rides, it is an uncomfortable truth that some are diving in deeper and beginning to live dangerously, exposing themselves to immediate or longer-term physical harm. Research confirms that a small percentage of eight- or nine-year-olds are trying alcohol, cigarettes, solvents or even cannabis in secret, away from the watchful eyes of adults, and some get lured to railway lines or motorway bridges to play dangerous games. We know from self-report studies that a significant minority of tweenies break the law, unbeknown to parents, and those who commit serious crimes as teenagers admit they were already dabbling in their pre-teens. While most dabblers give up as they grow up, we should not be complacent. Our little angels are capable of devilish things and we need to be on the look-out for any signs of potentially dangerous experimentation.

The challenge for parents in this area is to encourage only natural and healthy adventure and exploration that contributes to development and is therefore acceptable. Some healthy activities are patently risky, such as horse riding, abseiling or canoeing, and most parents have no problem with these provided correct safety procedures are followed. However, playing by motorways, railways, rivers or particular streets or areas is clearly downright dangerous and must be prevented. Our task is twofold: to encourage sufficient exposure to safely managed excitement that real dangers do not become attractive, and to prepare them for any likely uninvited or unanticipated danger so they know how to behave if things get out of hand.

This chapter will consider how we can encourage a developmentally healthy attitude to risk-taking while protecting them from real danger. It will also suggest how to gauge whether any worrying behaviour is normal or has reached a point where we need to seek help. It starts with a section on smoking, alcohol and drugs, moves then to look at the range of criminal behaviour pre-teen children typically engage in and ends with a practical focus: how to encourage healthy attitudes to, and safe encounters with, risk, danger and daring as children spend more time outside our direct control.

Smoking, drink and drugs

We might think that our eight- to twelve-year-old is far too young to be indulging in anything illegal so this is something that need not concern us. Though we might be right about him not having started to smoke or drink, we'd be wrong to ignore the possibility. If we're right about our nine-year-old, three years on we should be less complacent; and even if our twelve-year-old is still seemingly innocent and fully and constructively occupied with football, swimming club or in a youth club we should still be keeping the communication cables humming and active for the potentially rocky years that follow. Some ten-year-olds binge drink. Twelve is the start of the high-risk period for children's first use of illegal drugs. What we do know is that it's never too early to watch out for signs of risk-taking and certainly never too early to talk about it.

Talking is so important. We know that comfortable communication reinforces those protective family bonds. By talking during the tweenie years, we take the first important step to keep our children free of harmful substances longer term. If these subjects are discussed comfortably and frequently at home when there's no hidden agenda, resentment or suspicion, it is far easier to raise them later without causing a defensive upset when more might be at stake. Talking also shows you care, enjoy their company and means you spend enough time together to find the right moment to do so; for these are not topics you raise on the way to the bathroom in the morning, mid-grocery shop or while they grab an after-school snack. It helps to have enough time and to be armed with relevant facts. We focus first on smoking because it is a clear danger to health and very young smokers are more likely to experiment subsequently with alcohol and drugs, to truant and then offend.

Taster tips on talking to tweenies about smoking, alcohol and drugs

✓ The earlier children start to smoke or drink, the deeper the trouble they're likely to end up in. Our prime aim should be to delay their first use through talking and persuasion. Keep harm reduction as a second priority at this stage.

✓ If you have any worries about what they're up to, talk; don't stalk or spy. Be straightforward and caring, not critical. Focus on your concern for them, not on their 'unacceptable' behaviour.

✓ Try not to be horrified by and react strongly to any stories they tell you, otherwise they may clam up and you'll learn nothing. Just listen.

✓ Don't ask for any names of those whose activities you are told about. You are being told in confidence and your child will not want to be seen to 'sneak'.

✓ Ask instead questions such as, 'Why do you think some children need to smoke or drink?' 'Is this behaviour generally accepted in your group?' 'Why do you think Carly smokes?' 'Is it possible that Ben is pretending – claiming that he does these things but actually does not?' These leads will encourage discussion and increase awareness.

✓ Invite them to reflect on the consequences of making choices now that could harm their future health and plans.

SMOKING TOBACCO

Studies show that up to half of all ten- to twelve- year-olds have tried a cigarette. In one American project, one in seven eight- to twelve-year-olds admitted to being a habitual smoker. Nicotine is highly addictive, but until the addiction is obvious, it is easy to say, 'Well, I'm not hooked, so I can carry on doing it.' The earlier a person starts smoking, the harder it is to quit. Even then, the ill effects are not felt for many years, which is why 'scare tactics' are rarely effective. Children don't look that far ahead and anyway claim they'll quit long before then.

Teenage smoking is more likely to start through peer pressure and wanting to be part of the group. Tweenies, though, are more likely to be introduced to smoking through a sibling or a particular friend and will try it to satisfy their curiosity and feel 'cool'. Someone who is shorter than average and self-conscious of this may be tempted to smoke to show off, to make himself feel and look older or to be considered 'hard', and some may smoke to gain popularity or friends. At no age is the act of smoking illegal, though it is illegal for anyone under sixteen to buy cigarettes. The difficulty is that the more we disapprove of smoking the more attractive it may become. Any child who smokes or supplies another with cigarettes will need to break the law in order to obtain them. These children may also be willing to challenge parents or the law in other areas and explains the association with other high-risk behaviour.

Persuading your tweenie not to take up tobacco

Before the thought of trying a cigarette enters his consciousness:

- Make it clear to all visiting adult friends that smoking is not welcomed in your house. The same rules should apply to any child of ours and to their friends.
- Discuss his attitude to financial incentives, which can work for those insufficiently committed to stay tobacco-free without

help. To be effective, any reward should be staged and not over-delayed; for example, £10 if he has not smoked by the age of fourteen, £20 by sixteen, and £50 when he reaches eighteen.

• Focus on positive health – sensible eating and exercise – rather than on damage. Once children know we care and they learn to respect and look after themselves they'll be less willing to inhale anything harmful.

If we smoke, we can explain our regret and the power of addiction, spell out the cost and how it feels to be dependent on cigarettes, tell how it spoils our breath, teeth, fingers, clothes and physical stamina. And, of course, we should not leave cigarette packets lying around. If, at the end of all this, our child still takes no notice he should still be accepted; a good relationship with him is more important than ending the smoking and is, long-term, the best protector against adopting any other potentially self-harming behaviour. But it would be wise to try to re-route him: to encourage healthy pursuits, other friends to enjoy, and perhaps a hero who espouses healthy attitudes, not defiance or deviance.

USE AND ABUSE OF ALCOHOL

A study undertaken for the Youth Justice Board of England and Wales found that 7 per cent of eleven-year-olds drink alcohol once a week or more often, including at home. Twelve-year-olds now admit to binge drinking, defined as having more than five units of alcohol in close succession. In a recent survey of accident and emergency departments, three-quarters of the hospitals questioned said they believed the age of young people being admitted for alcohol problems was decreasing. One hospital reported treating a child of six, while others said that the average age of the youngest children they were seeing was ten. Alcohol damages health, increases the likelihood of injuring yourself and others and makes children more likely to offend. Early drinking increases the chance of later trouble so it is sensible to be concerned and watchful.

Eight- to twelve-year-old boys may be especially inclined to use alcohol and drink it to excess to prove their manliness, to gain popularity and notoriety, especially if they wish to feel older. Fathers may even encourage this, seeing the drinking as 'manly' and forging a father-son bond, but it perpetuates the assumption that boys are expected to drink and get drunk and implies that fathers have no other way to feel close.

Although there is a strong argument in favour of introducing children to alcohol slowly within the family to demystify it, through having the occasional drink diluted with water or lemonade on special occasions, any child under the age of ten or eleven is too young to be so included. Their bodies are small, still forming, alcohol could easily 'go to their head' and there is time enough to learn in a gradual way about the effects of alcohol and their own limits. Young children can develop a taste for it, and enjoy the easy 'buzz' that might blur or block any distress. Younger tweenies can celebrate special occasions with non-alcoholic fizzy grape juice, cola and other sodas, fruit juice cocktails and alcohol-free lager if preferred, but not the real thing and certainly not 'alcopops', that are too readily available and reckoned to be responsible for the rise in binge drinking among the very young. Around the age of twelve, a child may be ready to be offered the occasional, single alcoholic drink (a small lemonade shandy rather than straight lager or beer) but celebratory non-alcoholic alternatives should always be available; and certainly no child should be forced to try alcohol if he does not like the taste. No alcohol should be taken from our cupboards for their use and any instance firmly scotched.

Every parent should be clear about the dangers to young (or, indeed, all) bodies of excessive intake of alcohol. We also need to alert our tweenie to the particular danger of mixing paracetamol and alcohol. Some young people swallow two or three tablets after a binge session because they think they will wake with a clearer head the next morning and parents won't therefore know: they do not realise that paracetamol can intensify alcoholic poisoning with potentially dangerous consequences that will require hospital treatment.

Ben's story

When Ben went on a residential school trip aged twelve, he packed a full bottle of whisky that he had taken from home without his parents' knowledge, despite the school's warnings about alcohol being forbidden. He wasn't the only one, for it had been well planned. Needless to say, one evening the boys got drunk and the teachers noticed. His parents were contacted and he missed the next day's events.

However he was not sent home – too many individuals were implicated; instead, his punishment was to be dropped from the school's forthcoming music tour. Ben's parents discussed what they should do. They felt the school's punishment was not only appropriate but also sufficient, that it would be unfair to punish Ben twice. They expressed their strong disapproval and made him pay for a replacement bottle, but they also wanted to show their trust that he had already learned his lesson so they left it there. However, they assured him that any similar flaunting of school authority or misuse of alcohol would be treated far more strictly.

Whether we like it or not, parents teach by example. Our tweenie is far less likely to start drinking too young or go too far if we don't habitually drink to excess. It is also important to keep sufficiently sober to enable us to intervene and take responsibility if they get into difficulty and need our help. It is, of course, vital to insist that they contact us if ever they fear a situation that involves alcohol is getting out of hand.

TWEENIES, ILLEGAL DRUGS AND SOLVENTS: THE FACTS

The largest and most comprehensive studies of young drug takers in the UK were carried out in Scotland in the mid-1990s. These suggested that by the age of eleven to twelve about one in ten pupils would have already used an illegal drug. Boys were more likely to be using drugs than girls – 13.7 per cent compared with 8.8 per cent of girls. Drug use was not confined to any one social class but was spread across all income groups. Strong links were found between illegal drug use and a range of other experiences. The drug users were, for example, more likely than the rest to have had a whole alcoholic drink, have drug-using family members and have had behaviour problems when they were younger. The friends of these very young drug users were particularly likely to truant, sell drugs, be in trouble with the police, vandalise property, ride in stolen cars and run away from home.

Younger children have been interviewed more recently in a smaller survey for the Youth Justice Board (YJB) of England and Wales. The findings indicate strongly that the age of twelve marks an important watershed when the balance tips towards the appearance of longer-term social, educational and drug-related problems. Children who are excluded from school start taking drugs earlier, at aged twelve for cannabis and solvents, thirteen for amphetamines and LSD, and fourteen for cocaine. Eight per cent of thirteen-year-olds have taken ecstasy and tried cannabis, which implies that a few twelve-year-olds will also have done so. We know that children as young as seven smoke cannabis and sniff solvents and those who sniff can die on the first occasion, and our tweenie should know this is possible.

Perhaps more important, early drug use is now being linked with later mental disorders. In chapter nine, we saw that the brain does not settle to its adult state until a child is well into his teens; and the onset of puberty is marked by a period of particularly intense electrical activity and turmoil in the brain.

Regular drug use during this critical time is now thought to cause a permanent derangement that will show later as psychosis. If we suspect or find our child has been smoking, drinking inappropriately or taking drugs, we should talk it through calmly rather than make threats that could drive him away or the activity deeper underground.

Taster tips on responding to early drinking, smoking or drug taking

✓ Invite him to admit it, and thank him for being honest if he does.

✓ Ask him what he knows about how easy or hard it is to become dependent.

✓ Check his awareness of various issues and dangers – of harming others through passive smoking, of possible mental health problems, alcoholic poisoning, the cost and sources of funding.

✓ Encourage him to describe how he got into this, and where the cigarettes, glue, drink or other substances come from. This will tell us if he's mixing with kids we'd rather he left alone and if there might be more trouble to come.

✓ If he feels he needs to do this to remain accepted by his friends, ask why this activity is central to being friends with them; whether his idea of friendship involves giving people choices; and discuss how far he might go if they wanted to do something else that seemed more obviously wrong.

✓ Offer suggestions about how to say no convincingly but non-aggressively, if he'd find this helpful.

✓ Make clear our views on smoking, alcohol or drugs, if we have not already done so.

Dishonesty and law-breaking

We have already considered some aspects of dishonesty in chapters three and four. This section looks at when and why some children go beyond token lying, cheating and minor shoplifting to engage in more regular law-breaking. Children aged eight to twelve do commit crimes, more than parents or law officers ever realise. It is hard to know exactly when, how often or what because children do not always get caught and it is a rare one who owns up voluntarily. However, there are certain patterns. The most useful studies of child law-breaking are those that ask children to report what they have done, instead of relying on official figures recorded by the police or courts after children have been apprehended. Two national self-report studies in the United States that followed groups of children from birth onwards have found the figures for offending have remained level over the last twenty years. One found that by the age of twelve, only one-third of seven- to twelve-year-olds had steered clear of all wrongdoing. Of the remaining two-thirds that had behaved unlawfully, just over eight in ten admitted to minor aggressive acts, 5 per cent reported engaging in serious violence and almost one in ten had committed a burglary. There is no reason to think that children in the United Kingdom would behave very differently.

If our tweenie has a brush with the law, it is important to respond sensitively yet decisively, to back up the police but not punish harshly or aggressively because it could be a one-off. It will not mean he is destined for a life of crime. Although official figures suggest young law-breakers who are caught are two to three times more likely than older first-time law-breakers to develop a serious criminal career, the self-report figures show that messing about on the streets, even doing wrong, is a stage many young and not-so-young children go through, and then stop. If we review common tweenie crimes, we can keep a sense

of perspective and respond more appropriately should our tweenie stray.

COMMON TWEENIE CRIMES

In the UK, the two most common types of offences committed
by ten- to fifteen-year-olds are 'non-violent property' crimes –
vandalism in particular – and shoplifting. Children who commit
non-violent property offences may also engage in fire-setting
(arson) and burglary, though some will tend towards car crimes
and aggressive property offences instead. Shoplifting is more
likely than any other offence to be both a 'once-only' act and
be the 'offence of choice' of less aggressive and challenging children who never experiment with other crimes. In support of this,
a teacher friend has observed that stealing seems to be becoming increasingly acceptable among children, with many believing that there is nothing morally wrong in taking items of small
value, only expensive ones.

Taster tips on effective responses to children's early offending

✓ Assume, when you first find out, that it was a first
offence. It could be a bad move to go ballistic and get
heavily punitive if it was.

✓ Make it clear that what took place was wrong and
that they were wholly responsible, even though friends
might have influenced them.

✓ Ensure that there is an appropriate level 'consequence'
– appropriate to the offence and a possible first
offence that might have been an error of judgement.

✓ Don't humiliate them: instead, separate what they did
from who they are and focus your disappointment on
their behaviour.

> ✓ If you go overboard, you could drive them closer to possibly wayward friends.
>
> ✓ If you have been troubled for a while and the discovered offence a repeat one, be tougher. Say a firm no to other activities that could suggest a deeper rebellious attitude – smoking, body piercing, too much time unsupervised on the streets, and consider how to restrict their time with current friends (see chapter five).
>
> ✓ Consider whether any recompense might be appropriate and, if so, arrange it.
>
> ✓ After the whole matter is over, let it lie. Don't continually revisit the shame and rub their nose in it; or laugh about it after, for it was serious.
>
> ✓ Clear support for the law and the police, clear statements of right and wrong, clearly agreed penalties that acknowledge the distress caused, combined with a clear attempt to understand why and how it happened, are the most effective strategic response.

Boys are more likely to offend in this age group than girls. Boys are assumed to express their discontent and aggression directly while girls express it indirectly (for example by spreading malicious rumours). As one teacher said, girls simply don't make their anger or frustration public: 'When a girl gets mad at someone, she becomes friends with another girl for revenge.' In a study that followed girls born in the United Kingdom in 1953, there was little offending under the age of sixteen, and most of this was shoplifting. But times change, and in the US offending among female child delinquents (eight- to twelve-year-olds) has increased by 69 per cent over the last fifteen years. Now one in four of tweenies who engage in crime are female. In the UK, single or pairs of girls now hang out with boy gangs, and girl gangs are now more common and thought to behave more aggressively than they used to. What we do know is that nine out of ten juvenile fire-setters are boys. As this is one of the more common tweenie crimes, we shall explore how and why a natural fascination with fire can tip into criminal activity.

PLAYING WITH FIRE: UNDERSTANDING ARSON

Children are drawn to fire. It is fascinating to watch, linked to birthdays and excitement, cosy and compelling, yet also forbidden and dangerous. It can cook and it can kill. One moment there's nothing, and the next it's there, alive, dancing, daring. It is pretty yet powerful; and those who control it acquire power. Playing with fire becomes more common as children progress through the tweenie years, for it readily satisfies the need to savour danger. Fascination with the forbidden combines with both a desire to master what previously frightened them and an intellectual curiosity about how it changes colour, changes smell, glows, grows and then peters out. Widespread central heating means the full danger of fire is often not understood. Worse, gas log fires with neutered flames teach that fire is not even hot.

Boys start in the home and garden – finding out, usually with friends, what materials burn, which burn brightest, for how long the flames last, whether the smells emitted are pleasant or obnoxious, and what items, such as aerosol cans, explode and bang loudest. Girls enjoy fire, too, though their interest is often more domesticated, focusing on candles as they tell stories or chat. Tents, real ones or created by draping sheets over bushes or furniture, become even more exciting with candles inside, though close supervision would be essential especially if they then explore what melts or what food can be toasted in the flames.

Much of this experimentation with fire is natural and will go no further. However, some children get hooked on fire. For some, the habit can be well established by the age of eight, having been setting light to scraps of paper using matches or cigarette lighters since the age of five. For the later starters, if they get a taste for setting fires, they will then move out into the neighbourhood – into the streets, parks and playgrounds and look for a bigger impact each time.

According to an educational psychologist and arson expert, the young, habitual fire-setter is often angry, finds it hard to express himself verbally and will come from a family that doesn't talk much. When he finds that the flames seem to burn away the anger, he will do it again. Often he will set light to buildings and belongings associated with the source of his anger, but not necessarily so. So fire-raising might get out of hand when a child:

- Feels put upon and ignored, having no say in what is happening around him.
- Has little else to occupy him.
- Gets angry frequently but is not allowed to express it so the pressure builds.
- Does not talk much.

If our tweenie is burning things in play frequently and it feels unhealthy, think about what else is happening in his life and consider if there may be reasons for it. The local fire service is usually very willing to help; fire prevention officers are trained to help children develop a realistic and respectful attitude to fire and its consequences and the advice given later in this chapter is based on professional guidance.

WHY DO YOUNG CHILDREN GET INVOLVED IN CRIME?

Children get drawn into criminal behaviour for a variety of reasons. It relieves boredom, gives them an adrenaline rush, gives them status in the eyes of their peers and makes them feel they belong to a group. It can be a statement of anger or resentment against particular people or hardships, or a denial that they care about these; and of course crime can be seen as 'normal' if others – friends or family – around them overtly flout the law for personal financial gain. Children may also simply drift into it, starting with mucking about but finding the danger thrilling and repeating the act when they discover they get away with it. Although middle childhood, the age range with which we are concerned, has been thought of as a quiet period, it is also the time when children begin to gain independence, seek rank and status over their peers and gather in groups to hang out on the streets and in malls. They push at the boundaries and chance that they won't get caught.

If home is fraught and a child is either reprimanded regularly or ignored, he may see little point in staying in; but the more he wanders feeling antagonistic, the closer he'll get to serious trouble. School failure and lack of self-esteem are associated with child delinquency, but friends and family matter too. Influential family factors, all of which have been addressed in earlier chapters, are:

- Family dynamic (loving and warm or rejecting and hostile).
- Effective supervision.
- Reactions to challenging behaviour (predictable and positive or arbitrary and harsh).

It may be helpful to reread chapter four on the benefits to children of clear boundaries, positive discipline and how to avoid harmful confrontations. Given that our tweenies are most at risk of criminal or self-abusive behaviour when we take our eye off the supervision ball, we discuss it next.

MONITORING AND SUPERVISION
A few years ago a group of inmates in a young offender institution were asked about their earlier childhood experiences. Though many referred to violence, mental illness, abuse and

alcohol, the only feature everyone mentioned was feeling un-important to their parent or caregiver. The excessive freedom almost all of them had was experienced as neglect; no one cared enough about them to monitor their comings and goings or watch over them. They felt ignored and insignificant: cut off and cut out. Of course, the unsupervised will have more opportun-ity to get into trouble, but more important longer term is what children read into it: that parents who maintain rules, set sens-ible guidelines and take the time and trouble to check their chil-dren out actively demonstrate love and care and seek their safety – even if at times it feels irritating and untrusting.

Taster tips on how to supervise and monitor

✓ Start early by modelling good practice: always let them know in a friendly way where we've been, what we did and whether we enjoyed it.

✓ When they start to play out close to home, ask them to return every twenty to thirty minutes to confirm they're safe. Between report backs they simply cannot wander very far.

✓ Make very clear those places you are happy for them to be, and those they should not visit.

✓ Always check, and confirm wherever possible, who they are playing or going out with.

✓ Insist on being kept up to date with any last-minute changes in plans and make a fuss if you are not.

✓ Be friendly and curious about what they did so they know they may have to account for themselves.

✓ If we can't be at home when we've asked them to return from longer absences, call them up or ask them to call in to report safe arrival.

✓ Show interest, but don't be intrusive. If we appear

---

nosey our child may clam up. If he objects, respond that it's our job to ensure his safety – and we care.

✓ Be vigilant about receiving the change back from any money given to finance an activity. If you are seriously worried about any discrepancy, ask for receipts.

✓ Strike a balance between requiring information yet showing trust. If they feel you put them under a microscope and mistrust them, discuss other ways to settle your worries that are acceptable to everyone concerned.

Of course it is harder to keep tweenies at home if our accommodation is cramped and we have little to amuse them; and it is certainly more difficult to retrieve them from friends or the streets if we have younger children in tow. When we are frustrated and angry – understandable in this predicament – any defiance from a wandering child will be hard to handle calmly; but exploding doesn't help. Instead, we can:

• Explain the safety reasons for wanting to know their whereabouts and what it is like to be so worried.

• Enquire about any local sporting or play schemes that could be within your budget during difficult times such as school holidays.

• Talk to other parents who may have the same problem and share the care, advice or monitoring.

• Ask someone to mind any younger children to create time to have with our tweenie, doing something to keep the relationship active.

• Discuss possible ideas for things to do if he stays in, or activities you feel happy about him engaging in if he spends time with friends out of the home.

- Perhaps ask him to pick up some shopping for you while he is out or to help with other chores so he is encouraged to return more speedily.
- Say you trust him to be sensible; however any breach of the conditions agreed would have to be followed by a 'consequence', and you will discuss the nature of this with him if it becomes necessary.

AND IF THE POLICE DO GET INVOLVED ...

The police and other law enforcement agencies treat children and young people with increasing sensitivity. They also like to involve parents closely, not to blame or punish them but to get their backing for the intervention chosen as this helps the young person to take the experience seriously, reflect on his actions, feel sorry and mend his ways. Children are given two formal chances to change through, first, a Reprimand then a Final Warning, before full charges are brought that will lead to court proceedings. The police issue both of these in the police station and parents must attend and hear their child discuss the offence and how to make amends having had their circumstances assessed, part of the restorative justice approach discussed in chapter four. If a parent undermines the police's authority at any stage, this process is less likely to prevent further offending.

Thrills and spills: safer alternatives

Children's increasing freedom terrifies most parents. After all, we are biologically programmed to protect our children when they are babies and it can be hard to move on; but keeping youngsters behind closed doors or cocooned in the safety of our homes or cars metaphorically cuts their legs off and skews normal development. One mum who lived by a public common kept such tight reins on her daughter that when, come fourteen, she told her she could go out alone the daughter refused, saying she was too scared to do so. Of course, a child's safety is paramount, but it is every parent's task, as their child enters the pre-teens or even before, to let him grow wings and then use them, gradually. It is a difficult balance to achieve: when worried and frightened kids can't face the world or take risks in any part of their lives it becomes a form of disability. Over-concern creates an additional problem; the more adults exert control and limit exploration and experience, the more likely children are to be drawn to the forbidden, not simply as a de-fiant expression of frustration and anger but also to preserve their self-respect. Tweenies need to have adventures and take risks that are contained yet thrilling and creative, not harmful and death-defying. We must take care not to bring about that which we fear.

This section suggests how we can help tweenies to experience risk and excitement in relative safety, look out for themselves on the streets and have suitable strategies at the ready in the event of sexual harassment.

HAVING ADVENTURES, CREATING STORIES

Eight- to twelve-year-olds, like teenagers, need to have adventures and fun. Even simple activities can satisfy their need to feel they are growing up and, like the explorers of old, discovering new personal as well as geographical territory. Tweenies love camping, for example; if they cannot do it through an organised youth group, they can camp in a secure back garden, in a back shed or even in an indoor camp created in a room in the house, sleeping under a sheet 'tent'. Torches are a must-have part of this adventure. Night walks, always with torches and in the company of an adult, are also guaranteed to produce ex-aggerated shrieks and howls and can be spiced up with ghostly games and horror stories. As a calming device towards the end, biscuits and hot chocolate, served from insulated flasks, go down well and become part of the familiar and expected routine that's not only fun but can also prevent children from developing a paralysing fear of the dark.

How much risk do you let your child face?

Which of the following do you let them do, with friends or alone?

In the house: Use penknives, craft or other knives; check the wiring in an electrical plug; cook; light matches or candles; stay in the house alone for one or two hours.

Outdoors: Go to your local park or swimming pool; build and light a bonfire, barbeque or campfire; cross main roads; ride a bike in local streets; travel on public buses or trains; stay out after dark; try out higher-risk activities such as abseiling, horse riding.

Personal safety: Does your child know . . . emergency telephone numbers; your work telephone number; how to use a public pay phone; carry a phone card or mobile phone; know about 'good sense defence'; have clear coming home times that stick, even during daytime?

Funfairs and theme parks are not everyone's cup of tea, but most growing children adore them, and the scarier the ride, the better. Unfortunately, many have become so exhilarating that they make the average travelling traditional funfair seem tame. If we take other people's children with us on an outing, accept that each one will have a different thrill threshold. Under-twelves can still be truly frightened. They should be free to decline any ride and not teased about it. For those ready to relish conquering fear, adventure holidays that offer canoeing, windsurfing, abseiling, go-karts, wall climbing and quad bikes can test and develop both physical skill and mental determination.

An interest in lighting fires is, as acknowledged earlier, normal and part of growing up. Tweenies can experiment, for example, with holding a magnifying glass in the sun's rays to char paper or leaves, or light little outdoor bonfires under supervision, collecting their own twigs and cooking things like sausages. It is better to satisfy any pyromaniac tendencies safely than to make all fires forbidden. Youth groups such as Cubs, Brownies and the Woodcraft Folk teach children how to enjoy fire in a safe and respectful manner.

Taster tips on fire safety at home and the positive use of fire

✓ Teach fire safety: a match or lighter is a tool, not a toy. Show your child other tools – gardening or DIY, in the house to get the message across in a practical way. Show them how to use matches, tapers, lighters or other lighting devices safely when they are old enough.

✓ Make sure they understand what fire can do: that houses can burn down in just a few minutes; that it can kill adults, children and, of course, pets, very quickly; that smoke is responsible for more deaths than flames.

✓ If space allows, family barbeques and bonfires enable us to demonstrate sensible precautions. Supervise their first attempts before handing over responsibility.

✓ Keep all matches, cigarette lighters and lighting fuels and blocks away from curious fingers until you feel they are of an age to manage them responsibly. (We keep pills or medicines away from children, so why be less vigilant with matches?)

✓ Use candles in the home carefully and responsibly,

---

explaining any safety measures. Keep matches out of sight and mind. Rules for bedroom use will include: always have the window shut; remove all paper from the area; place candles on an incombustible plate or tray, especially if used at floor level; avoid tall candles or holders that may topple over (the low, round tea lights are safest) and have a fire-retardant or wet cloth at the ready in the event of accident.

Three ideas have been suggested so far for supervised excitement – activities that will help to meet tweenies' need for adventure and daring and encourage them to become risk-aware and safety-conscious and feel more grown up. Here are some additional ones:

- Adventurous sports such as canoeing, dry slope skiing, wall climbing, ice-skating, motorised quad bikes or supervised stunt or track skateboarding and bike riding.
- Helping to do heavy gardening jobs, such as chopping down shrubs and trees.
- Local environmental management or young person's natural history programmes offer something different and extend general knowledge. Evening bat walks, building birds' nesting boxes, clearing overgrown areas or pond and river dipping feel exciting to most young people whose lives are generally quite restricted.
- Survival projects. There are some simple books available for children on how to assemble a survival kit and manage in the great outdoors without mod cons. Water purification tablets (available from any camping shop or chemist), stock cubes, a penknife and first-aid essentials are examples of things that fit into small tins or boxes that can fire the spirit and imagination in a practical way.

SAFETY ON THE STREETS: TIPS FOR BECOMING STREETWISE

When our children begin to go out with friends or get themselves to school on their own, we need to feel sure that they know what to do to keep themselves safe. Older tweenies will increasingly want to be out and about but some under-tens also use the streets close to home as an important meeting place and somewhere to skateboard or play football. One study of young people's attitudes to using public places for socialising and play found that the street is an important social venue for many young girls just as much as boys, that they gravitate to the streets often because there is nowhere else to go away from prying adults, and for children whose families are less affluent the street becomes the main social forum. The study found that young people are not out looking for trouble, and they viewed traffic as the greatest danger, not bullies, gangs, strangers or being attacked. However, trouble does occasionally arise, so our tweenie does need to be aware of sensible practices to follow that will help to increase his confidence and safety. Older brothers, sisters or cousins will be able to help, but it is our responsibility to check tweenies know what to do, such as:

- Always stay in public view and in populated areas – play on open land close to paths, not near bushes.
- Always avoid back stairs and subways.
- Always cross the road at designated places.
- Create safety in numbers. Don't get separated.
- Stay in a small-sized group, because larger ones can get out of hand.
- Always travel downstairs on a double-decker bus, in the guard's carriage on a train if possible and never travel in an empty carriage.
- Carry money safely – a small amount in a purse and the rest elsewhere.

- Keep mobile phones out of view – in a pocket, not on the front of a bag or on a belt.
- Don't be reluctant to call or return home if there is any development that concerns them, that feels wrong. It's okay to be in a minority of one.
- How to call the police from a public telephone in an emergency.

Talking about 'good sense defence' is a useful way to discuss sensible reactions in the unlikely event of being approached by or followed in an uncomfortable or threatening manner by someone unknown to them. These will include screaming, biting the person's hand or finger and running away or taking a diversion. If other adults are nearby, it is generally better to seek help from a female with young children than a single man. It is fine to go into a shop if there is one close to report the problem or for sanctuary. It can be useful to discuss some 'what if . . .' situations so they can rehearse various reactions if difficulties present themselves.

What would you do if . . .
You felt someone in a parked car was watching you.

You believed someone was following you – down a street with houses, in a shopping centre.

You saw someone commit a crime, for example, kick someone viciously, pick someone's pocket, sell what could be drugs, cause damage to public property.

An unknown older teenager asked if you wanted to have a smoke or try a sweet.

Someone in a friend's house started to behave and talk in a manner that felt uncomfortable.

A man exposed himself to you.

A drunk lurched and asked you for money.

It is not helpful to get obsessed about the potential dangers;

it could make our children over-fearful. Provided children stick together, watch the road and their surroundings and keep their heads, the chance of serious injury is very small. Remember that young girls are in fact more likely to be molested in their own homes than on the streets and those most likely to be assaulted are boys aged fifteen to twenty-five, not tweenies.

Sexual approaches

Taster tips on alerting tweenies to sexual dangers

✓ Point out that while surprises are fine, secrets can be dangerous. If secrets involve hugs and kisses from other adults or older kids, it is very important to tell someone else.

✓ Make it clear that their body is private and no adult or older teenager should touch it in strange places or ways, or ask to be touched inappropriately as an alternative.

✓ Warn that threats could be made about dire consequences should a child tell. Reassure that these are almost never carried through and it is vital to speak out.

✓ It's okay to be rude. Here's an instance when offence is the best form of defence. Rehearse some phrases that could be useful.

✓ Be normally attentive and affectionate. Younger children are more vulnerable to inappropriate advances if they feel starved of love and attention.

Pre-teens are known to be sexually curious and may look and compare with same-age friends and sometimes touch each other non-intrusively. Occasionally, it goes further or crosses acceptable age boundaries. If we suspect our eight- to twelve-year-old is interfering sexually with a much younger child, or has been approached by an older teenager, we should seek immediate professional advice to arrange specialist support. Again, neither of these situations is common, but we should be aware that adults who display disturbing patterns of sexual behaviour often develop those patterns during puberty.

DRAWING THIS TOGETHER

Next to discipline, getting the balance right between security and independence, risk and creativity, and autonomy and certainty as children grow is the hardest part of parenting. We can never be sure our children will not bite off a little more than they can chew, or choose a path we, or they, might regret. What we do know is that the tweenie years are exactly the time to lay the groundwork for sensible attitudes and healthy experiences. Children are more likely to take unsafe risks and court danger prematurely if we either over-protect them or, at the other extreme, seem indifferent to their safety, care and welfare. The best protection we can supply against either predatory adults or wayward friends is to maintain a warm, active, affectionate, constructive, communicative and trusting relationship that sanctions safe, or at least appropriate and measured, encounters with playful excitement and daring. Our tweenies should be able to enter their adolescent years with their curiosity, confidence and optimism intact; yet protected by an emerging good sense, some practical life skills, and the knowledge that if they do make a mistake, we are there to back them up.

Ten top take-out tips

- Stay affectionate and involved but avoid over-control: don't see tweenies' growing desire for independence as a green light to cut off and cut out.
- Build children's self-esteem: it gives children the power to say 'No!' – to their friends or to any adult whom they find frightening or strange.
- Encourage autonomy: then children have the confidence to act to manage a situation.
- Allow the expression of feelings. If it's okay to feel sad, excited or angry at home, it will be easier to respond honestly and decisively to feelings of uncertainty, fear or suspicion when they face possible danger.
- Encourage them to be physically fit as this contributes to self-confidence and enables them to wriggle free or run for help.
- Help them develop good road and street sense. Walk, take them on public transport and practise crossing roads together.
- Listen to them properly when they want to tell you something. Believe them, so they are never frightened to talk about problems or difficult experiences.
- Give them an excellent tip – that applies to us all – : 'Trust your instincts; which means if you hesitate, don't do it!'
- Tweenies are still very young and they mature at different rates. Any remaining uncertainty about the best course, having weighed up all factors, and we should err on the side of safety, not risk.
- Enter the no-go area of talking about drugs, drink, sex and smoking: be truthful, catch the moment, be repetitive (once isn't enough), don't scaremonger and seek, listen to and respect their views.

And Remember!

Indoors plus in cars equals inexperience.

Tweenies are at more risk from accidents and abuse indoors than out.

Boosting their self-worth helps protect them: doing them down makes them vulnerable.

12
FACING FORWARD:
A Final Word to Keep Tweenies Right on Track

B ETWEEN THE AGES OF EIGHT and twelve, our tweenies change from being young, inward-looking children to emergent young adults very conscious of the wider world in which they now move. Over these five years their brains change, enabling them to think in more complex and 'adult' ways; their bodies respond to hormonal beckoning and begin to fill out and strengthen; and their identity is ready to flourish free of family. With the right kind of encouragement and support, they realise they can manage a great deal more, which fuels their pride and feeds their sense of self-worth. At any age, children are as old as they've ever been; and each one will feel capable on occasions because of this aware-ness alone. Tweenies' self-respect is, however, notably invested in feeling effective and competent. It is our prime task to nurture our child's self-belief, not to undermine it or put her down during this important stage of development.

Children are our future; tweenies are already influencing their future, and now is never too soon to reflect upon the values we want to share, promote and bequeath. These five years present the last easy opportunity to model and bed in values, attitudes, modes of behaviour and expectations before the rocky years ahead, during which time our children are likely to become more self-focused and we are less likely to be listened to. It is not always easy getting the balance right but we have seen that it is possible: between encouraging a healthy self-assuredness yet avoiding selfishness, between the freedom to choose and the capacity to show self-restraint, between the pleasure of giving and the joy of owning, and between self-determination yet acknowledging the needs of others and the importance of reciprocity in relationships. We are more likely to get most of it right and have our guidance and support taken seriously if we show we understand events and experiences from our tweenie's perspective, and if we then intervene sensitively, judiciously and appropriately. Our overall aim must be to keep the relationship strong, active, positive and open, which takes time, real effort and commitment. Communication is key. The potential reward is the joy of living with a growing person who is loving, generous, sensible and fun, vocal and independent-minded, able to ride the waves of self-doubt, can enjoy challenge and fulfilment and who will be sufficiently confident to hold on to her essential self on the sometimes rocky road ahead through those infamous teens.

The ten most telling take-out tips

- It is better for children to be relationship rich and possession poor, than possession rich and relationship poor; time and attention are far more valuable than money and goods, so give of these generously!
- Raise their self-esteem: treat them with dignity and respect; value and enjoy their company; understand and validate their view of the world; give them opportunities to achieve and praise and appreciate effort and success.
- Letting children grow wings and learn to use them involves sharing power and letting go, but we must firmly retain ultimate parental responsibility and authority.
- Always listen to what they have to say. Respect their views and contributions and believe them and act immediately if they report being hurt in any way.

- Remember to consult them when making any decision that might affect them; treat them as the source of authority about their wishes and preferences.
- Encourage autonomy. Create clear and safe domains over which they have self-determination, but retain overall responsibility for their health, safety and care.
- Avoid constant conflict by appreciating their developmental stage: sympathise with their drive to be different, their fascination with the forbidden and their need to experiment with risk as they explore greater independence. Be firm, but don't retaliate, be harsh, sarcastic or cause humiliation.
- Show trust and think positive. Always assume that they can and will, not that they can't or won't. Strong self-belief is their passport to the future.
- Separate yourself from them – any failure is theirs, not yours, any success is theirs to keep too; and don't take everything they say and do personally, even if you feel it personally.
- Take them seriously – treat them as important, valuable, lovable, trustworthy, reliable and responsible – and be reliable.

And Remember!

Tweenies need to believe in their possible selves: don't put them down or let them down.

Take the pressure off: love them for who they are, not for what they can do.

Give them a voice so they learn who they are, they can stand up for themselves and they see they can make a difference.

STAY CLOSE and invite them to reflect, WHILST BEGINNING TO LET GO.

References and Resources

THIS RESOURCES SECTION IS ARRANGED under topics that reflect those covered in the text of this book, though it starts with suggested organisations and books that either offer general support or give a general overview of the eight-to-twelve age group. Each topic provides information on useful reading material (books, articles, booklets and information sheets), organisations and specialist websites, in that order. Where books, helplines and websites have been written or provided especially for children and young people, these have been indicated with the prefix *Tw*. In addition, the Joseph Rowntree Foundation's *findings* series, listed at *www.jrf.org.uk* and the National Children's Bureau's *Highlight* series, *www.ncb.org.uk/resources*, summarise issues and research on a wide range of relevant topics.

Providing a general overview

John Coleman and Leo Hendry (1999), *The Nature of Adolescence* (third edition), London: Routledge

Elizabeth Hartley-Brewer (1994), *Positive Parenting: Raising Children with Self-esteem*, London: Vermilion

Jennie Linden (1996), *Growing Up: From Eight years to Young Adulthood*, London: National Children's Bureau

Nicola Madge et al. (2000), *9–13: The Forgotten Years?*, London: National Children's Bureau

Brigid McConville (2002), *Where to Look for Help: A Guide for Parents and Carers of Teenagers*, Brighton: Trust for the Study of Adolescence

General contact organisations, websites and telephone helplines

BBC parenting website www.bbc.co.uk/parenting (has a pre-teen section)

Council for Disabled Children Tel: 020 7843 1900 www.ncb.org.uk/cdc

National Family and Parenting Institute Tel: 020 7424 3460 *www.nfpi.org, www.e-parents.org* Unit 430, Highgate Studios, 53–79 Highgate Road, London NW5 1TL

NSPCC Tel: 020 7825 2500 National Helpline: 0808 800 5000 *www.nspcc.org.uk*

Parenting Education and Support Forum Tel: 020 7284 8370 Information Service: 020 7284 8389 *www.parenting-forum.org.uk* Unit 431, Highgate Studios, 53–79 Highgate Road, London NW5 1TL

Parentline Plus Tel: 020 7284 5500 National Helpline: 0808 800 2222 *www.parentlineplus.org.uk* Unit 520, Highgate Studios, 53–79 Highgate Road, London NW5 1TL

Young Minds Tel: 020 7336 8445 Helpline: 0800 018 2138 *www.youngminds.org* 102–108 Clerkenwell Road, London EC1M 5FA

Other www.raisingkids.com (has a pre-teen section)

Tw Childline: *www.childline.org.uk* Tel: 0800 1111

Tw NSPCC: *www.There4me.com*; *www.nspcc.org.uk/kidszone*

Tw Young Voice: *www.youngvoice.org.uk*

Child development, identity, gender issues

Jo Adams (2002), *Go Girls! Supporting Girls' Emotional Development and Building Self-esteem*, Sheffield: Centre for HIV and Sexual Health

Simon Blake, Rob Brown (2003), *Boys' Own: Supporting Emotional Resourcefulness and Self-esteem of Boys and Young Men*, Sheffield: Centre for HIV and Sexual Health

Erik H. Erikson (1950), *Childhood and Society* (second edition), London: Vintage

Erik H. Erikson (1980), *Identity and the Life Cycle*, New York: Norton

Claire Gillman (2003), *The Best of Boys: Helping Your Sons Through Their Teenage Years*, London: Pan Books

Susan Harter (2000), *The Construction of the Self*, New York: Guilford Press

Elizabeth Hartley-Brewer (2000), *Self-esteem for Boys: 100 Tips for Raising Happy and Confident Children*, London: Vermilion

Elizabeth Hartley-Brewer (2000), *Self-esteem for Girls: 100 Tips for Raising Happy and Confident Children*, London: Vermilion

Tim Kahn (1998), *Bringing up Boys: A Parents' Guide*, London: Piccadilly Press

Rob Pattman, Stephen Frosh and Ann Phoenix (2002), 'Boyzone: Boys Talk about Girls and Masculinity', *YoungMinds Magazine* (59)

Mary Pipher (1995), *Reviving Ophelia*, New York: Ballantine

Ann Treneman (2002), 'Sugar, Spice and All Things Nasty', *The Times*, 6 August 2002

Sibling Rivalry

Adele Faber and Elaine Mazlish (1999), *Siblings Without Rivalry*,
London: Piccadilly Press
J. Parker and J. Stimpson (2002), *Sibling Rivalry, Sibling Love*,
London: Hodder Mobius
Richard Woolfson (1995), *Sibling Rivalry*, Wellingborough:
Thorsens

Home alone

SPECIALIST WEBSITE
www.pbskids.org/itsmylife/family/homealone

Commercialism and pester power

Simon Caulkin (2003), 'A Brand New Kind of Advert', *Observer*,
6 April 2003
Axel Dammler and Astrid V. Middlemann-Motz (2002), 'I Want
the one with Harry Potter on It', *Advertising & Marketing
to Children*, vol. January–March, 2002
Margaret Driscol (2003), 'Stealthily Stealing their Innocence',
Sunday Times, 19 January 2003
Andy Fry (2001), 'Hit Me Baby One More Time', *Mediaweek*,
25 May 2001
Shannon Maughan (2002), 'BeTwixt and Be'Tween', *Publishers
Weekly (US)*, 11 November 2002
Ben Summerskill (2001), 'Generation Gimme', *Observer*, 5
August 2001

Discipline, Morals and Manners

Kate Cairns (2002), *Attachment, Trauma and Resilience: Therapeutic Caring for Children*, London: British Association for Adoption and Fostering (BAAF)

F. Clark Power (1991), *Lawrence Kohlberg's Approach to Moral Education*, Columbia University Press

William Damon (1988), *The Moral Child*, New York: Free Press

Sheila McName, Kenneth J. Gergen et al. (1999), *Relational Responsibility*, London: Sage Publications

Elizabeth Thompson Gershoff (2003), 'Parental Corporal Punishment and Associated Behaviour and Experiences', *Psychological Bulletin*, July 2003

Rowan Boyson (2002), *Equal Protection for Children: An Overview of the Experiences of Countries that Accord Children Full Protection from Physical Punishment*, London: NSPCC information sheet

Eileen Hayes (2002), *Encouraging Better Behaviour: A Practical Guide to Positive Parenting*, London: NSPCC booklet

Penelope Leach (1997), *Getting Positive about Discipline: A Guide for Today's Parents*, London: Barnardo's booklet

National Family and Parenting Institute (2002), *Over the Top Behaviour in the Under Tens*, London: NFPI booklet

---

Organisations and their websites

Attention Deficit Disorder Information Service Tel: 020 8906 9068 *www.addis.co.uk*

Friendships and Bullying

J. Alexander (1998), *Your Child Bullying: Practical and Easy to Follow Advice*, London: Element Books

A. Katz, A. Buchanan, and V. Bream (2001), *Bullying in Britain: Testimonies from Teenagers*, Surrey: Young Voice

A. Mellor (1993), *Bullying and How to Fight It: A Guide for Families*, Glasgow: Scottish Council for Research in Education

J. Pearce (1989), *Fighting, Teasing and Bullying: Simple and Effective Ways to Help Your Child*, Wellingborough: Thorsens

Rosalind Wiseman (2002), *Queen Bees and Wannabes*, London: Piatkus

Tw Michelle Elliott (1997), *Willow Street Kids: Beat the Bullies*, London: Macmillan

Tw Graham Gardner (2003), *Inventing Elliot*, London: Dolphin

Tw Althea and Karin Littlewood (1996), *The Bullies*, London: A&C Black

Tw Michael Morpurgo (1993), *The War of Jenkins' Ear*, London: Egmont Children's Books

Tw Jacqueline Wilson (1996), *Bad Girls*, London: Corgi Yearling

Tw Jacqueline Wilson (2001), *Sleepovers*, London: Young Corgi

Organisations and their websites

Anti-Bullying Alliance Tel: 020 7843 6000
www.ncb.org.uk/aba

Kidscape www.kidscape.org.uk 152 Buckingham Palace Road, London SW1W 9TR

Young Voice www.youngvoice.org.uk/bullying 12 Bridge Gardens, East Moseley, Surrey KT8 9HU

SPECIALIST WEBSITE
Tw www.pupiline.net

School, Work and Play

Guy Claxton (1997), *Hare Brain, Tortoise Mind: Why Intelligence Increases When You Think Less*, London: Fourth Estate

Peter Downes and Carey Bennett (1997), *Help Your Child Through Secondary School*, London: Hodder and Stoughton

Howard Gardner (1993), *The Unschooled Mind: How Children Think and Schools Should Teach*, London: Fontana Press

Elizabeth Hartley-Brewer (2004), *Raising a Self-starter*, New York: Da Capo Press

John Holt (1982), *How Children Fail*, London: Penguin

A. Osler, C. Street, M. Lall and K. Vincent (2001), *Not a Problem? Girls and Exclusion from School*, London: National Children's Bureau

Mariaemma Willis and Victoria K. Hodson (1999), *Discover Your Child's Learning Style*, Roseville, CA: Prima Publishing

Warren Clark (2003), 'The Dangers of Safe Play', *Recreation*, April 2003

Rosalind Edwards and Pam Alldred (2000), 'A Typology of Parental Involvement in Education Centring on Children and Young People', *British Journal of Sociology of Education*, vol. 21, no. 3

Tim Gill (1999), 'Play, Child Care and the Road to Adulthood', *Children and Society*, vol. 13, pp. 67–9

Diane Reay and Dylan Wiliam (1999), '"I'll be a Nothing": Structure, Agency and the Construction of Identity Through Assessment', *British Educational Research Journal*, vol. 25 (3)

Sue Summers (2003), 'Look Mum, No Hands!' *Observer Magazine*, 1 June (school trips)

Tw In School, Stay Cool A YoungMinds Booklet

Tw Bel Mooney (1998), *I'm Bored!*, London: Mammoth

Organisations and their websites

Advisory Centre for Education (ACE) *www.ace-ed.org.uk*

Campaign for State Education (CASE) *www.casenet.org.uk*

Children's Play Information Service, *www.ncb.org.uk/library* National Children's Bureau, 8 Wakley Street, London EC1V 7QE

National Association for Gifted Children Tel: 0870 770 3217 *www.nagcbritain.org.uk*

SPECIALIST WEBSITE
www.dfes.gov.uk/parents

Healthy Eating

R. Bryant-Waugh and B. Lask (1999), *Eating Disorders: A Parents' Guide*, London: Penguin

Caroline Braet (1999), 'Treatment of Obese Children: A New Rationale', *Clinical Child Psychology and Psychiatry*, vol. 4(4) pp. 579–91

The Children's Society (2001), *My Child Still Won't Eat.* Booklet that contains useful general tips and insights despite being focused on younger children. London

The Eating Disorders Association (2002), *It's Not About Food . . . It's About Feelings.* An educational resource. Norwich: EDA

Tw A. Naik (1999), *Wise Guides Eating: Improve Your Body Image*, London: Hodder Children's Books

Mental and emotional health

Sally Burningham (1994), *Young People Under Stress: A Parent's Guide*, London: Virago

David Lewis (1993), *Helping Your Anxious Child*, London: Cedar

Sarah McNamara (2000), *Stress in Young People: What's New and What Can We Do?*, London: Continuum

Nicci Gerrard (2002), 'Why Are So Many Teenage Girls Cutting Themselves?', *Observer*, 19 May 2002

K. Hawton, J. Fagg, S. Simkin, E. Bale, A. Bond (2000), 'Deliberate Self-harm in Adolescents in Oxford, 1985–1995', *Journal of Adolescence*, vol. 23

Philip Graham and Carol Hughes (1995), *So Young, So Sad, So Listen*, London: Royal College of Psychiatrists booklet

Rob Long (1999), *Understanding and Supporting Depressed Children and Young People*, Tamworth: Nasen (To obtain this booklet, contact *www.nasen.org.uk*)

Tw Alison Faulkner (2000), *Self-Harm: Hurting Yourself Less*, London: National Self-harm Network

---

Organisations and their websites

Eating Disorders Association (EDA) *www.edauk.com* Helpline: 01603 621414

Youth line Tel: 01603 765 050 Wensum House, Prince of Wales Road, Norwich NR1 1BR

National Self-Harm Network *www.nshn.co.uk* PO Box 16190, London NW1 3WW

YoungMinds See above

Sex and Puberty

John Coleman and Leo Henry (1999), *The Nature of Adolescence* (third edition), London: Routledge

Tw Nick Fisher (1994), *Living with a Willy: The Inside Story*, London: Macmillan Children's Books

Tw Robie H. Harris (1995), *Let's Talk About Sex*, London: Walker Books

Tw www.gurls.com

Tw www.sistersunlimited.com

Tw www.thehormonefactory.com for children 10–12 explaining sexual and reproductive development and the physical, emotional and social changes associated with puberty. Clear, straightforward and light-hearted information answering the questions this age group often ask . . . and the ones they don't (but still wonder about)

Family Upsets

Judy Dunn and Kirby Deater-Deckard (2001), *Children's Views of their Changing Families*, York: YPS

ChildLine (1997), *Listening to Ten-Year-Olds: A ChildLine Study*, London

David Knox and Kermit Leggett (2000), *Divorced Dad's Survival Guide: How to Stay Connected with Your Kids*, Massachusetts: Perseus Books

A. Mullender, S. Burton, G. Hague, U. Imam, E. Kelly, E. Mallos and L. Regan (2002), *Children's Perspectives on Domestic Violence*, London: Sage

A. Mullender, et al (2003), *'Stop Hitting Mum!' Children Talk about Domestic Violence*, Surrey: Young Voice

Bren Neale and Amanda Wade (2000), *Parent Problems! Children's Views of Life When Parents Split Up*, Surrey: Young Voice

Amanda Wade and Carol Smart (2002), *Facing Family Change: Children's Circumstances, Strategies and Resources*, York: YPS

Dan Court, Shauna Kearney and Andrew Rogers (2003), 'Attention Deficit: Living in a Sick Sibling's Shadow', *YoungMinds Magazine* (64)

YoungMinds (2003), *Keeping in Touch: How to Help Your Child After Separation and Divorce*, London: YoungMinds booklet

Working With Stepfamilies, information sheet published by Parenting Education and Support Forum, London (2002)

Tw Judy Bloom (1998), *It's Not the End of the World*, London: Macmillan Children's Books (on divorce and separation)

Tw Khadj Rouf (1989), *Secrets*, London: Children's Society (picture strip-style book dealing with sexual abuse for 8–16-year-olds in alternative versions for black and white families)

Tw Jacqueline Wilson (2002), *The Worry Website*, London:Corgi Yearling

Tw Suzie Hayman (2001), *Hands Off!* NSPCC booklet (on abuse)

Tw Worried? Need to Talk? (2002), NSPCC pocket guide (on abuse) , London

Video: Joined up Families, Leeds Animation Workshop Tel: 0113 248 4997

Organisations and their websites

National Association of Child Contact Centres Tel: 0870 770 3269 Offers neutral meeting places for children to have contact with a non-resident parent

National Family Mediation Helpline: 011 7904 2825 or *www.nfm.u-net.com* Alexander House, Telephone Avenue, Bristol BS1 5BS

One Parent Families Tel: 020 7428 5400 Helpline: 0800 018 5026 or *www.oneparentfamilies.org.uk* 225 Kentish Town Road, London NW5 2LX

> *Refuge* Tel: 020 7395 7700 Helpline: 0870 599 5443
> (domestic violence) 2–8 Maltravers Street, London
> WC2R 3EE

Bereavement

Tw Tim Bowler (1997), *River Boy*, Oxford: OUP

Tw Alan Gibbons (2004), *The Lost Boys Appreciation Society*, London: Orion

Tw Alex Shearer (2001), *The Great Blue Yonder*, London: Macmillan Children's Books

Tw Susan Varley (1984), *Badger's Parting Gifts*, London: Picture Lions

---

Organisations and their websites

Child Bereavement Network 01159 118070 or e-mail *cbn@ncb.org.uk* Video available: *A Death in the Life of . . .*

Cruse Bereavement Care Tel: 020 8940 4818 Helpline: 0870 167 1677 *www.crusebereavementcare.org.uk* Cruse House, 126 Sheen Road, Richmond, Surrey TW9 1UR

Winston's Wish Tel: 01452 394 377 Family Helpline: 0845 20 30 40 5 The Clara Burgess Centre, Gloucestershire Royal Hospital, Gloucester GL1 3NN

SPECIALIST WEBSITES

www.grief-recovery.com

Tw www.winstonswish.org.uk supports bereaved children and young people

http://www.shb.ie Guidance for parents on supporting bereaved children, from the Scottish Health Board

Risk, danger and keeping safe

Sonia Livingstone (2002), *Children's Use of the Internet: A Review of the Research Literature*, National Children's Bureau

Rolf Loeber and David Farrington (eds.) (2001), *Child Delinquents*, London: Sage Publications

Viv Armstrong (2003), 'Step Back and Relax: Every Child Needs to Take Risks and Live a Little Dangerously Once in a While', *Junior* (June), pp. 14–17

J. Harden, K. Backett-Milburn, S. Scott, S. Jackson (2000), 'Scary Faces, Scary Places: Children's Perceptions of Risk and Safety', *Health Education Journal*, vol. 59, pp. 12–22

National Children's Bureau (2002), *Cannabis: Its Effect on Children and Young People*, information sheet: *Highlight* No. 189, London: NCB

Tw Michelle Elliott (1997), *The Willow Street Kids: Be Smart, Stay Safe*, London: Macmillan

Tw Anita Naik (forthcoming, 2005), *Wise Guide: Drugs* (new edition), London: Hodder Children's Books

---

Organisations and their websites

Alcohol Concern Tel: 020 7928 7377 *www.alcoholcon cern.org.uk* Waterbridge House, 32–36 Loman Street, London SE1 0EE

Crime Concern Tel: 01793 863 500 *www.crimeconcern.org.uk* Beaver House, 147–150 Victoria Road, Swindon SW1 3UY

SPECIALIST WEBSITES ON INTERNET SAFETY

www.bbc.co.uk/webwise/basics
www.fkbko.net
.www.getnetwise.org
www.nch.org.uk/itok
www.nspcc.org.uk/kidszone

INDEX

Index

motorway games 283
music systems 42

name-calling 133, 134
National Society for the Prevention
   of Cruelty to Children 49
needs, genuine 68–9
neglect 19, 21, 54, 298
negotiation 31

obesity 206, 207–9
objectivity 83
openness 28, 89, 117, 246, 276,
   312
optimism 28, 250, 308
oral sex 238, 247
ordinariness 32, 33
outdoor environment 216–17
over-indulged children 15

paedophiles 226, 236
paracetamol, and alcohol 289
Parent Problems! 266, 270
parental break-up 261–8
   if you are living apart from your
      tweenie 264
   managing relationship break-up
      267–8
   tuning in to tweenies 265
   what research shows is best for
      children 262
   where to live, which parent to live
      with? 265–6
Parentline Plus 241
parties 3, 122, 123
peer pressure 1, 2, 5, 10, 56, 121–4,
   243, 244
periods 228, 230, 231–2, 242, 263
personal care 46
pester power 56–80
   dealing with shoplifting 76–8
   learn to say no 66–9
   managing choices 70–71

the marketing power of companies
   57–9
parental power: tactics to stay
   ahead 65–6
pocket money 71–5
tweenies' perseverance and
   persistence 59–65
   assessing their pleas and ploys
      60–65
   the pester power ladder 59–60
ten top take-out tips 79
pets 231, 238, 242
   death of 260–61
physical abuse 25, 39, 90, 92, 126,
   248, 261
play schemes 299
playing out 2–3
pocket money 26, 57, 69, 71–5, 79,
   91, 108, 109, 238
police 292, 294, 300, 306
politeness 81–2
pop bands 9, 58, 238
popularity 117, 123, 134, 139
positive recognition 17, 18
possessions
   frequent loss of 138
   respecting 29, 39, 40
praise 17, 19, 29, 89, 111, 173–5
pregnancy, teenage 244, 246
presents 33, 269
pressures
   academic 10, 12, 160
   peer 1, 2, 5, 10
   and self-belief 199
   social 10, 12
privacy 18, 42–3, 45, 54, 139, 233
puberty 6, 8, 9, 13, 24, 28, 213,
   242, 247
   see also sex and puberty
punishment 82, 90–93, 103, 109

quad bikes 302, 304

335

Index

**Transform your life
with Hodder Mobius**

For the latest information on the best in
Spirituality, Self-Help,
Health & Wellbeing and Parenting,

visit our website
www.hoddermobius.com